David J. Phillips is the Author of USA in Decline, Bush Hate and On This Day (two volumes).

"President Obama has declared war on prosperity through income redistribution."

http://thoughthead.blogspot.com

First 100 Days of President Obama

Left Wing Populist Spin Master

David J. Phillips

iUniverse, Inc.
New York   Bloomington

First 100 Days of President Obama
Left Wing Populist Spin Master

iUniverse books may be ordered through booksellers or by contacting:

iUniverse
1663 Liberty Drive
Bloomington, IN 47403
www.iuniverse.com
1-800-Authors (1-800-288-4677)

ISBN: 978-1-4401-4894-1 (sc)
ISBN: 978-1-4401-4893-4 (ebk)

Printed in the United States of America

iUniverse rev. date: 5/27/2009

Contents

INTRODUCTION

DO NOT INTERFERE WITH MOTHER NATURE

In 1930, Congress passed a massive tariff increase, in hopes of protecting American jobs. Hoover signed it. But it simply accelerated the economy's slide. The Federal Reserve contracted the money supply, taking a recession and making it into a depression. By 1932, real GDP was 25% lower than three years earlier.

Hoover increased federal spending steadily, including an increase in real terms of about 40% in 1932. At the same time, fearful that deficits were harmful, Hoover raised income taxes.

Nothing worked. So Franklin Roosevelt came into office pledging stronger medicine. His recipe was even bigger increases in government spending, government nationalization and government-organized cartels. Unions were strengthened. Crops and livestock were destroyed to raise prices. It was a whirlwind of activity without any real plan. The consequence was bigger deficits.

It worked for a while, but then, in 1938, the economy turned sour again. Unemployment, which had been falling, spiked again, reaching 19%. Consumption didn't recover to its prewar levels until 1945.

Obama is trying to emulate the New Deal: a massive accumulation of power in Washington justified by the need to save the nation with a whirlwind of activity. He is recklessly over-compensating, throwing vast quantities of money around for a quick fix which will be a millstone around the necks of future generations. He then dishonestly claims that the USA will arise stronger than before. There is no way that he can believe his own words. His own populist cult status is his personal justification. Just as in the 1930s, there is no evidence that the Liberal policy makers have any understanding of what they are doing.

They are interfering with the natural forces of repair. They need to let housing prices fall. They need to let firms go bankrupt. They need to let firms that are healthy thrive. They need to let healthy firms buy the sick firms. It is time to let the imprudent fail and the prudent pick up the bargains. They are making the recession worse and will hasten the decline of the USA.

By acting without rhyme or reason, Liberal politicians have destroyed the rules of the game. There is no reason to invest, no reason to take risk and no reason to be prudent. Everything is up in the air and as a result, the only prudent policy is to wait and see what the government will do next. The frenetic efforts of FDR had the same impact: Net investment was negative through much of the 1930s.

Worst of all are the political incentives that are unleashed when Washington decides to spend trillions of dollars. Government cannot spend such money wisely. The information about who needs to be bailed out and who needs to fail is too complicated. Inevitably, such decisions are more about Liberal politics and ideology than economics.

The banks were first, then the insurance companies, then the car makers. Now federal agencies are being bolstered, welfare and free handouts are being increased and extended. The governors are next in line with delinquent homeowners right behind. Now free loading individuals and companies know that they do not need to try to save themselves as they can maneuver to be saved by government. Those who are hard working, frugal and successful will pay the bill increasingly for the free loaders. If they are young up and comers, they will be prevented from achieving their potential as they are dragged down. They are understandably angry. The resulting downward spiral will be devastating.

In the 1940s the USA was saved economically and embarked on the right path to prosperity by a world war which barely touched these shores but left most of the rest of the world ruined. That enabled the USA to prosper as it benefited from needs throughout the world from countries no longer able to help themselves. What will save us this time?

GOODBYE AMERICA

The swooning frenzy over Barack Obama as President of the United States must be one of the most absurd waves of self-deception and swirling fantasy ever to sweep through an advanced civilisation. This cult following is like the one which grew up around Britain's Princess Diana, bereft of reason and devoid of facts.

The newspapers which recorded Obama's victory have become valuable relics. You may buy Obama picture books and Obama calendars and there is even a pre-school TV version of his story.

The real story recording his sordid associates, his cowardly voting record, his astonishingly militant commitment to unrestricted abortion and his blundering trip to Africa, are little-read and hard to find. If you can believe that this undistinguished and conventionally Left-wing machine politician is a sort of secular saviour, then you can believe anything. He plainly doesn't believe it himself. His cliche-stuffed, clunker of an acceptance speech suffered badly from nerves. It was what you would expect from someone who knew he'd promised too much and that from now on the easy bit was over.

He needn't worry too much. From now on, the rough boys and girls of America's Democratic Party apparatus, many recycled from Bill Clinton's stained and crumpled entourage, will crowd round him, to collect the rich spoils of his victory and also tell him what to do, which is what he is used to.

Just look at his sermon by the shores of Lake Michigan. He really did talk about a 'new dawn', and a 'timeless creed' (which was 'yes, we can'). He proclaimed that 'change has come'. He revealed that, despite having edited the Harvard Law Review, he doesn't know what 'enormity' means. He reached new depths of oratorical drivel never before plumbed, burbling about putting our hands on the arc of history (or was it the ark of history?) and bending it once more toward the hope of a better day.

No wonder that awful hack Jesse Jackson sobbed as he watched. How he must wish he, too, could get away with this sort of stuff. Perhaps though he was sobbing because he knew that his son was in line to take Obama's senate seat.

And it was interesting how the President-elect failed to lift his admiring audience by repeated – but rather hesitant – invocations of the brainless slogan he was forced by his minders to adopt against his will – 'Yes, we can'. They were supposed to thunder 'Yes, we can!' back at him, but they just wouldn't join in. No wonder. Yes we can what exactly? Go home and keep a close eye on the tax rate perhaps. He'd have been better off bursting into 'I'd like to teach the world to sing in perfect harmony' which contains roughly the same message and might have attracted some valuable commercial sponsorship.

Perhaps, being a Chicago crowd, they knew some of the things that 52.5 per cent of America prefers not to know. They know Obama is the obedient servant of one of the most squalid and unshakeable political machines in America. They know that one of his alarmingly close associates, a state-subsidised slum landlord called Tony Rezko, has been convicted on fraud and corruption charges.

They also know the US is just as segregated as it was before Martin Luther King – in schools, streets, neighbourhoods, holidays, even in its TV-watching habits and its choice of fast-food joint. The difference is that it is now done by unspoken agreement rather than by law.

If Mr Obama's election had threatened any of that, his feel-good white supporters would have scuttled off and voted for John McCain, or practically anyone. But it doesn't. Mr Obama, thanks mainly to the now-departed grandmother he both praised as a saint and denounced as a racial bigot, has the huge advantages of an expensive private education. He did not have to grow up in the badlands of useless schools, shattered families and gangs which are the lot of so many young black men of his generation.

Washington DC, America's capital and Obama's new home, has a sad secret. It is perhaps the most racially divided city in the world, with 15th Street, which runs due north from the White House, the unofficial frontier between black and white. But, like so much of America, it also now has a new division. Less than a mile away from the smart white area is a suburb where Spanish is spoken as much as English, plus a smattering of tongues from such places as Ethiopia, Somalia and Afghanistan. Among the Mexicans, Salvadorans and the other Third World nationalities, Obama has been greeted with ecstasy.

They grasped the real significance. They knew it meant that America had finally switched sides in a global cultural war. Forget the Cold War, or even the Iraq War. The United States, having for the most part a deeply conservative people, had until now just about stood out against many of the mistakes which have ruined so much of the rest of the world. Suspicious of welfare addiction, feeble justice and high taxes, totally committed to preserving its own national sovereignty, unabashedly Christian in a world part secular and part Muslim, suspicious of the Great Global Warming panic, it was unique.

These strengths had been fading for some time, mainly due to poorly controlled mass immigration and to the march of political correctness. They had also been weakened by the failure of Republicans to fight with conviction on the cultural and moral fronts, instead trying to appease Liberals. Indeed this bipartisan spirit was George W. Bush's undoing. And now the US, like Britain before it, has begun the long slow descent into the Third World. How sad for those of us who saw Britain in decline and came to the USA with the audacity of hope (sorry, we will all resort to talking drivel before long). Where now can we go?

CHAPTER 1 ... ... ADORATION

DREAMS FROM MY FATHER

"Dreams From My Father" was written with a political motive, not just the itch to write for writing's sake. It reveals to some extent what makes Obama tick. He is essentially an intelligent, well educated, blank canvas on which others can see what they want to see.

Obama had come to Chicago by way of Hawaii, California and New York, and had to establish his credentials in the world of Chicago politics. Obama was intent on staking out a claim to having put down deep and permanent roots in Illinois's First Congressional District.

The long midsection of the book, set among the housing projects of the South Side, where Obama spent less than three years as a community organizer, is a love letter to the people of Chicago and to Harold Washington, the city's first black mayor. "Dreams" came out in 1995; the next year, Obama successfully ran for the state senate; three years later he challenged Bobby Rush on his home turf for his congressional seat. Although he lost that primary, his presence in the race would have been unthinkable had he not so convincingly transformed himself into a full-blooded Chicagoan in the pages of "Dreams."

To build a political base in his adopted city, Obama had to write a book, but it's a measure of his seemingly unbounded confidence in his abilities that he set his sights on making the book a work of literary art. "Dreams" is less of a memoir than it is a novel: Most of its characters are composites with fictional names; its total-recall dialogue is as much imagined as remembered; its time sequences are intricately shuffled. It has an old-fashioned plot, as it charts the progress of its hero, first met as a 21-year-old loner for whom "my solitude" was "the safest place I knew," on a quest for identity and community. Like a Trollope novel, "Dreams" ends with a wedding scene, in which all the warring fragments of Obama's life -- black and white, Hawaii and Indonesia, Kenya and Chicago -- finally cohere into one like pieces of an elaborate jigsaw puzzle. Married to a South Side native, and, by inference, to the South Side itself, the wandering hero has at last come home, in -- as it so happens -- the very heart of Bobby Rush's political bailiwick.

Obama is a skillful novelist. He is a vigilant listener and watcher, a hoarder of contingent details, who hugs his observations to himself, then weaves them into a tale. Alone with his burning cigarette, he figures out his world in passages of eloquence. Three o'clock in the morning is a recurring time in "Dreams," the hour at which patterns reveal themselves, resolutions are made and the reader enjoys the illusion of unhindered intimacy with the author.

The book really takes off when Obama wriggles out of the constraints of the first person singular and, like a novelist, imagines his way into the heads of other people. Early on, he tries to see Kansas in the 1930s through the young eyes of his white grandparents, "Toot" and "Gramps," when they were courting. Later, his 7-year-old self is playing with Lolo, his Indonesian stepfather, in the backyard of their house in a Jakarta suburb when Obama catches sight of his mother, watching them from behind a window. For the next five pages, he observes himself and Lolo through her eyes. He expresses the pain of his mother's expatriation and her budding estrangement from her second husband, so troublingly different in his native Indonesia from the student with whom she fell in love in Honolulu. Obama paints the scene as he would like us to see her. The truth is irrelevant.

In Kenya, Obama, who speaks only a few words of Luo, interrogates "Granny," his black grandmother, with the help of his English-speaking half-sister. From that single, halting conversation, he constructs for Granny a 28-page recitation, in formal English like the language of translated Greek myth, in which she takes over the narrative reins of the book and tells the story of his family from the perspective of her African village.

Obama's promised style of governance chimes with his style of writing. In naming his cabinet and organizing his inauguration, he incorporates into the narrative characters and voices quite different from his own (like Hillary Clinton's and Rick Warren's), Obama has demonstrated a consistency between his instincts as a writer and his performance as president-elect. In both, Obama is in the business of community organizing. "Dreams" is frequently fiction. Its very title is nonsense. Obama's father was a gifted person, who was given opportunities but who used others, including affirmative action for a subsidized education in the USA and threw off relationships once they had served their usefulness. He had no relationship with his son, except for the one visit back to Hawaii, exaggerated out of proportion in "Dreams." He abused his wives both physically and emotionally and died a hopeless unsuccessful loner and drunk, in a car accident.

Now Obama employs a team of ghostwriters, led by the 27-year-old wunderkind Jon Favreau. He's said to have input into his own speeches, and to edit and modestly rewrite them - a far cry from the time when he was composing "Dreams." We are now seeing how Obama the novelist transforms and fares as Obama the President. Acting out the words of others, reading from a teleprompter, Obama will continue to woo the masses, but is not what the job is all about.

HOW OBAMA WON

Barack Obama's presidential campaign raised $104 million in the weeks around Election Day, a grand finale to a successful bid that shattered fundraising records. Overall, Obama raised nearly $750 million during his odyssey to the presidency.

The campaign said more than 1 million contributors donated during the period, with more than half donating for the first time. Throughout the campaign, more than 3.95 million contributors gave to Obama.

The Democrat's fundraising and his spending eclipsed that of his Republican rival, John McCain. Obama was the first presidential candidate since the campaign finance reforms of the 1970s to raise private donations during the general election. McCain opted to accept public financing. That limited him to $84 million to spend from the beginning of September.

By comparison, Obama spent $315 million since Sept. 1, a huge disparity that McCain tried to narrow by relying on millions of dollars worth of help from the Republican National Committee. Obama's expenditures during the final period alone totaled more that $136 million. He ended with a cash balance of nearly $30 million.

Obama's prowess at attracting money was one of his campaign's defining characteristics. What distinguished him from his successful predecessors was his ability to motivate donors to give repeatedly. Obama persuaded an unusually large number of people to give more than once. 212,000 people were repeat givers of $200 or more, averaging $490 each. Obama had a total of 580,000 individual donors as of mid-October.

Overall Obama collected about 26 percent of his total haul from people who gave less than $200, about the same as President George W. Bush did in his 2004 campaign, but less than Democrat Howard Dean's small-donor take of 38 percent in his unsuccessful primary bid that year. Obama's campaign relied for nearly half of its fundraising on big donors, who gave $1,000 or more. They were the financial engine of the Obama campaign.

WHO IS OBAMA?

There is nothing overwhelmingly striking about Barack Obama. There is a cerebral quality to him, and an air of detachment. He has eloquence, but within bounds. He speaks in generalities without actually saying anything. His political genius is that he is a blank slate. The devotees can project onto him what they wish. The coalition that has propelled his quest - African-Americans and affluent white Liberals - has no economic coherence. But for the moment, there is the illusion of a common undertaking – a false sense of equality within the crowd. Once Obama has to act, the crowd will discover its own fissures and the euphoria will be shattered. The affluent will have to pay for the programs promised the poor. The redistribution agenda that runs through Mr. Obama's vision is anathema to the Silicon Valley entrepreneurs and the hedge-fund managers now smitten with him. Their ethos is one of competition and the justice of the rewards that come with risk and effort. All this is hidden, as the devotees sustain the candidacy of a man whose public career has been a steady advocacy of reining in the market and organizing those who believe in entitlement and redistribution.

A creature of universities, left wing community groups and nonprofit institutions, the former Illinois senator, with the blessing and acquiescence of his upscale supporters, has glided past these hard distinctions. On the face of it, his affluent devotees would seem ready to foot the bill for the new order, or are convinced that after victory the old ways will endure, and that Mr.

Obama will govern from the center. Ambiguity has been a powerful weapon of this gifted candidate. He has been different things to different people, and he has not obligated himself to tell this coalition of a thousand discontents, and a thousand visions, the details of his political programs.

Chapter 2 ... ... AIG

AIG

While taxpayers were still absorbing the shock of having to foot an $85 billion bill (a tab that later grew to $144 billion) to bail out American International Group, executives at the insurer headed straight for the exclusive St. Regis resort in Southern California just days after their company got the money. The $440,000 tab for their eight-day stay at the Tuscan-style resort included $150,000 for meals, $23,000 in spa charges and $7,000 for golf outings. AIG says the event was held mainly to reward performance of independent insurance agents and brokers who were not company employees.

Should taxpayers pay to keep executives who steered a company into a ditch? American International Group thinks so. It then agreed to pay retention bonuses to 130 executives, including $3 million for Jay Wintrob, who heads the division that sells annuities. Last year, he earned $2.5 million in salary, bonus, stock and options. Other AIG execs will get more than $500,000, or about 200% of their salaries, to stay through 2009. The insurer had previously promised to forgo bonus payouts as part of the bailout plan. AIG says retention bonuses are needed to keep execs from leaving while it restructures and that departures could cause the company's reinsurers to cancel contracts.

The latest earnings report underscores AIG's worsening condition with its total loss for the quarter exceeding $60 billion. AIG is seeking an overhaul of its $150 billion government bailout package that would substantially reduce the insurer's financial burden, while further exposing U.S. taxpayers. One of the restructuring plan's central goals is to safeguard AIG's credit ratings, which, if cut, would force it to make billions of dollars in payments to its trading partners, further weakening its already precarious financial position. The new plan is being structured in close consultation with major credit-rating agencies.

AIG'S FINANCIAL PRODUCTS DIVISION

After Congress passed a law in 2000 deregulating the kind of paper bets AIG was making, the company was free to write as much of this insurance as it wanted without demonstrating it could cover any and all bets that went bad. The company made $500 billion in paper bets with little or nothing to back them up.

What the Obama government is hoping to do now is keep AIG afloat long enough to sell it off in pieces. But time is running out. As AIG's financial problems continue, its customers will likely look elsewhere for insurance as their policies expire.

Members of Congress now expressing the loudest outrage were among those who approved the rules that let AIG get into the casino business in the first place.

The failure of Government to act more responsibly and effectively is not surprising. AIG was one of the biggest contributors to Obama and key members of Congress in charge of making the rules. The company, like the rest of the financial services industry, has some of the best laws money can buy.

THE CLINTON ERA

If President Barack Obama wants to find a scapegoat for the mess at American International Group, it is legislation enacted by The Clinton administration that laid the groundwork for AIG's collapse and the Bailout itself.

"It's hard to understand how derivative traders at AIG warranted any bonuses, much less $165 million in extra pay," Obama said. "How do they justify this outrage to the taxpayers who are keeping the company afloat?"

AIG has taken out $170 billion in federal funds, and more will be required. The company, now 80 percent owned by U.S. taxpayers, locked into paying $165 million in bonuses to key executives for retention bonuses agreed eighteen months ago before the bailout. They cannot be broken legally. Challenging these contracts will cost AIG and the government even more money including legal fees.

The employment contracts became so complex, with pay packages consisting of stock options and other forms of deferred compensation, because of Congress' previous attempts to control salaries. In 1993, Congress limited the tax deduction that companies could take for cash payments to $1 million. The result was a cottage industry of lawyers, consultants and advisors who structure even bigger pay packages with creative legal strategies that now make the AIG bonuses difficult to rescind.

Congress played an even bigger role in the mess which led the government into the taxpayer-funded bailout of AIG in a misguided attempt to stem a potential global financial meltdown.

AIG and the counterparties it did business with are reeling because of a type of insurance policy known as credit default swaps. Sellers of these securities promise to pay any losses to bondholders in the event bond issuers default and fail to pay back the original investment. In return the buyer pays a premium to the issuer of the policy, just as a homeowner pays a premium for fire insurance.

That's where the similarity ends. Unlike your homeowners insurance, credit default swaps are unregulated. Investors were allowed to buy insurance on bonds they didn't even own, and companies like AIG were allowed to write credit insurance many times over on the same bond. These bonds, many of them backed by subprime mortgages, often were rated triple-A, so no one expected them to default. Collecting premiums looked like easy money.

But when the housing market began to unwind, AIG had to begin making good on those credit default swaps. Worse, instead of just paying once, it had to pay many times over for the same defaulted bond. That became the financial equivalent of paying a dozen people for the full cost of replacing each home wiped out by a hurricane.

Because these risky bets were unregulated, none of the government agencies that were supposed to make sure the financial system was sound, from state insurance regulators to the Federal Reserve, were aware of just how much risk was in the system. There were also no regulations to prevent AIG from making all kinds of unconscionable bets.

It was a law approved by Congress in 2000 that allowed companies to place tens of trillions of dollars of these risky credit default swap bets. After the 1998 collapse of Long Term Capital Management, a giant hedge fund that pioneered the use of derivatives, the Fed engineered a rescue to prevent the unwinding of risky bets from spreading to the larger financial system. That brought calls for tighter regulation of derivatives, including a push for greater derivatives regulation at the Commodity Futures Trading Commission.

Strong opposition to the proposal from then-Fed Chairman Alan Greenspan and senior Clinton administration officials sank the idea. On Dec. 21, 2000, President Clinton signed into law the Commodity Futures Modernization Act, which further eased restrictions on derivatives like credit default swaps. In so doing 150 years of insurance regulation and derivatives regulation were eliminated.

The new law cleared the way for an explosion in credit default swaps. In the first half of 2001, there were $632 billion in credit default swaps outstanding. By the second half of 2007, that number was up 100-fold to more than $62 trillion. Now, as the government tries to unwind the mess at AIG, much of the tax money pumped into AIG has quickly flowed out to dozens of counterparties, which are the companies, investment funds, municipalities and others who bought credit default swaps from the insurance giant. Effectively, AIG entered into speculative derivatives gambles with banks that were operating in the role of a bookie that made bad bets. Taxpayer funds went to pay off the bookies through the government bailouts.

GOVERNMENT INCOMPETENCE

Former AIG chief executive, Hank Greenberg questioned the U.S. government's approach to the insurance giant's massive credit default swaps business. Greenberg ran AIG for nearly four decades before leaving in 2005.

Speaking before the House of Representatives Committee on Oversight and Government Reform, Greenberg told lawmakers the U.S. should have "walled" off AIG Financial Products Group, the business unit involved with the CDS activities, and provided guarantees to counterparties instead of cash. Also, he questioned why AIG continued to be a large presence in the swaps market after it lost its "AAA" rating. The loss of the "AAA" rating forced it to post more collateral to counterparties in swap agreements.

"Approximately $50 billion of taxpayer cash has been paid to U.S. and foreign firms who were AIG's counterparties in its credit default swaps business, another $44 billion was paid over to counterparties in the securities lending business," Greenberg said. "These cash payments should never have occurred."

Greenberg came out against the U.S. government's plan to liquidate AIG because there is not much of a market for the insurer's assets. "Fire-sale prices will bring taxpayers, who now own almost 80% of AIG, only pennies on the dollar for their investment in AIG," Greenberg said.

Greenberg said plans to liquidate the firm have destroyed AIG's value because its professionals are leaving the firm. "Employees do not want to remain in a company being liquidated; they will simply move to competitors and take business with them," Greenberg said.

AIG'S RIVALS OPPOSE BAILOUT

AIG's competitors oppose the federal bailout since it is unfairly tilting the commercial-insurance playing field. AIG is using the government bailout to secure an advantage, particularly by cutting prices. Since the government stepped in, AIG has slashed insurance prices by more than 30% in some cases to keep or win contracts. This tack has helped AIG insure customers ranging from the U.S. Olympic Committee and an Arizona airport to an Illinois nursing home and a Florida town government.

When the Fed stepped in to save AIG in September, its primary focus was on a small outpost of the company's sprawling empire: It wanted to prevent soured bets on subprime mortgages from draining AIG's resources. The government bailout led to payments of tens of billions of dollars to AIG's trading partners, including big banks in the U.S. and Europe. But the bailout spurred by these exotic financial bets has also politicized the nuts-and-bolts insurance business. Merely by propping up the ailing insurer, the government transformed the competitive landscape, blunting efforts by AIG's rivals to pick off its customers.

The Fed needs AIG's business to remain competitive because that could help the company repay the government. But if AIG charges too little for policies to keep from losing business, it could run up big losses on insurance claims years down the road which is bad news for tax payers.

Insurance executives who managed their businesses prudently object to having to compete with a government-supported AIG. If you have an implicit federal backstop, you can do that.

AIG has been able to hold onto many clients and fend off rivals. A big part of AIG's business, its property and casualty lines, has held up remarkably well for a company that was headed for disaster. AIG had a 6.5% share of the U.S. market last year, according to the National Association of Insurance Commissioners, down from 7.3% in 2007. Still, AIG remains the second-largest player in this field in the U.S., and sells protection against property damage and liability to many of the nation's largest corporations.

The bailout leaves the government with a difficult oversight task. AIG has 116,000 employees, 74 million customers, $860 billion in assets and operations in about 130 countries. The Fed does not have the staff or expertise to manage the far-flung businesses.

WORST LOSS EVER

American International Group (AIG), the world's biggest insurer, made it into the record books as it reported losing $61.7 billion in the last three months of 2008. That is the largest quarterly loss in the history of U.S. companies.

As a response the Obama administration will provide the troubled company another $30 billion. The existing loan package from tax payers, as mandated by government, totals some $150 billion.

Under the new deal, the U.S. Treasury and the Federal Reserve will provide about $30 billion in fresh capital to the insurer, lower the interest rate on a $60 billion loan and ease the terms of a $40 billion preferred share investment.

AIG will repay much of the $40 billion it owes the Federal Reserve with equity stakes in two AIG overseas units — Asia-based American International Assurance Co. and American Life Insurance Co., which operates in 50 countries. Repayment was originally supposed to be made in cash with interest.

In addition, AIG will securitize $5 billion to $10 billion in debt, backed with life insurance assets, to further reduce its debt burden. And the $60 billion Federal Reserve credit facility AIG received in November will be reduced to $25 billion. AIG has already drawn down about $38 billion of those funds.

Major credit rating agencies have already signed off on the deal. Without the support of the credit rating agencies, AIG would have faced crippling cuts to its ratings.

Problems at AIG did not come from its traditional insurance operations, but instead from its financial services units, and primarily its business insuring mortgage-backed securities and other risky debt against default. AIG specialized in credit-default swaps, which was insurance for securities tied to home mortgages. Shares of AIG closed at 42 cents. The stock, which traded at $49.50 a year ago, has lost nearly all of its value since the market meltdown began in September. Taxpayers now own 80% of AIG.

The taxpayer bailout of AIG mandated by the Obama administration will eventually exceed $250 billion without any realistic expectation that it will be repaid. The ugly truth is that if AIG was allowed to go bankrupt, major damage would be inflicted on those foreign institutions which buy US debt, without which we could not continue to feed our debt addiction. We cannot afford to anger those upon whom we depend to supply the money we crave for our consumer driven addiction. Obama is the conduit. The cost is destructive Liberal ideology and the accelerating decline of the USA which is the lot of all addicts.

AIG PRETENSE

AIG has expressed optimism that it will repay about $34.5 billion to the government over the next several months. It plans to do so partially with equity stakes in two large overseas insurance companies and partially with securities backed by cash flow from the U.S. insurance business. The government could then sell those stakes to raise money toward the $170 billion it's owed.

The reality is that the AIG wind-down inevitably will cost taxpayers even more money up to an additional $200 billion so that its core businesses can be sold off. That is sinking money into a hole.

The problems stems from AIG's obligations to its trading partners. So far, the hobbled insurance giant has honored in full its contracts with U.S. and foreign banks. It has paid out more than $90 billion in taxpayer money to keep some of the biggest names in finance from losing money on bad bets linked to subprime mortgages and other risky assets.

No bailout recipient has burned through more taxpayer money than AIG, which is now about 80 percent owned by the government. A 90-year-old insurer, it was listed as recently as last year as the world's 18th largest publicly traded company. Back then, AIG's stock traded for about $40 a share. Today, you can buy one share for just under a buck.

The government has made four separate attempts to save the company, including a $30 billion cash injection when AIG reported a $62 billion fourth-quarter loss, the worst three-month performance in U.S. corporate history.

STOKING PUBLIC ANGER

Troubled insurance giant American International Group has paid bonuses of $1 million or more to 73 employees, including 11 who no longer work for the company.

New York State Attorney General Andrew Cuomo has subpoenaed information from AIG on Monday to determine whether the payments constitute fraud under state law. He says contracts written in March 2008 guaranteed employees 100 percent of their 2007 pay for 2008.

President Barack Obama and Congress have blasted AIG for paying more than $160 million in bonuses to employees of its Financial Products division, the unit primarily responsible for the meltdown that led to a federal bailout of the company, while the company has received billions in taxpayer bailout funds.

The company and federal regulators have said it was obligated by contract to make the payments. Cuomo tried to argue that the bonuses might have been fraudulent if AIG officials knew the company couldn't afford them.

In a letter to Rep. Barney Frank, chairman of the House Committee on Financial Services, Cuomo outlined the bonus and contract information and asked the panel to take up the issue at a Congressional hearing with the intention of stoking public anger.

"These payments were all made to individuals in the subsidiary whose performance led to crushing losses and the near failure of AIG," Cuomo wrote. "Thus, last week, AIG made more than 73 millionaires in the unit which lost so much money that it brought the firm to its knees, forcing a taxpayer bailout. Something is deeply wrong with this outcome."

What is not discussed is the nature of the bonuses. AIG agreed to pay these retention bonuses in March 2008 to keep employees who were unwinding its Financial Products division. Retention bonuses are necessary so that key people do not leave. Expert knowledge is required not to only to create but also unwind the complex trades in which AIG was involved. The honorable way to void these contracts would have been to let AIG go into bankruptcy. It is dishonorable to prop up AIG with tax payer money and then to distort the law, stoke public anger against AIG and its executives, bully bonus recipients to pay back bonuses and even to enact laws in Congress specifically to claw back the bonus money by imposing 100% taxation. Unfortunately Obama and his cronies are without honor and do not understand its meaning.

OBAMA TRASH TALK

President Obama has instructed Treasury Secretary Timothy Geithner in addition to what he should be doing, however ineptly, to "pursue every legal avenue" to block $165 million in bonuses to American International Group executives who were in part responsible for the company's near collapse.

"This is a corporation that finds itself in financial distress due to recklessness and greed," Obama was scheduled to say according to prepared remarks released by the White House. "Under these circumstances, it's hard to understand how derivative traders at AIG warranted any bonuses, much less

$165 million in extra pay. How do they justify this outrage to the taxpayers who are keeping the company afloat?"

This repeated posturing by the President in attempts to promote himself continues to damage our economy, driving down the stock market and causing harm throughout the USA. Is he capable of positive action or is the blame game all that he knows?

AIG PAY BACK

New York Attorney General Andrew Cuomo said that 15 of the top 20 retention bonus recipients in AIG's Financial Products unit have agreed to give back their bonuses -- amounting to returned cash in excess of $30 million.

Mr. Cuomo says of the $165 million in controversial bonuses, 47%, or about $80 million of it, was given to Americans, and he is aiming to recoup that amount to AIG. Mr. Cuomo says his office is working both with AIG executives and with individual bonus recipients to get the bonus money back. Fear of harm to self and family is a powerful motivator as was learned in Nazi Germany.

NAZI STATE TACTICS

New York Attorney General Cuomo said he has received the list of AIG bonus recipients and is working with AIG to determine who has kept or returned their bonuses. He has said that he will publish names. Recipients who do not willingly comply will be subject to hate from their local communities. One has already received a death threat. Death was also suggested by a US Senator.

AIG EXODUS

An American International Group Inc. executive who received a retention bonus worth more than $742,000 after taxes has resigned publicly in an Op-Ed column in The New York Times.

Jake DeSantis, an executive vice president at AIG's Financial Products Division, said he is leaving the company and will donate his entire bonus to charity. The letter, addressed to AIG's CEO, Edward Liddy, criticized Liddy for, among other things, agreeing to the payments but then calling the bonuses distasteful as he testified before disapproving members of Congress.

"We in the financial products unit have been betrayed by AIG and are being unfairly persecuted by elected officials," wrote DeSantis, who was head of business development for commodities. "In response to this, I will now leave the company and donate my entire post-tax retention payment to those suffering from the global economic downturn. My intent is to keep none of the money myself."

He added: "I take this action after 11 years of dedicated, honorable service to AIG. I can no longer effectively perform my duties in this dysfunctional environment, nor am I being paid to do so."

The bonuses were promised in contracts with employees that AIG signed early last year.

AIG has expressed concern that the company may not be able to attract and retain talented employees if they believe their compensation is subject to adjustment by the government. An AIG spokesman said Monday that a "handful" of senior-level executives have resigned from the financial products division, and that there will likely be more resignations to come.

RESIGNATION LETTER

Dear Mr. Liddy,

It is with deep regret that I submit my notice of resignation from A.I.G. Financial Products.

I am proud of everything I have done for the commodity and equity divisions of A.I.G.-F.P. I was in no way involved in — or responsible for — the credit default swap transactions that have hamstrung A.I.G. Nor were more than a handful of the 400 current employees of A.I.G.-F.P. Most of those responsible have left the company and have conspicuously escaped the public outrage.

After 12 months of hard work dismantling the company — during which A.I.G. reassured us many times we would be rewarded in March 2009 — we in the financial products unit have been betrayed by A.I.G. and are being unfairly persecuted by elected officials. In response to this, I will now leave the company and donate my entire post-tax retention payment to those suffering from the global economic downturn. My intent is to keep none of the money myself.

I take this action after 11 years of dedicated, honorable service to A.I.G. I can no longer effectively perform my duties in this dysfunctional environment, nor am I being paid to do so. Like you, I was asked to work for an annual salary of $1, and I agreed out of a sense of duty to the company and to the public officials who have come to its aid. Having now been let down by both, I can no longer justify spending 10, 12, 14 hours a day away from my family for the benefit of those who have let me down.

You and I have never met or spoken to each other, so I'd like to tell you about myself. I was raised by schoolteachers working multiple jobs in a world of closing steel mills. My hard work earned me acceptance to M.I.T., and the institute's generous financial aid enabled me to attend. I had fulfilled my American dream.

I started at this company in 1998 as an equity trader, became the head of equity and commodity trading and, a couple of years before A.I.G.'s meltdown last September, was named the head of business development for commodities. Over this period the equity and commodity units were consistently profitable — in most years generating net profits of well over $100 million. Most recently, during the dismantling of A.I.G.-F.P., I was an integral player in the pending sale of its well-regarded commodity index business to UBS. As you know, business unit sales like this are crucial to A.I.G.'s effort to repay the American taxpayer.

The profitability of the businesses with which I was associated clearly supported my compensation. I never received any pay resulting from the credit default swaps that are now losing so much money. I did, however, like many others here, lose a significant portion of my life savings in the form of deferred compensation invested in the capital of A.I.G.-F.P. because of those losses. In this way I have personally suffered from this controversial activity — directly as well as indirectly with the rest of the taxpayers.

You also are aware that most of the employees of your financial products unit had nothing to do with the large losses. And I am disappointed and frustrated over your lack of support for us. I and many others in the unit feel betrayed that you failed to stand up for us in the face of untrue and unfair accusations from certain members of Congress and from the press over our retention payments, and that you didn't defend us against the baseless and reckless comments made by the attorneys general of New York and Connecticut.

My guess is that in October, when you learned of these retention contracts, you realized that the employees of the financial products unit needed some incentive to stay and that the contracts, being both ethical and useful, should be left to stand. That's probably why A.I.G. management assured us on three occasions during that month that the company would "live up to its commitment" to honor the contract guarantees.

You've now asked the current employees of A.I.G.-F.P. to repay these earnings. As you can imagine, there has been a tremendous amount of serious thought and heated discussion about how we should respond to this breach of trust.

As most of us have done nothing wrong, guilt is not a motivation to surrender our earnings. We have worked 12 long months under these contracts and now deserve to be paid as promised. None of us should be cheated of our payments any more than a plumber should be cheated after he has fixed the pipes but a careless electrician causes a fire that burns down the house.

Many of the employees have, in the past six months, turned down job offers from more stable employers, based on A.I.G.'s assurances that the contracts would be honored. They are now angry about having been misled by A.I.G.'s promises and are not inclined to return the money as a favor to you.

The only real motivation that anyone at A.I.G.-F.P. now has is fear. Mr. Cuomo has threatened to "name and shame," and his counterpart in Connecticut, Richard Blumenthal, has made similar threats — even though attorneys general are supposed to stand for due process, to conduct trials in courts and not the press.

That is why I have decided to donate 100 percent of the effective after-tax proceeds of my retention payment directly to organizations that are helping people who are suffering from the global downturn. This is not a tax-deduction gimmick; I simply believe that I at least deserve to dictate how my earnings are spent, and do not want to see them disappear back into the obscurity of A.I.G.'s or the federal government's budget. Our earnings have caused such a distraction for so many from the more pressing issues our country faces, and I would like to see my share of it benefit those truly in need.

On March 16 I received a payment from A.I.G. amounting to $742,006.40, after taxes. In light of the uncertainty over the ultimate taxation and legal status of this payment, the actual amount I donate may be less — in fact, it may end up being far less if the recent House bill raising the tax on the retention payments to 90 percent stands.

Sincerely,

Jake DeSantis

TO THOSE WITH COURAGE

Employees at the insurer gave a standing ovation for Jake DeSantis, an executive in AIG's financial-products division, who was the first to publicly refuse to return his retention bonus despite an outcry over the payments.

Five other employees of the unit quit the same day. The departures and refusals to return bonuses have compounded the turmoil within a division that still had an estimated $1.6 trillion in its portfolio of derivatives instruments as of March 14, according to the company.

The risks overseas are even greater. Amid the rage over retention bonuses at AIG two of the company's top managers in Paris have resigned. Their moves have left the giant insurer and officials scrambling to replace them to avoid an expensive situation in which billions in AIG trading contracts could default.

In recent days, employees have huddled in small groups in conference rooms off the division's main trading floor in Wilton, Conn., debating what to do. Some have expressed worries about retaliation. One employee said he had instructed his wife to call the police in the event his identity became known and a news truck appeared at his home. Others commiserated that their children have been verbally abused in school.

Mr. DeSantis and other employees argued that they did not work in the part of the business that produced the problem. The losses stemmed from credit-default swaps, insurance-like contracts that protected banks and others holding mortgage-related assets.

Obama led vilification and harassment of AIG employees is grossly unfair and unwarranted. Employees have reduced risk in the business by cutting outstanding trading positions by 36%.

AIG employees have criticized an opponent of the bonus payments, New York Attorney General Andrew Cuomo, arguing that he had supported the bonuses in October by backing the need for retention plans at the parent company. Cuomo has subpoenaed AIG to get the names of the bonus recipients. The retention bonuses were approved in early 2008 by the board of AIG's financial-products unit, which included Harvard economist Martin Feldstein.

PILING ON

Some of the same banks that got government-funded payouts to settle contracts with AIG also turned to the insurer for help cutting their income taxes in the U.S. and Europe.

The IRS is now challenging some of the tax deals structured by AIG Financial Products.

THE REAL AIG OUTRAGE

President Obama and the rest of the Liberal political class are deflecting attention from the larger outrage, which is the five-month cover-up over who benefited from the AIG bailout. Taxpayers have already put up $173 billion, or more than a thousand times the amount of those bonuses, to fund the government's AIG "rescue." This federal takeover, never approved by AIG shareholders, uses the firm as a conduit to bail out other institutions. Since September 16, AIG has sent $120 billion in cash, collateral and other payouts to banks, municipal governments and other derivative counterparties around the world. This needless cover-up is one reason Americans are becoming angrier as they wonder about the extent that Washington is lying to them about these bailouts.

Obama and his cohorts have never defined what systems American taxpayers are paying to protect. It is not capitalism, in which risk-takers suffer the consequences of bad decisions. In some cases it is not even Americans. The U.S. government is now in the business of distributing foreign aid to offshore financiers, laundered through AIG which it continues to prop up through more and more taxpayer money.

Liberal politicians prefer to talk about AIG's latest bonus payments because they deflect attention from Washington's failure to supervise AIG. The Beltway crowd has been selling the story that AIG failed because it operated in a shadowy unregulated world and cleverly exploited gaps among Washington overseers. President Obama parrots, "This is a corporation that finds itself in financial distress due to recklessness and greed." He should talk instead about his own greed and that of his fellow travelers in the political class as that is perhaps the only form of greed that he understands, but putting that to one side, he is deliberately ignoring the real issue. Various arms of Liberal government approved, enabled and encouraged AIG's disastrous bet on the U.S. housing market.

Contrary to media myth, AIG's infamous Financial Products unit did not slip through the regulatory cracks. The whole of AIG, including this unit, was regulated by several agencies and by many global bureaucrats.

Additionally, AIG's Financial Products unit has been overseen for years by an SEC-approved monitor. AIG also made the same bets on housing using money in its securities lending program, which was heavily regulated at the state level. State, foreign and various U.S. federal regulators were all looking over AIG's shoulder and approving the bad housing bets.

Most of AIG's troubles began in 2005 when the company's board buckled under pressure from then New York Attorney General Eliot Spitzer, driven by his personal animosity, when it fired longtime CEO Hank Greenberg. Almost immediately, Fitch took away the company's triple-A credit rating, which allowed it to borrow at cheaper rates. AIG subsequently announced an earnings restatement. The restatement addressed alleged accounting sins that Mr. Spitzer trumpeted initially but later dropped from his civil complaint.

Other elements of the restatement were later reversed by AIG itself. But the damage had been done. The restatement triggered more credit ratings downgrades. Mr. Greenberg's successors seemed to understand that the game had changed, warning in a 2005 SEC filing that a lower credit rating meant the firm would likely have to post more collateral to trading counterparties. But rather than managing risks even more carefully, they went in the opposite direction. Tragically, they did what Mr. Greenberg's AIG never did, which was to bet big on housing.

Current AIG CEO Ed Liddy was picked by the government in 2008. It is on Mr. Liddy's watch that AIG has lately been conducting a campaign to stoke fears of "systemic risk." To mute objections to taxpayer cash infusions, AIG's lobbying materials suggest that taxpayers need to continue subsidizing the insurance giant to avoid economic ruin. Among the more dubious claims is that AIG policyholders won't be able to purchase the coverage they need. In truth, it is a competitive market place. Regarding those infamous bonuses, AIG can argue that it needs to pay top dollar to survive in an ultra-competitive business, or it can argue that it offers services not otherwise available in the market, but not both.

Obama and other Liberal politicians want to focus on bonuses because it aims public anger on private individuals who cannot defend themselves, not the Liberal political class who kicked off AIG's demise by ousting Mr. Greenberg, for failing to supervise its bets, and then for blowing a mountain of taxpayer cash on their AIG nationalization.

HALL OF SHAME

Whatever its contempt for the upper middle class that acquires wealth through salaried work and bonuses, Obama still has eyes for the hedge fund class, which will be ladled out taxpayer dollars to make one-way bets on problematic bank assets.

Geithner should have quelled this furor before it ever got started. Instead he played dumb and climbed aboard the outrage bandwagon and Obama did the same.

There is not a shred of justice in the hysteria that followed. As AIG Chief Ed Liddy explained on the Hill last week, the people receiving retention bonuses were not the same people who launched AIG's housing bets that brought the company down. Those people were gone.

Those who remained had been asked a year ago to stay and work themselves out of a job. In accepting the terms offered to them, they committed no offense (say, failing to pay taxes). Their only crime was possessing marketable knowledge -- all the more marketable because of the opportunity for hedge funds and other counterparties to profit from AIG's distress. Had the company submitted to Chapter 11 rather than a government takeover, a bankruptcy judge might well have authorized identical incentives to minimize losses and maximize recovery for legitimate stakeholders.

In numerous internal AIG e-mails and memos there were many months of assurances to Financial Products employees that the insurance giant would honor those contracts. The retention plan had been disclosed over and over in public filings. As far back as October, New York Attorney General Andrew Cuomo had summoned the Treasury-appointed Liddy to hammer out a deal on AIG's pay practices. Cuomo said in a statement afterwards: "These actions are not intended to jeopardize the hard-earned compensation of the vast majority of AIG's employees, including retention and severance arrangements, who are essential to rebuilding AIG and the economy of New York."

Obama's one honorable choice was to insist on the bonuses' legality. However politically inopportune the bonuses may be, the President has forever destroyed his credibility by authorizing a feel-good, bipartisan hate storm aimed at innocent AIG employees.

Barney Frank bullied Liddy into violating the privacy rights of his employees. Liddy, who is doing his job with personal sacrifice, is blamed by Congress too cowardly to do anything but place blame on others and throw away taxpayer money.

The biggest lesson is the old one that the price of freedom is eternal vigilance, beginning with insistence on the rule of law. Americans clearly cannot trust their elected officials to defend their rights and interests, or care whether justice is served, when the slightest political risk might attach to doing so.

Cuomo has been threatening to publish names of AIG employees who don't relinquish pay they were contractually entitled to have. Cuomo is a thug but so are his Liberal fellow travelers in this Hall of Shame including the President of the USA. He is also manipulative and week kneed and easily manipulated himself, a point that will not be lost on our foreign adversaries.

PAYMENTS FROM AIG

In 2008, Barack Obama was paid $104,332 and Christopher Dodd $103,900 by AIG. How can we respect these people?

Chapter 3 ... ... Bailouts

WHERE HAS PRIVATE EQUITY GONE?

Vikram Pandit of almost nationalized Citigroup says: "We have gone from arm's length, free market, just-in-time availability of funding to a system where big credit-reliant businesses now have only one place to turn, government." He is parroting from a play book that will delight his new masters in Congress.

The original Troubled Asset Relief Program (TARP) is now considered to be idiocy. The debate never progressed beyond whether Washington would pay face value or discount value for the bad mortgages it would have taken off banks' books. Instead the money was spent on more bad loans and continued wasteful operating excesses.

Now Washington is trying a Hail Mary being executed in taxpayers' name by the federal government. The hope is that all the money ($8 trillion or so) being printed to acquire or insure mortgages, student loans, credit card receivables, commercial paper and banking shares will be seamlessly withdrawn once those assets are sold back to willing parties in the private sector when the Liberal induced panic has passed.

The reality was that a deep recession was always unavoidable by government action. It was created by government excesses over decades and when the bubble burst, a painful deleveraging had to occur. Trying circumvention makes it worse. TARP is now to become TAMP (the Troubled Asset Multiplication Program) as public money is shoveled at mortgages that will continue to go bad and failing companies that will continue to fail. Detroit will have increasing company.

The U.S. was not like Japan when we started but it will be like Japan after Liberal government has destroyed free enterprise. The Japanese had a much more closed financial system when entering their post-bubble lost decade of the 1990s. We have venture capital, private equity, hedge funds, and an entrepreneurial tradition. The problem is that government interference, government fear mongering and cheap government credit has driven financial entrepreneurs to the sidelines. We may be able to roll over the resulting mounting federal debt at cheap rates for a while if international markets and the Chinese in particular continue to support us, but it is inevitable that the bailout's end result will be towering tax rates, drastic spending cuts and crippling inflation.

EXACTLY HOW DOES STIMULUS WORK

The President and his team espouse intellectual arrogance. David Axelrod claims that people are not concerned about "this detail or that detail".

Coming after four months of the TARP's dizzying billions spent in futility, we have a President spending nearly $1,000,000,000,000 on what he calls "stimulus." In the White House and in Congress, the "stimulus" has become a magical incantation, requiring no explanation beyond that it is "necessary".

The theory beneath the $800 billion of spending is called the Keynesian multiplier, first posited around 1931. Barnstorming in Elkhart, Ind., Mr. Obama took a shot at explaining it, calling the weatherization of homes "an example of where you get a multiplier effect."

The administration's primary technical explanation for how this spending revives an economy is in a paper prepared during the transition by Mr. Obama's economic advisers Christina Romer and Jared Bernstein. To arrive at the number of new jobs the bill would create, the Romer-Bernstein paper attempted to "simulate the effects of the prototypical (stimulus) package on GDP." The multiplier, as they explain, is applied to a given amount of federal spending to arrive at the likely effect on GDP. On the basis that 1% of GDP equals 1 million jobs, they conclude that 3,675,000 jobs will be created.

These voodoo economics ignore that without any stimulus, market forces will bring about a recovery from the recession later this year according to the normal trend of past cycles.

Much of the spending is a massive cash transfer to the Democratic Party's union constituencies and a percentage of that cash will flow back into the 2010 congressional races. The bill is a Trojan horse of Liberal policies not related to anyone's model of economic stimulus.

MORE FREE HANDOUTS OBAMA STYLE

Obama is promoting a recovery plan that would feature spending on roads and other infrastructure projects, energy-efficient government buildings, new and renovated schools and environmentally friendly technologies.

There would also be some form of tax relief, according to the Obama team, which is well aware of the political difficulty of pushing such a large package through Congress, even in a time of recession. Any tax cuts would be aimed at middle- and lower-income taxpayers, and aides have said there would be no tax increases for wealthy Americans.

While some economists consulted by Obama's team recommended spending of up to $1 trillion over two years, a more likely figure seems to be $850 billion. There is concern that a package that looks too large could worry financial markets, and the incoming economic team also wants to signal fiscal restraint.

In addition to spending on roads, bridges and similar construction projects, Obama is expected to seek additional funds for numerous programs that experience increased demand when joblessness rises. Among those programs are food vouchers and other nutrition programs, health insurance, unemployment insurance and job training programs.

Obama's goal is to preserve or create 2.5 million jobs over two years.

Obama is still living with "Dreams." He will claim success by the jobs that he preserves since there is no way that this number can be verified.

David J. Phillips

$787 BILLION STIMULUS BILL

Friday, February 13, 2009, Congress passed a $787 billion stimulus package designed to jump-start the U.S. economy for immediate signature by President Obama. Most of the stimulus package is a mystery even to the people who wrote it and certainly to the people who approved it. Some aspects are as follows -

Timelines for Appropriations

The bill is designed to provide funding for projects that are "shovel ready"; that is, ready to be implemented immediately. President Obama's stated goal is to create jobs as quickly as possible in order to boost consumer spending and consumer confidence. The final version of the bill implements this goal by setting deadlines for all appropriations: Unless otherwise indicated by a specific provision, all funding made available by the bill will expire on September 30, 2010.

Businesses, states, local governmental entities, and individuals should act quickly to position themselves to receive grants of stimulus funding or the funding will expire.

General Provisions

"Buy American" provision that requires the use of American iron, steel, and manufactured goods whenever economical and consistent with international trade agreements

Requirement that competitive bid and grant procedures be used

All appropriations will expire at the end of the current fiscal year unless otherwise designated.

Energy Efficiency and Renewable Energy Programs—$16.8 billion total

$3.2 billion for energy efficiency and conservation block grants to States
$2.5 billion for applied research, development, and demonstration and deployment activities for renewable energy technology

$5 billion for the Weatherization Assistance Program
$2.1 billion for competitive grants to States with green building energy codes for residential and commercial buildings
$2.0 billion for grants for the manufacturing of advanced batteries

Fossil Energy Research and Development

Note: The stimulus bill appropriates the $3.4 billion as a block grant to the Department of Energy. The conference report provides insight into Congress's intent regarding how the Department of Energy should allocate the funding. The following items are drawn from the conference report.

$1 billion for fossil energy research and development programs
$800 million for Clean Coal Power Initiative program
$1.52 billion for competitive solicitation for a range of industrial carbon capture and energy efficiency improvement projects, including a small allocation for innovative concepts for beneficial CO_2 reuse
$50 million for competitive solicitation for site characterization activities in geologic formations
$20 million for geologic sequestration training and research grants
$10 million for program direction funding

Innovative Technology Loan Guarantee Program—$6 billion total

Three types of projects are eligible: (1) Renewable energy systems; (2) Electric power transmission systems; and (3) leading edge biofuels projects currently performing at the pilot or demonstration scale

Department of Energy to consider several factors in making loan guarantees, including (1) viability of project without guarantees; (2) availability of other federal and state incentives; (3) importance of the project in meeting reliability needs; (4) effect of the project in meeting a State or region's environment (including climate change) and energy goals

Maximum of $500 million to be allocated to leading edge biofuels projects

Program will expire on September 30, 2011

David J. Phillips

Energy Tax Incentives

Extension of renewable energy production tax credit for certain renewable technologies, including wind, closed-loop biomass, open-loop biomass, geothermal, small irrigation, hydropower, landfill gas, waste-to-energy, and marine renewable facilities

Opportunity for entities eligible for the renewable energy production tax credit to instead elect to claim an investment tax credit

Some limitations repealed on credits for renewable energy property

Additional allocations provided for issuance of new clean renewable energy and qualified energy conservation bonds

Incentives extended and expanded for non-business energy property, e.g. energy efficient building property

New credit created for qualified investments in advanced energy projects, i.e., projects that re-equip, expand, or establish a manufacturing facility for the production of products that generate or facilitate the generation of renewable energy or clean fossil technology

Several new credits created for plug-in electric vehicles

Other Energy Funding and Provisions

$4.5 billion for electricity delivery, energy reliability programs, and smart grid programs

$400 million to fund the Advanced Research Projects Agency–Energy, as authorized by the America COMPETES Act.

$483 million for non-defense environmental cleanup

$390 million for uranium enrichment decontamination and decommissioning fund

$330 million for Department of Energy science projects

Supplemental borrowing authority granted to the Bonneville Power Administration and the Western Area Power Administration

Interior, Environment, and Related Agencies

$5.127 billion for Defense Environmental Cleanup
$600 million for Hazardous Substance Superfund
$200 million for Leaking Underground Storage Tank Trust Fund Program
$6.4 billion for assistance grants to States and Tribes to administer environmental programs
$750 million for National Park Service operation and construction
$280 million for United States Fish and Wildlife Service resource management and construction
$1.15 billion for Forest Service capital improvement, maintenance, and wild land fire management

A TRILLION DOLLARS

Abandoning any pretence of bipartisan behavior, Barack Obama and his Liberal fellow travelers have blasted through an economic stimulus package which will exceed $1 trillion after the inevitable corrupt add-ons.

$1 trillion is about one-third of annual U.S. government spending and 13% of the U.S. economy. It is more than the GDP of all but 12 countries in 2007 (America, Japan, Germany, China, the U.K., France, Italy, Spain, Canada, Brazil, Russia and India, in that order). A trillion dollars is also:

- The difference between George W. Bush's budgets of 2002 and 2008 -- the former being the first in U.S. history to exceed $2 trillion, the latter being the first to exceed $3 trillion.
- The minimum deficit expected for 2009.
- One-sixth of the entire outstanding U.S. federal debt held by the public, one-tenth including intragovernmental debt such as Social Security IOUs.
- The drop in market capitalization of the American financial industry since last October.
- The cost that Al Gore attaches to his plan to liberate the U.S. of carbon-based energy.
- Not even close to the unfunded liability of Medicare, which is $36 trillion over the next 75 years.

In comparison in inflation-adjusted dollars:

- The Apollo space program cost $140 billion between 1961 and 1972, while the Manhattan project to develop the atomic bomb to ensure victory in World War 2 cost $29 billion.
- Thomas Jefferson purchased Louisiana for $261 million ($15 million in 1803).
- The Panama Canal opened in 1914 after the U.S. had spent $7 billion.
- The New Deal cost $500 billion ($32 billion in the 1930's).
- Eisenhower's interstate highway system, which still remains the largest public works project in the U.S., took 35 years and cost $800 billion. (It was originally estimated to take 12 years and cost $25 billion at that time).

BARACK TO THE RESCUE

President Obama said his plan to prevent home foreclosures will not rescue the unscrupulous or irresponsible by throwing good taxpayer money after bad loans and it will not reward folks who bought homes they knew from the beginning they would never be able to afford.

Wrong Again. The only certainty of this latest Obama gamble is that it will do all of the above. The good news is that the plan will help some struggling homeowners who deserve help. But by investing in failure, the Administration will also prolong the housing downturn and make financing a home purchase more difficult for future borrowers.

Meanwhile, the plan isn't likely to slow the continuing decline in housing prices.

Anyone with mortgages owned or guaranteed by Fannie Mae and Freddie Mac will be able to refinance to lower rates if his mortgage is between 80% and 105% of the value of the home. This sweet deal is not available to renters looking to buy homes now. For those who deferred home ownership until they could afford it, the 20% down payment has now once again become the industry standard. Galling to them is also that their taxes will allow other people to stay in homes they can't afford.

Existing borrowers who may not qualify for Fan/Fred refinancing can still receive loan modifications that move their mortgage payments down to 31% of monthly income. In either case, no effort will be made to verify that recipients of aid were truthful on their original mortgage applications.

Given that mortgage fraud skyrocketed during the housing boom, and that the Obama Administration intends to assist up to nine million troubled borrowers, the unscrupulous will be among those rescued. Obama is not truthful.

Under the previous plan, the number of loans modified in the first quarter that were 30 or more days delinquent was 37 percent after three months and 55 percent after six months. Re-default rates increase each month and showed no signs of leveling off after six months. The magical figure of 31% will lower re-defaults but at a substantial cost to taxpayers. Only by putting an astronomical price tag on this plan, will the Administration fix most of the loans for the long term.

The program encourages mortgage servicers to keep the payments low only for five years, after which rates will rise. These are the problematic "teaser" rates once again. Modifications also may extend the term of, say, a 30-year mortgage to 40 years, but still leave the borrower underwater. Borrowers without equity are not a good bet to stay current.

Mr. Obama's mortgage plan is his third big economic rescue proposal in a month. The financial markets will once again react with scorn. As one analyst said, "Obama speaks, market listens, sells off."

What investors, businesses and working Americans want to hear is a President with ideas to spur economic recovery. They do not want another bailout for freeloaders which will make the problem worse and more prolonged for everyone else. Unfortunately freeloaders will become an increasing majority under Obama. That will ensure a perpetuation of him and Liberal ideology and will mean a smaller pie for everyone to share. That though is still a better deal if you are a free loader so long as the fat cats can be made to take an increasingly smaller share.

THE FED AS ATM

With the country sinking deeper into recession, the Federal Reserve is making additional risky moves to revive the economy. The Fed will spend $300 billion to buy long-term government bonds and an additional $750 billion in mortgage-backed securities guaranteed by Fannie Mae and Freddie Mac. The Fed has decided to be the ATM for the credit markets. In response the stock market posted gains and government bond prices soared. Heralding a coming drop in mortgage rates, the yield on the benchmark 10-year Treasury note dropped to 2.50 percent from 3.01 percent which was the biggest daily drop in percentage points since 1981. The dollar, meanwhile, fell against other major currencies, signaling that the Fed's intervention will spur inflation over the long run. That means that we will all pay the price for the dollar being worth less and being able to buy even less. That is the inevitable cost of increasing the supply of money by printing without producing more goods or value.

NO SHORTAGE OF LIQUIDITY

There is no shortage of liquidity. It is just moving to safety from those who will misappropriate it, namely crooks and Liberal government.

Investors traumatized by the Bernard Madoff scandal will continue to redeem hedge fund shares in droves, shrinking the industry by 30% this year to as low as $1 trillion. That was the size of the industry in 2005. Hedge funds averaged declines of 19% last year. At the end of 2008, the hedge fund industry stood at $1.4 trillion, after being hit with $152 billion in redemptions, or 9% of assets, in the fourth quarter. Last June, the industry was much larger—$2.7 trillion.

Money market funds netted $10.71 billion in the week ended March 11, even as the seven-day simple yield fell to a record low of 29 basis points. Assets in money funds now total $3.835 trillion. Taxable funds took in $7.06 billion, hitting a record $3.35 trillion. Within this category, prime funds rose by $9.21 billion, and government funds lost $2.15 billion. Tax-free funds reaped $3.65 billion.

Data for the week ended March 4, shows that long-term mutual funds lost $21.17 billion, fueled by $19.75 billion in withdrawals from stock funds.

THE REAL STIMULUS BURDEN

We will pay for it in many ways, for many years.

The stimulus bill will mark the largest single-year increase in domestic federal spending since World War II; it will send the budget deficit to heights not seen in 60 years; and it will establish a new and much higher spending baseline for years to come. We are about to test the limits of our national balance sheet.

The original economic theory behind this bill was to spend the money quickly to create jobs fast. But even the most talented spenders on Capitol Hill couldn't find enough projects to fund in such a rush. So they spread out the largesse over several years -- long after everyone hopes the recession is over. Some of these stimulus payments won't hit the economy until after the 2016 Olympics.

Our Liberal Congress wants us to believe that the money which will be spent on their favorite programs will vanish after two or three years. This chicanery ignores the last half-century of budget politics. Spending never declines; at best it merely fails to grow as fast as the economy.

Far more plausibly, our Liberal Congress will take the stimulus increases and make them part of a new, higher baseline for future spending growth. Anyone who proposes to cut from that amount will be denounced as a non-compassionate conservative.

Now that President Obama has opened the floodgates does he really believe that he can persuade his colleagues in Congress to stop spending? He is not that naïve. His dishonesty is clear.

If Congress continues to fund the most politically untouchable programs at their new stimulus levels, deficits will soar. These programs include Pell Grants, Head Start money for poor children, nutrition programs for seniors, Medicaid, special education and food stamps.

The stimulus bill will increase the 2009 budget deficit dramatically. It is already the largest in modern history. In the Reagan years, the peak deficit was only 6% of GDP in 1983. At the start of the Clinton presidency, the peak deficit was 3.9% of GDP. CBO estimates the 2009 deficit will reach 8.3% of the economy, not including the stimulus or bank bailout cash. With these included, the deficit could hit nearly $2 trillion, or 13.5% of the U.S. economy.

These levels are uncharted territory, especially if the economic recovery is weak as it probably will be. The new spending means new federal debt in the trillions of dollars over the next few years, which will test the limits of America's credit-worthiness. To the extent that taxes rise to pay for it all, the

U.S. will become less desirable as a destination for the world's capital, its people and its companies. Theft through inflation will only make matters worse.

BANK BAILOUTS ARE DOOMED

Fed Chairman Ben Bernanke and Treasury Secretary Tim Geithner were, as Fed officials, among the chief architects of easy money and are therefore largely responsible for the credit bubble that created the mess that we are in. Worse, their commitment to meddling in markets has only intensified with the adoption of near-zero interest rates and massive bank bailouts. They are the wrong people to lead us out of the present crisis.

The best policy response would be to do nothing and let the free market correct the excesses brought about by unforgivable policy errors. Further interventions through ill-conceived bailouts and bulging fiscal deficits are bound to prolong the agony and lead to another slump -- possibly an inflationary depression with dire social consequences.

From the beginning, the handling of the U.S. crisis has been politicized. The partisanship is as toxic as the bad assets on bank balance sheets. President Obama is now coming up with schemes to impede the process of foreclosing on homeowners who can't afford their homes, which would get those homes into the hands of new owners who can afford them. Does anyone believe that a government controlled bank will squeeze homeowners?

We know how the government runs financial institutions. We only have to look at Fannie Mae and Freddie Mac or IndyMac, whose management by the FDIC has inflated the rescue costs through its Liberal loan-modification program. A money-center bank in the hands of Liberal government is a conduit for politicized lending and grants disguised as loans. That's what's happened at Fannie and Freddie. Liberal government will never let go of its political ATM from a bank such as Citi.

Mr. Geithner wants a public-private partnership to buy toxic assets from banks. All that government has done thus far has only scared private money off. As bankers now realize, when you turn to the government for financial assistance you take on an untrustworthy partner. Outside money will not come in only to see its investment diluted later on when the government injects additional funds.

Rather than focusing on ways in which we can further involve the government in the financial system, we need to find ways to extricate banks from government's deadly embrace. Banks, at least the behemoths, were public-private partnerships before the crisis. Deposit insurance, access to the Fed's lending, and the implicit (now explicit) government guarantee for banks "too big to fail" all constituted a system of financial corporatism. It must be ended not extended.

If a bank is too big to fail, then it is simply too big. Those institutions need to be downsized until their failure would no longer constitute a systemic risk. Then we can discuss how to untangle the government and the major banks, and create a banking system of genuinely private institutions.

Liberals would like to believe that more money will fix the messes of our financial institutions, ignoring the unpalatable truth that the system is insolvent. In the past 12 months, taxpayers, sovereign wealth funds and private investors have sunk $1 trillion into failing U.S. and British financial institutions, while central banks have slashed their cost of funds to nothing and their collateral standards even lower. Yet major banks continue to collapse. The hole at the bottom of bank vaults is simply too big to fill even by governments that can mass-produce money with the press of a button. The math is not complicated. Bank losses from the write-offs of bad loans and busted derivatives tally up to $1.5 trillion so far. In addition, $5 trillion to $10 trillion worth of off-balance-sheet businesses such as structured investment vehicles - leveraged lending vehicles used by big banks to fatten their profits in boom times - are being forced back to banks' balance sheets by regulators. Rules require banks to keep a base of real shareholder capital amounting to 10% of those funds. So banks need to find up to $1 trillion within the next year to meet that objective. Add the $1.5 trillion in losses to $1 trillion in needed new reserves, and it is clear that banks need as much as $2.5 trillion in new capital to remain solvent under current rules.

In aggregate, the entire system is simply insolvent, as liabilities are greater than assets. Obama does not want to face the truth assuming that he understands it. Investors are not so gullible and that is why big banks' shares have lost most of their value. The Obama administration in trying desperately to help banks plug the gap will continue to come up short. $500 billion from sovereign wealth funds plus the $500 billion from the first tranche of the Troubled Assets Relief Program is $1 trillion. That still leaves a gap of $1.5 trillion.

It is difficult to understand why the Bush administration created TARP in the first place. The problem was that to do nothing would have been political suicide with an election looming and a Liberal bandwagon in motion, so $500 billion basically bought time until the election was over. Unfortunately the only answer that Liberal government knows is more of the same drugs that caused the fatal addiction. It is the worst of times to have a Liberal government.

The banking system simply has no capital. All the money that's been allocated so far has been like pouring water into a bucket with a hole in the bottom. We cannot have a bankrupt banking system and so the market has priced in the inevitable: nationalization of most large banks. If your owner can print money, you don't need to keep any reserves. Problem solved.

Nationalization is only radical in that banks would have to issue equity to the government, a process that wipes out current shareholders. Most bank stocks would go to zero. Such banks will be run completely differently going forward in that they will not have to answer to shareholders on a quarterly basis, they will not be able to pay high salaries to executives and they will only make loans that the government believes to be in the public interest. Of course, our Liberal government will say the banks will be privatized eventually, but realistically we are on course for decades of government ownership. Government bureaucrats will make even more inane lending mistakes, like giving mortgages to low-income families with inadequate means of repayment. They would almost certainly not support lending to hedge funds or providing money for leveraged buyouts, or do much merger-and-acquisition financing at all. Nor provide money to entrepreneurs to create the giants of to-morrow like Microsoft and Hewlett Packard.

A flavor of what is to come is in our present nationalized businesses such as Amtrak, the government-run rail system. We already have mortgage lenders Fannie Mae and Freddie Mac under federal control. We also have the post office. Enough said.

The best course of action, which would have been the most painful in the short term but beneficial in the long term, would have been to force banks to open all their books to regulators and investors, allowing us to see which were solvent and which were not. Then the FDIC could have closed the bad banks and merged their assets into strong banks.

CHAPTER 4 ... ... BANKS

FANNIE AND FREDDIE

Congress has completed its self-absolution through its own Hearings where it released some papers but not others that would be damaging to the hypocrites undertaking the investigation.

The two government-sponsored mortgage giants have long maintained they were merely unwitting victims of a financial act of God. That is, while the rest of the market went crazy over subprime and "liar" loans, Fan and Fred claimed to be the grownups of the mortgage market. There they were, the fable goes, quietly underwriting their 80% fixed-rate 30-year mortgages when they were blindsided by the greedy excesses of the subprime lenders who lacked their scruples.

Internal documents tell a different story. Memos and emails at the highest levels of Fannie and Freddie management in 2004 and 2005 paint a picture of two companies that saw their market share eroded by such products as option-ARMs and interest-only mortgages. The two companies were prepared to walk ever further out on the risk curve to maintain their market position.

The companies understood the risks they were running. But squeezed between the need to meet affordable-housing goals set by HUD and the desire to sustain their growth and profits, they took the leap anyway. As a result, by the middle of this year, the two companies were responsible for some $1.6 trillion worth of subprime credit of one form or another. They were the central players, in the creation of the housing boom and the credit bust.

Fannie and Freddie spent millions on lobbying to ensure that regulators did not get in their way. Freddie spent $11.7 million in lobbying in 2006 alone. Documents prove beyond doubt that Fan and Fred turbocharged the housing mania with a taxpayer-backed, congressionally protected business model that has cost America dearly.

FANNIE AND FREDDIE BONUSES

Fannie Mae and Freddie Mac expect to pay about $210 million in retention bonuses to 7,600 employees over 18 months, according to a letter from the mortgage companies' regulator. The maximum retention bonus for any individual executive under the plan will total $1.5 million during the 18 months ending in early 2010. $51 million of the payouts were made in late 2008 and the rest are to be made this year and early in 2010.

Freddie's retention-bonus program involves 4,057 employees, or about 80% of the total head count, while Fannie is making the payments to 3,545 employees, or 61%.

During 2009, 92 Freddie employees are due to receive retention bonuses of at least $100,000 and one person will receive more than $675,000. At Fannie, 121 employees will get bonuses of at least $100,000 and the maximum payout will be $705,000. The bonuses this year are to be paid in two installments, one in April and the second in November. Hundreds of other Fannie employees also are eligible for retention awards, but the company disclosed only the largest of the bonuses.

These organizations lost more than $100 billion in a year and bonuses to these Government run enterprises were made with an infusion of cash from taxpayers. Washington has so far not vented the anger that it directed at AIG. That presumably is because these quasi- Government behemoths are beloved by Liberals.

Both companies, which are a continuing sink for tax payer dollars, have enormous losses as a consequence of Liberals in government, using them as a mechanism to achieve home ownership for people who were not credit approved for conventional loans. They are essentially nationalized entities propped up by taxpayers.

FANNIE MAE

On Feb. 26, 2009, Fannie Mae posted a fourth-quarter net loss of $25.2 billion amid massive fair-value losses and credit-related expenses. In addition, the company submitted a request for an additional $15.2 billion from the U.S. Department of the Treasury in order to help reduce Fannie's net worth deficit.

FREDDIE CEO RESIGNS

Less than six months after the government installed him as Freddie Mac's leader, David Moffett resigned as chief executive on March 13th. Freddie Mac is still making big losses and will draw between an additional $30 billion and $35 billion from a line of credit at the Treasury Department.

CITIGROUP

As Citigroup unveiled its third government bailout in five months, the embattled New York Company offered little hope that it will return to ongoing profitability any time soon. On Feb. 27, 2009, Citigroup reached a deal for the US government to take a larger stake in the bank. Under the plan, Citigroup will exchange up to $27.5 billion of existing preferred securities for common stock at a conversion price of $3.25 a share. The company will reconstitute its board to include a majority of new directors beholden to Liberal government. It said of the 15 current directors, three will not stand for reelection, two will reach retirement age and it will announce new directors soon.

The federal government has now taken a 36% stake in the $2.02 trillion-asset company CEO Pandit said: "In the end, our business is about confidence. Investors seemed anything but confident, sending Citi's shares down to less than a dollar. In March 2006, the company's shares changed hands at $45 a share.

The company is now worth about $ 5 billion, down from $244 billion two years ago. Waves of layoffs have accompanied that slide, with about 75,000 jobs already gone or set to disappear from a work force that numbered about 375,000 a year ago.

The bank's downfall was years in the making and involved many in its hierarchy, particularly Charles O. Prince III, Citigroup's chief executive and Robert E, Rubin, an influential director and senior adviser. Mr. Prince and Mr. Rubin played pivotal roles in the bank's current woes, by drafting and blessing a strategy that involved taking greater trading risks to expand its business and reap higher profits.

When he was Treasury secretary during the Clinton administration, Mr. Rubin helped loosen Depression-era banking regulations that made the creation of Citigroup possible by allowing banks to expand far beyond their traditional role as lenders and permitting them to profit from a variety of financial activities. During the same period he helped beat back tighter oversight of exotic financial products. Since joining Citigroup in 1999 as a trusted adviser to the bank's senior executives, Mr. Rubin, who was an economic adviser on the transition team of President-elect Barack Obama, has sat atop a bank that has been roiled by one financial miscue after another.

Citigroup was ensnared in murky financial dealings with the defunct energy company Enron, which drew the attention of federal investigators; it was criticized by law enforcement officials for the role one of its prominent research analysts played during the telecom bubble several years ago; and it found itself in the middle of regulatory violations in Britain and Japan.

For a time, Citigroup paid off handsomely, as it rang up billions in earnings each quarter from credit cards, mortgages, merger advice and trading. When Citigroup's trading machine began churning out billions of dollars in mortgage-related securities, it courted disaster. As it built up that business, it used accounting maneuvers to move billions of dollars of the troubled assets off its books, freeing capital so the bank could grow even larger.

Robert Rubin helped push Citigroup along this new path. He has responded lamely that his role was peripheral to the bank's main operations even though he was one of its highest-paid officials making ten million dollars a year for ten years.

Robert Rubin has moved seamlessly between Wall Street and Washington. After making his millions as a trader and an executive at Goldman Sachs, he joined the Clinton administration. Then Citigroup's chief executive at the time Sandy Weill wooed Mr. Rubin to join the bank as chairman of Citigroup's executive committee, serving on the Board after Rubin left

Washington. Subsequently Mr. Weill was a key influence in the financial services industry's lobbying to persuade Washington to loosen its regulatory hold on Wall Street.

GOLDMAN SACHS

Goldman Sachs has been working for months to overcome the government's restrictions on executive pay for TARP recipients.

Last year, 953 Goldman employees were paid in excess of $1 million apiece. The restrictions have severely crimped Goldman's ability to offer such lavish pay this year.

Goldman has taken fresh steps to break free: It has announced, as expected, that it plans to raise $5 billion by selling new common shares to investors, and that it would like to use the money to repay government bailout money received last year. The firm also reported stronger-than-expected first-quarter earnings of $1.81 billion.

The problem is that Obama does not want and might not allow Goldman Sachs to escape his leash.

UBS BONUSES

UBS has eliminated cash bonuses for the managing directors of its investment bank

Cracking down on bonuses appeases governments and the public, but also raises questions about a commitment to investment banking. UBS's investment bank has already been decimated by bad gambles on securities underpinned by mortgage loans.

Nevertheless successful bankers in other areas have individually earned tens and hundreds of million dollars for the bank this year and rely on the expected compensation from bonus payments, commensurate with this performance as the major part of their pay. That though was Capitalism.

The new Liberal power elite want to punish all bankers irrespective of their positive contributions. As a consequence, top bankers will go elsewhere, when they can find new jobs, while clients will fret about the potential loss of talent and they will also go elsewhere for their investment banking needs.

The lack of a cash bonus will create difficult financial situations for many bankers who will be unable to meet their obligations. That though will evoke little sympathy in comparison with the plight of the chronic unemployed where a kiss and a hug from President Obama is such a good media photo opportunity.

BANKING PROBLEMS

Foreclosures and bad loans raced through the banking industry in 2008, with the more than 8,000 U.S. banks registering a 149 percent increase in troubled assets, according to a new analysis of bank financial reports to the federal government.

While a large majority of banks were still healthy, 163 ended the year with more troubled loans than capital, up from only 13 a year earlier.

Nationwide, seven out of every 10 banks had less capital to cover potential loan losses than a year earlier. The analysis relies on information reported quarterly to the FDIC, calculating each bank's troubled asset ratio, which compares troubled loans against the bank's ability to withstand losses.

Although attention has focused on the largest banks, which hold the lion's share of deposits, the analysis shows how widespread the problems in the banking industry became in 2008 as the mortgage meltdown and broader recession unfolded.

REGULATORY MISSTEPS FUEL CRISIS

Washington's preferred stake in Citigroup might convert to common stock which will expand regulators' reach deeper into the company. That raises a disturbing question: Does the government know what it is doing?

There are few answers to an ever growing list of questions. The vacuum is undercutting the government in various ways, which is worsening the industry's problems. No one trusts regulatory capital standards anymore, so in their place analysts are using a much harsher yardstick, tangible common equity. This measure makes the banks look even weaker than they are.

With every twist of the bailout, government regulators have lost credibility. Regulators assured the market that Fannie Mae and Freddie Mac were well-capitalized just before putting both companies into conservatorship. They tried to fix what was wrong at Wachovia by merging it into Citi. Two merged disasters, both inadequately understood, would have created an even bigger mess. Fortunately Wells Fargo took over Wachovia saving the government from itself. The new administration is even more out of its depth than the previous one.

Political ideology is a big obstacle to taking the steps needed to resolve the crisis. There is uncertainty as to what to do next, with some Liberal politicians wanting to partially nationalize banks and others saying more capital injections are the answer.

The plan unveiled by Treasury Secretary Timothy Geithner on February 10th was not a plan. Short on details, Geithner said he wanted to stress-test large institutions to determine whether they had sufficient capital. He left it unclear how the stress tests would work. When the stress tests were announced, the idea was that regulators would examine which institutions were healthy enough to get more capital. Those that failed the test would be subject to supervisory action. Now it seems that the only consequence of failing a stress test would be to receive yet more money from the government.

Far from sorting out the healthy from the sick, the stress tests now appear geared to determining how much money an institution should receive. The conclusion is that the Obama administration is lost when it comes to fighting the financial crisis.

The government took too long to address mark-to-market accounting rules that have forced massive write-downs at banks and other financial companies. As a consequence short-sellers are able to spread rumors of an institution's impending collapse, so that pressure continues to build around a financial institution while the government finally decides to intervene or not.

Then those that get help—such as Citigroup and Bank of America—continue to be caught in a net of expectations on Wall Street. As regulators have provided unprecedented assistance to these two banking companies, including billions in capital and hundreds of billions in loan guarantees, the unanswered concern is the possibility that they will soon be taken over by the government. Unwillingness by government regulators to state policy turns investors away as they are concerned about being diluted.

OBAMA CONTROL

There's a reason Obama refuses to accept repayment of TARP money. Obama wants to control the banks, just as he now controls GM and Chrysler, and will surely control the health industry in the not-too-distant future. Keeping them TARP-stuffed is the key to control. And for this intensely political president, mere influence is not enough. The White House wants to tell them what to do.

By managing the money, Obama can steer the whole economy even more firmly down the left fork in the road. If the banks are forced to keep TARP money, which was often forced on them in the first place, the Obama team can work its will on the financial system to an unprecedented degree.

A bank with TARP money can be told where to lend. Special loans and terms can be offered to favored constituents, favored industries, or even favored regions. The Obama administration will be able to dictate pay for anyone working in any company that takes TARP money.

Class warfare has come to the USA.

CEO PAY

On Feb. 4, 2009, Obama unveiled a series of pay curbs, including a strict new limit on executive salaries for companies that receive "exceptional assistance." Under the new rules, companies that receive "exceptional assistance" from taxpayers may not pay any top executive more than $500,000 a year, an administration official said. Any additional compensation would have to be in restricted stock that will not vest until taxpayers have been repaid, the official said. It's not clear yet what counts as "exceptional assistance."

Moreover, all banks receiving help will face tougher restrictions, including requirements that shareholders have a say on compensation, and will face tougher disclosure rules on items such as aviation services, holiday parties and golden parachutes.

CHANGING THE RULES

The Financial Accounting Standards Board (FASB) rule makers have approved a plan to ease "mark-to-market" (MTM) accounting, allowing companies more leeway in valuing their investments. The revised rules allow companies to use their judgment to a greater extent in determining the "fair value" of their assets. The board also made it easier for companies to avoid having to take impairment charges against earnings when they suffer losses on their investments. Stocks jumped on the news, pushing the Dow Jones Industrial Average up more than 250 points as bank stocks rose.

MTM accounting isn't perfect, but it did provide a compass for investors to figure out what an asset would be worth in today's market if it were sold in an orderly fashion to a willing buyer. Before MTM took effect, the Financial Accounting Standards Board (FASB) produced much evidence to show that valuing financial instruments and other difficult-to-price assets by "historical" costs, or "mark to management," was folly. Pleas now to bubble-wrap financial statements run counter to increased calls for greater financial-market transparency and ongoing efforts to restore investor trust.

A group of investors and former regulators, the Investors' Working Group (IWG) have simultaneously voiced concerns about the independence of FASB. Specifically, IWG, which has in its ranks former Securities and Exchange Commission chiefs William Donaldson and Arthur Levitt, raised concerns about Liberal political and special interest groups pressuring FASB and how it sets accounting standards. It is critical to the well being of the USA that such standards are politically neutral and faithfully represent economic reality.

In a letter to Robert Herz, chairman of FASB, IWG voiced opposition to how changes were being made to accounting procedures. "We reiterate the concerns about the absence of adequate due process and failure to provide the basis for conclusions when amending a standard that has been applied for 15+ years, contrary to FASB's mission."

President Obama ignores the principle that justice must be done. When he has made that leap he can start to think that justice must also be seen to be done.

BANKS IN REVERSE GEAR

Lending at the nation's biggest banks has fallen, despite the Federal government pumping billions of dollars into them.

The biggest recipients of taxpayer aid made or refinanced 23% less in new loans in February, the latest available data, than in October, the month the Treasury kicked off the Troubled Asset Relief Program.

Small community banks are complaining loudly that they had nothing to do with the excesses of the big government controlled banks (notably Fannie Mae and Freddie Mac), freewheeling deals in the mortgage market and risky investments that precipitated the economic crisis.

In the meltdown's wake, community banks find themselves under tighter scrutiny from federal regulators. They say the $700 billion financial bailout has favored large institutions. And they are upset about a special assessment the government wants to charge to shore up the Federal Deposit Insurance Fund, which failed banks are draining.

CHAPTER 5 ... ... BLACKS

BLACK RACISM

Inevitably it was only a matter of time before the Obama administration would step up black racist rhetoric.

With the federal government's annual African American History Month celebrations as a backdrop, the attorney general, the first lady and the head of the Environmental Protection Agency have started to beat the racist drum.

Lisa P. Jackson, the EPA administrator and a native of New Orleans, told her staff about having grown up in an area where she would have had to drink from unsafe water fountains because of her race. "Now in 2009, I am, along with you, responsible for ensuring that all Americans have clean water to drink," Jackson said. "Change has certainly come to this agency."

First lady Michelle Obama hosted middle-school children in the White House East Room and taught the children about African Americans and their roles in the executive mansion: the slaves who built it, the signing of the Emancipation Proclamation there, the meetings held with civil rights leaders.

Attorney General Eric H. Holder Jr., used a key speech as an admonition that "to get to the heart of this country, one must examine its racial soul."

"Though this nation has proudly thought of itself as an ethnic melting pot, in things racial we have always been and continue to be, in too many ways, essentially a nation of cowards," Holder said. "Though race-related issues continue to occupy a significant portion of our political discussion, and though there remain many unresolved racial issues in this nation, we, average Americans, simply do not talk enough with each other about race."

CHIMPANZEE

The New York Post is apologizing for a cartoon that critics say links President Barack Obama to a raging chimpanzee shot dead by police in Connecticut. The paper said the cartoon was meant to mock the federal economic stimulus bill.

The drawing shows a dead chimp, with the caption reading: "They'll have to find someone else to write the next stimulus bill." The cartoon depicts police shooting an ape and plays on the real shooting of an enslaved chimpanzee which attacked the friend of its owner in Connecticut. Police shot and killed the 200-pound chimpanzee. The chimp, named Travis, had once starred in television commercials and was taking medication for Lyme disease.

Al Sharpton chanted "End racism now!" outside the parent company's offices in midtown Manhattan and called for the jailing of Rupert Murdoch who owns the Post.

We should be much more concerned about the derogatory references to chimpanzees, likening them to the bizarre behavior of people, including politicians. President Obama fits right into the Washington scene, having learned the tricks of the trade in Illinois. The one certainty already demonstrated, is that he has no clue how to resolve the economic issues in the USA and instead is continuing to inject fear into the Washington rhetoric which is making the situation worse. We need a commander-in-chief who projects confidence not a political opportunist who is a smart lawyer and nothing else.

JOCELYN FRYE

At Harvard Law School, they supported student demands for more professors of color and talked about how two black women might make their mark.

Jocelyn Frye became a proponent of affirmative action and workplace equity and an advocate for women and families in Washington. Michelle Obama became a Chicago community organizer and a hospital administrator working on free health care. Ms. Frye is now the first lady's policy and projects director, helping Mrs. Obama develop a policy platform and a presence in Washington. Ms. Frye, who also works for President Obama's domestic policy team, was granted a waiver to work for the administration despite rules that ban the employment of lobbyists.

Ms. Frye and Mrs. Obama share a passion for policies that affect black women and families. Charles J. Ogletree Jr., the black activist Harvard law professor mentored both Ms. Frye and Mrs. Obama.

A native Washingtonian, Ms. Frye has taken the lead in helping the Obamas integrate themselves into her community. Ms. Frye is the daughter of government workers; her mother worked for the Library of Congress and her father worked for military intelligence. She attended private schools and still lives in the predominantly black neighborhood where she grew up. At Harvard, she and others took over the dean's office to draw attention to the lack of faculty diversity. She is now arguing for equal pay for women in struggling families, particularly as growing numbers of women have become primary breadwinners.

Ms. Frye has organized visit by Mrs. Obama to various community institutions such as Mary's Center, a health clinic that serves poor immigrants, Howard University, a historic black college and Miriam's Kitchen, a nonprofit group that feeds the homeless.

She has also supported Mrs. Obama's decision to promote the President's legislative agenda, at odds with how first ladies have conducted themselves traditionally in avoiding discussing legislation.

GEORGE HUSSEIN ONYANGO OBAMA

You probably do not want to know as much as you already do about Obama's extended family in Kenya that he knew nothing about until he wanted to burnish his credentials and so made them a bizarre part of his life.

The White House has declined to comment on reports that U.S. President Barack Obama's half-brother was arrested in Kenya in January after police found him in possession of marijuana. Substance abuse is a topic about which President Obama is knowledgable but it is not now a topic that he would like to discuss.

George Hussein Onyango Obama, who is in his mid-20s, was arrested on the outskirts of Nairobi. He is the youngest half-brother of Barack Obama that we know of, born c.1982, son of Barack Obama Sr. and Jael (now a resident of Atlanta, Georgia). George was six months old when his father died in an automobile accident, after which he was raised in Nairobi by his mother and a French step-father. George Obama slept rough for several years, until he was given a six-by-eight foot corrugated metal shack in the Nairobi, Kenya slum of Huruma Flats.

KEZIA

Barack Obama's stepmother Kezia lives on welfare in England. She is now using the Obama name to make money on bingo on-line gaming.

She was married to his father, Barack Snr, in Nairobi when she was sixteen. Barack Sr, a Muslim, would go on to marry three or so more women - including Barack Jr's mother Ann Dunham, an American he met while on financial aide in Hawaii, and an American teacher Ruth, both of whom he married bigamously unless the rationale that Africans can marry multiples of woman prevails (as will be the case for the next President of South Africa).

Barack Obama's mother died in 1995 and Kezia now takes pride of place at special family gatherings. Kezia who was there to celebrate Barack Jr's 2005 inauguration as an Illinois senator and his inauguaration as President, even though she barely knows the President.

She met Barack Jr when he came to Kenya in 1985. As well as Auma, her eldest child and daughter, Kezia has three sons by Barack Snr. Her two youngest, Bernard and Abo, live in Nairobi. Bernard sells mechanical parts while Abo runs an international telephone shop. Their eldest son Roy studied at a madrasah in Nairobi before moving to the States where he is an accountant.

Barack Snr was a bigamist and died a drunk.By the summer of 1959, he was bound for Hawaii, leaving Kezia three months pregnant with Auma. There he was sexually intimate with Barack Jr's mother, Ann, in Honolulu. She was an 18-year-old fellow student and within months they were in a bigamist marriage. Barack Jnr was born in August, 1961. Two years later, Barack Snr was accepted at Harvard and left Ann and their little boy behind. He then married Ruth. His return to Kenya with Ruth was in 1965. Ruth's two sons with Barack Obama, Sr., are Mark and David Ndesandjo.

Barack Snr lost both legs in a car crash coming back from a nightclub. Barack Snr went on to become an economist in Jomo Kenyatta's government. He continued to see Kezia and had son Abo with her in 1968, followed by Bernard in 1970. Kindergarten head Ruth divorced Barack after seven years and now has the surname Ndesandjo. He then fathered at least one more son by another woman.

By the time of the split, Barack had lost his job and he returned to Kezia. Barack Snr was killed in 1982 in another car crash, before his son made his first trip to Kenya.

OBAMA'S AUNT

Obama's aunt, who had been living in the country illegally, can stay in the USA at least until next year. The aunt of Barack Obama was denied asylum by a judge four years ago. The Kenyan woman has been living illegally in a Boston neighborhood.

Zeituni Onyango is the half-sister of Obama's late father. She had been instructed to leave the country four years ago by an immigration judge who rejected her request for asylum from her native Kenya.

An immigration judge stayed her deportation order on Dec. 17. The judge reopened her case requesting asylum on Dec. 30, and she had a hearing on April 1 in a Boston immigration court. Now nothing will happen for another twelve months when she will have another hearing. At the brief hearing, a judge set her case to be heard Feb. 4, 2010. Onyango wore a curly red wig to the hearing. She declined to comment to reporters as she was led away from court by her attorneys and Federal Protective Service police.

Onyango, 56, first applied for asylum in 2002, but her request was rejected and she was ordered deported in 2004. She did not leave the country and continued to live in public housing in Boston. Her lawyer, Cleveland immigration attorney Margaret Wong, said in a statement that Onyango first applied for asylum 'due to violence in Kenya,' but she did not reveal what grounds she has cited in her renewed bid for asylum. The court hearing was closed at her lawyer's request. Onyango, the half-sister of Obama's late father, first moved to the United States in 2000. People who seek asylum must show that they face persecution in their homeland on the basis of religion, race, nationality, political opinion or membership in a social group.

Obama has said he did not know his aunt was living here illegally even though he invited his aunt and her lawyer to his inauguration. Onyango traveled to Washington for her nephew's inauguration. She attended an inaugural ball with Margaret Wong.

CHAPTER 6 ... ... CONGRESS

LIBERAL SUPERMAJORITY

Liberals have a filibuster-proof Senate or very close to it. Without the ability to filibuster, the Senate will become like the House, able to pass whatever the majority wants, giving one of the most profound political and ideological shifts in U.S. history. Liberals will dominate the entire government in a way they haven't since 1965, or 1933. We will experience the restoration of the activist government that fell out of public favor in the 1970s.

The most important power of the filibuster is to shape legislation, not merely to block it. The threat of 41 committed Senators can cause the House to modify its desires even before legislation comes to a vote. Without that restraining power, all of the following have very good chances of becoming law in 2009 or 2010.

- Medicare for all. When HillaryCare cratered in 1994, the Democrats concluded they had overreached, so they carved up the old agenda into smaller incremental steps, such as Schip for children. A strongly Democratic Congress is now likely to lay the final flagstones on the path to government-run health insurance from cradle to grave.

Obama wants to build a public insurance program, modeled after Medicare and open to everyone of any income. The Obama plan will shift between 32 million and 52 million from private coverage to the huge new entitlement. Like Medicare or the Canadian system, it will never be repealed.

The commitments would start slow, so as not to cause immediate alarm. But as U.S. health-care spending flowed into the default government options, taxes would have to rise or services would be rationed, or both. Single payer is the inevitable next step, as Mr. Obama has already said is his ultimate ideal.

- The business climate. Look for a replay of the Pecora hearings of the 1930s, with Henry Waxman, John Conyers and Ed Markey sponsoring ritual hangings to further their agenda to control more of the private economy. The financial industry will get an overhaul in any case, but telecom, biotech and drug makers, among many others, can expect to be investigated and face new, more onerous rules such as regulatory overkill like Sarbanes-Oxley. Punitive windfall profits tax will be enacted.

- Union supremacy. One program certain to be given right of way is 'card check'. Unions have been in decline for decades, now claiming only 7.4% of the private-sector work force, so Big Labor wants to trash the secret-ballot elections that have been in place since the 1930s. The "Employee Free Choice Act" would convert workplaces into union shops merely by gathering signatures from a majority of employees, which means organizers could strong arm those who opposed such a petition. The bill also imposes a compulsory arbitration regime that results in an automatic two-year union "contract" after 130 days of failed negotiation. The point is to force businesses to recognize a union whether the workers support it or not. This would be the biggest pro-union shift in the balance of labor-management power since the Wagner Act of 1935.

- Taxes. Taxes will rise substantially, the only question being how high. Obama would raise the top income, dividend and capital-gains rates for "the rich," substantially increasing the cost of new investment in the U.S. He also wants to lift or eliminate the cap on income subject to payroll taxes that fund Medicare and Social Security. This would convert what was meant to be a pension insurance program into an overt income redistribution program. It would also impose a probably unrepealable increase in marginal tax rates and a permanent shift upward in the federal tax share of GDP.

- The green revolution. A tax-and-regulation scheme in the name of climate change is a top left-wing priority. Cap and trade would hand Congress trillions of dollars in new spending from the auction of carbon credits, which it would use to pick winners and losers in the energy business and across the economy. Huge chunks of GDP and millions of jobs would be at the mercy of Congress and a vast new global-warming bureaucracy. Without the GOP votes to help stage a filibuster, Senators from carbon-intensive states would have less ability to temper coastal Liberals who answer to the green elites.

- Free speech and voting rights. A liberal supermajority would move quickly to impose procedural advantages that could cement Democratic rule for years to come. One early effort would be national, election-day voter registration. This is a long-time goal of Acorn and others on the "community organizer" left and would make it far easier to stack the voter rolls. The District of Columbia would also get votes in Congress -- Democratic, naturally. Felons may also get the right to vote nationwide, while the Fairness Doctrine is likely to be reimposed. A major goal of the supermajority left would be to shut down talk radio and other voices of political opposition.

- Special-interest potpourri. Look for the watering down of No Child Left Behind testing standards, as a favor to the National Education Association. The tort bar's ship would also come in, including limits on arbitration to settle disputes and watering down the 1995 law limiting strike suits. New causes of legal action would be sprinkled throughout most legislation. The anti-antiterror lobby will be rewarded with the end of Guantanamo and military commissions, which probably means trying terrorists in civilian courts.

In both 1933 and 1965, liberal majorities imposed vast expansions of government that have never been repealed, and the current financial panic will give today's left another pretext to return to those heydays of welfare-state Liberalism.

The recession will temper some of these ambitions but for how long?

HUGE SPENDING BILL

Knowing they have a patsy in the White House, The Liberals have used their super majority to pass a $410 billion measure to fund the government, sending it to President Barack Obama for his signature, which he will obediently do immediately.

The $410 billion bill is chock-full of lawmakers' pet projects and significant increases in food aid for the poor, energy research and other Pelosi type (read bull) programs. The bill ran into a political hailstorm in Congress from conservatives after Obama's spending-heavy economic stimulus bill and his

2010 budget plan forecasting a $1.8 trillion deficit for the current budget year. And Republicans seized on Obama's willingness to sign a bill packed with pet projects after he assailed them as a candidate. The Liberal supermajority makes passage inevitable.

The 1,132-page spending bill has an extraordinary reach, wrapping together nine spending bills to fund the annual operating budgets of every Cabinet department except for Defense, Homeland Security and Veterans Administration.

At issue is the approximately one-third of the budget passed each year by Congress for the operating budgets of Cabinet departments and other agencies. The rest of the budget is comprised of benefits programs such as Social Security, Medicare and Medicaid — as well as interest payments on the swelling $11 trillion national debt.

Adding in spending bills passed last year for Defense, Homeland Security and the Veterans Administration — as well as $288.7 billion in appropriated money in the stimulus bill — total appropriations so far for 2009 have reached $1.4 trillion. And that's before the Pentagon submits another $75 billion for the wars in Iraq and Afghanistan.

Obama's budget for next year calls for $1.3 trillion in appropriations.

The bill should be an embarrassment to President Obama, who promised during last year's campaign to force Congress to curb its pork-barrel ways; the bill contains 7,991 earmarks totaling $5.5 billions. Among the many earmarks is $485,000 for a boarding school for at-risk native students in western Alaska and $1.2 million for Helen Keller International so the nonprofit can provide eyeglasses to students with poor vision.

Generous above-inflation increases are spread throughout, including a $2.4 billion, 13 percent increase for the Agriculture Department and a 10 percent increase for the money-losing Amtrak passenger rail system. Other big increases include a 14 percent boost for a program that feeds infants and poor women and a 10 percent increase for housing vouchers for the poor.

Congress also awarded itself a 10 percent increase in its own budget, bringing it to $4.4 billion.

LIBERALS GONE WILD

Fresh from passing its $787 billion stimulus, and then attending President Obama's "fiscal responsibility summit," the House approved a bonus hike in the 2009 budget for most domestic agencies of 8%.

The $410 billion omnibus bill gives federal programs an extra $32 billion to spend for the seven months left in this fiscal year. Then these increases are added to the spending baseline in setting future budgets.

In total the increase in spending across nine federal categories combining the stimulus bill and the omnibus bill will go from $378.4 billion in 2008 to $679.6 billion in 2009, which is an 80% increase. Federal spending as a share of GDP will be 28%, which is by far the highest level since World War II.

The omnibus bill is also replete with 9,000 earmarks. These are the parochial projects that Obama and House Speaker Nancy Pelosi said they were going to rein in.

EARMARK MADNESS

Barack Obama signed the $410 billion omnibus spending bill in private to avoid questions about the $14.3 billion in earmarks, which he had pledged to eliminate.

Pork may be nature's purest form of stimulus spending. Most of these earmark projects have been shovel-ready for so long the shovels are rusting. Instead of hiding, President Obama should have signed all 8,570 earmarks (16 per Member of Congress on average) on the White House lawn. He should have celebrated the $2 million earmark for the Steptoe Street Extension in Kennewick, Washington, the $2.8 million for the Cesar Chavez/Calexico West Port of Entry Congestion Improvements in California and the $4 million earmark for West Virginia's Coalfields Expressway. Keynesian economics tell us that new workers will soon be spending the multiplier at Wal-Mart.

Earmarks often have irresistible American names: the Codorus Creek Watershed Restoration, Dog Island Shoals, Blue River, the Emiquon Preserve, Winnapaug Pond, Shortcut Canal and even Pleasure Island (in Maryland). Others are more mundane but just as questionable: Integrated Predated

Management Activities, the Lake Worth Sand Transfer Plant, the Vermont Farm Viability Program, Sustainable Beef Supply in Montana and $3.45 million for the Maine Machias River project.

The only question is how much of this taxpayer money finds its way into the pockets of the Members of Congress from a grateful electorate in each of their districts – in addition of course to helping ensure their re-election.

GOVERNMENT BY FEAR

Since public shaming and Congress' hyperbolic outrage had failed to cow all of the bonus-receiving executives to return the money, House Financial Services Committee Chairman Barney Frank demanded their names. If Liddy doesn't provide them, Frank said, he'll subpoena them.

Naming the executives wouldn't just jeopardize their lives, Liddy said, but those of their children. "'All of the executives and their families should be executed with piano wire around their necks,'" Liddy read into the microphone, from the text of one of the threats his company had received since news of the bonus payments exploded into the headlines over the weekend.

Liddy read from another: "'My greatest hope is that if the government can't do this properly, we, the people, will take it in our own hands and see that justice is done. I'm looking for all the CEOs names, kids, where they live, etc.'"

Liddy said he has no doubt that some of the bonus recipients will return the money, but they likely will hand in their resignations, as well.

Frank said during Liddy's testimony before the House Financial Services subcommittee that concern doesn't outweigh the public interest. Liddy said he would provide a list of names "only if I can be sure" it would remain confidential. But Frank said he couldn't promise that. "I ask that you will submit those names without restriction," he added.

Bank of America has also been forced to turn over list of bonus-receiving Merrill Lynch executives

BARNEY FRANK

Massachusetts Rep. Barney Frank called Supreme Court Justice Antonin Scalia a homophobe in a recent interview.

The Liberal lawmaker was discussing homosexual marriage and his expectation that the high court would some day be called upon to decide whether the Constitution allows the federal government to deny recognition to same-sex marriages.

"I wouldn't want it to go to the United States Supreme Court now because that homophobe Antonin Scalia has too many votes on this current court," said Frank.

Scalia dissented from the court's ruling in 2003 that struck down state laws banning consensual sodomy. He has complained about judges, rather than elected officials, deciding questions of morality about which the Constitution is silent. Controversial topics like homosexual rights and abortion should not be in the hands of judges, he has said, calling on people to persuade their legislatures or amend the Constitution.

This background is important as it is clear that Frank is not a person who would be concerned about the safety of the families of people who work for AIG. Frank does delight in anal sex with young males. In 1985, Frank engaged the services of a male escort named Stephen Gobie, who had advertised his "hot bottom" in a personal ad. Over the next two years, he and Gobie carried on a clandestine affair, during which time Frank hired Gobie as a driver despite knowing Gobie was on probation for drug possession and for possession of child pornography. Frank used his House privileges to fix Gobie's parking tickets. He wrote a memo trying to clear Gobie from probation that was a deception. Gobie ran a homosexual prostitution service out of Frank's Capitol Hill apartment.

CHAPTER 7 ... ...
CORRUPTION

CORRUPTION

Corruption is endemic in US politics at all levels. One needs to be a lawyer to know how to do it legally.

Corruption has become a major industry in Illinois with a long history of scoundrels and scandals. Corruption and graft have become so entrenched over the decades that they've become part of the political culture, and experts cite a list of reasons why: Weak state campaign finance laws that have allowed influence peddlers to make big contributions, lawmakers who don't always get close scrutiny, a patronage system that makes employees beholden to political bosses and a jaded public that seems to accept chicanery as the cost of doing business.

The state's history of rogues and crooks ranges from a long-ago secretary of state who died leaving hundreds of thousands of dollars mysteriously stashed in shoeboxes in his hotel closet to a judge who took money to fix murder cases. Former governors, congressmen, aldermen, and state and city workers have all gone to prison.

Top competitors for the title of the most corrupt state seem to be New Jersey and Louisiana. More than 130 public officials in New Jersey have been found guilty of federal corruption in the past seven years. Louisiana more than holds its own. A congressman once described the state this way: "Half of Louisiana is under water, and the other half is under indictment."

Louisiana also is known from its flamboyant governors, from Huey Long to Edwin Edwards, who is now sitting in prison for his involvement in a scheme to rig riverboat casino licensing.

Nationwide, more than 1,800 federal, state and local officials have been convicted of public corruption in the last two years, according to FBI statistics released this spring. The number of pending cases has jumped by 51 percent since 2003, the agency said. In the last decade or so, the governors of Louisiana, Connecticut and Rhode Island have pleaded guilty or been convicted of wrongdoing.

Of even greater concern are the shenanigans in Washington. The only difference is that the corruption is more subtle and more institutionalized. In this one aspect of his job, President Obama is not a neophyte.

OBAMA AND REZKO

Obama had already installed himself in Chicago when he became the first African-American named editor of the Harvard Law Review. That got him on Rezko's radar screen. Rezko called Obama and offered him a job. Obama declined, but he and Rezko became friends, as did their spouses.

Obama became a lawyer and community organizer in Chicago, and Rezko got into the property development business seeking to take advantage of federal programs. Obama apparently never directly represented Rezko legally, though he did represent nonprofit groups that became partners with Rezko in development projects.

Rezko helped bankroll Obama's political campaigns. He did so first for the state Senate and then the U.S. Senate. When Obama wanted to buy his dream house in Chicago, he got Rezko to help him do so, only months after being elected to the U.S. Senate. Rezko, now a convicted criminal, acting through his wife, paid for part of a U.S. senator's home.

OBAMA TIMELINE TO POWER

When U. S. Senator Obama bought his 1.6 million dollar mansion in Kenwood on the South side of Chicago in the Spring of 2005, a time when Rezko was said to be under investigation by the Feds, Obama went to Rezko to help in the purchase and Rezko's wife did Obama the favor of purchasing the side lot from the seller, who wanted to sell the side lot and house simultaneously, and the joint purchase would have been a financial stretch at the time for Senator Obama. In 2006, Senator Obama bought a portion of the side lot back from Mrs. Rezko.

While Obama was still attending Harvard Law School in 1991, Antoin Rezko offers him a job. Obama declines in order to pursue grass roots activism to polish his credentials. From 1995 on Rezko contributes to Obama's campaign for the Illinois State Senate. Rezko raises at least $250,000 for Obama's state and federal campaigns over the span of the following nine years. Rezko's associates are contributors as well. Rezko also offers to help Obama to buy a house which was beyond his means by indirectly providing money for the purchase as a gift, with the expectation that he would get a good return on this money to further his criminal activity. During his 2004 campaign for the U. S. Senate, Obama speaks with now convicted felon, and then Obama fundraiser and finance guy, Rezko, almost daily.

In May 2005, Rezko was subpoenaed as part of investigation into whether Blagojevich fundraiser Christopher Kelly traded jobs for campaign contributions.

On May 26, 2005, the Chicago Tribune runs a profile of Rezko and controversies he's involved in: he "has been subpoenaed to supply any records he may have as part of a criminal investigation into allegations that the administration traded plum appointments for campaign cash.

On June 15, 2005, Obama purchases a home from Fredric Wondisford and Sally Radovick for $1.65 million. The purchase is $300,000 less than the asking price

On the same day, Rita Rezko - Antoin's wife – buys the plot next door for $625,000 asking price. During the six months following the purchase the Obamas look into putting up a fence between their property and Rezko's: consult with attorney, architect, city about regulations and permits.

On July 15, 2005, a city landmarks deputy commissioner, Brian Goeken, sent a long e-mail to Michelle Obama saying he had gone out one evening to look at the house. He listed suggestions for obtaining a permit for the fence.

On September 1, 2005, The Chicago Tribune reports that Rezko has been subpoenaed in investigation of scheme involving the state teachers' pension system.

On December 31, 2005, The Chicago Tribune reports that federal investigators have subpoenaed "the tollway authority for information about oases contracts with links to key political insiders" - including Rezko.

During this time, the Obamas have a portion of Rezko's yard appraised.

On January 2006, Rita Rezko sells the Obamas one-sixth of her lot for $104,500.

Rezko obtains a fence permit to build a fence between the Obama house and Rezko's useless vacant lot.

On May 5, 2006 in a story about a bank's lawsuit against Rezko over a bank loan, the Chicago Sun-Times reports that "Rezko's name also has surfaced as federal investigators probe whether state pension contracts were steered to companies contributing to Blagojevich's campaign".

On October 12, 2006, Rezko is indicted for fraud. Rezko is now a convicted felon serving time.

LEGAL CORRUPTION

In 2001 a Longtime Political Supporter, Chicago Entrepreneur Robert Blackwell Jr. Paid Obama An $8,000-A-Month Retainer To Give Legal Advice To His Growing Technology Firm, Electronic Knowledge Interchange." (Chuck Neubauer and Tom Hamburger, "Obama Donor Received A State Grant," Los Angeles Times, 4/27/08)

"It Allowed Obama To Supplement His $58,000 Part-Time State Senate Salary For Over A Year With Regular Payments From Blackwell's Firm That Eventually Totaled $112,000." (Chuck Neubauer and Tom Hamburger, "Obama Donor Received A State Grant," Los Angeles Times, 4/27/08)

"Blackwell Sr., Who Served With Michelle Obama For Years On The Board Of A Local Literacy Group, Said Her Diversity Program Is Critical Because Minorities Don't Always Enjoy The Informal Social Connections Available To Others." (Joe Stephens, "Contracts Went To A Longtime Donor," The Washington Post, 8/22/08)

"Blackwell And His Family, Records Show, Have Been Longtime Donors To The Political Campaigns Of Michelle Obama's Husband, Barack. Robert Blackwell Jr., A Former Partner In The Firm, Is A Major Fundraiser For Barack Obama." (Joe Stephens, "Contracts Went To A Longtime Donor," The Washington Post, 8/22/08)

"With Support From Obama, Other State Officials And An Obama Aide Who Went To Work Part Time For Killerspin, The Company Eventually Obtained $320,000 In State Grants Between 2002 And 2004 To Subsidize Its Tournaments." (Chuck Neubauer and Tom Hamburger, "Obama Donor Received A State Grant," Los Angeles Times, 4/27/08)

"A Few Months After Receiving His Final Payment From EKI, Obama Sent A Request On State Senate Letterhead Urging Illinois Officials To Provide A $50,000 Tourism Promotion Grant To Another Blackwell Company, Killerspin." (Chuck Neubauer and Tom Hamburger, "Obama Donor Received A State Grant," Los Angeles Times, 4/27/08)

OBAMA CORRUPTION

In 2005 the Obamas sold their ground-floor flat at 5450 South East View Park for $415,000. They moved into a spacious mock-Georgian mansion about a mile away at 5046 South Greenwood Avenue.

The sellers were Fredric Wondisford and his wife, Sally Radovick, both professors at the University of Chicago hospitals, where Michelle Obama served as head of external affairs. The sellers insisted that the two pieces of property be sold at the same time.

Instead of purchasing both the house and garden, the Obamas paid $1.65million for the mansion by itself with a $1.32million mortgage from Northern Trust The garden was sold by the same seller on the same day to Rita

Rezko, the wife of Barack Obama's longtime friend and fundraiser Antoin "Tony" Rezko, the corrupt criminal Syrian-born Democratic political fixer.

Mrs Rezko paid the full asking price of $625,000 for the garden, while the Obamas paid $300,000 below the asking price for the house. The Obamas bought the mock Georgian mansion in a trust that concealed their identity behind the name Northern Trust No 10209. Mrs Rezko subsequently sold a 10ft strip of the garden to the Obamas for $104,500 in January 2006.

OBAMA TACTICS

In News Conferences Obama pre-selects the people who can ask him questions and only selects those who are nice to him. This change of protocol by Obama is another in the wrong direction. In this way he can avoid the awkward questions where his speechwriters have not been able to put the right words in his mouth. In this way he can avoid the mess he made in handling the Blagojevich scandal.

It's clear he was unprepared for this circumstance - his hesitancy in answering questions, his claims that he knows of nothing wrong done by his staff, the Axelrod disconnect, the scrubbed meetings. The press still loves Obama with all the passion of an epic high school crush, but he will not get away with type of gaffe as it is too juicy for the media to ignore and it will not go away. It doesn't have any of the complexity of Tony Rezko or the hot-button issues of Jeremiah Wright - it's as simple and easy to explain as it gets, and has audio evidence that will leak eventually. Even Obama's media supporters can't help but point out that Obama confidants like COS Rahm Emanuel and National Campaign Co-Chair Jesse Jackson Jr. are up to their ears in connections to this scandal.

Mr. Emanuel was Obama's contact person with Mr. Blagojevich. There were calls between the Blagojevich and Obama camps about the Senate seat. It was not clear if any calls were recorded by federal agents, who had tapped the governor's phones.

News conferences will be rigged so that President Obama is not asked questions linking Blagojevich, Rahm Emanuel, Jackson, Jr. and Obama himself.

It is probable that Obama himself did nothing legally wrong. He is too smart to be recorded in anything connected to this matter. But this is exactly the sort of deal that Emanuel has been connected to in the past, and he has shared more staff with Blagojevich than any other politician.

Does the arrest of Gov. Rod Blagojevich, who was endorsed by Barack Obama two years ago, for trying to sell Obama's Senate seat to (among others) the national co-chair of Obama's presidential campaign:

Suggest that the press should have looked more closely at Obama's involvement in Chicago machine politics during the campaign?

Signal that Obama's background in Chicago machine politics will continue to haunt him, in much the way Arkansas scandals haunted Bill Clinton?

Represent the point at which the media starts asking Obama questions he can't or won't answer to their satisfaction?

BLAGOJEVICH

The words on the recording sound as if they were uttered by a mob boss. Instead, the feds say, it is the governor of Illinois speaking.

"I've got this thing and it's (expletive) golden, and I'm just not giving it up for (expletive) nothing. I'm not gonna do it," Democratic Gov. Rod Blagojevich says in a conversation intercepted by the FBI.

Federal prosecutors have accused the 51-year-old Blagojevich of scheming to enrich himself by selling Barack Obama's vacant Senate seat for cash or a lucrative job for himself. In excerpts released by prosecutors, Blagojevich snarls profanities, makes threats and demands and allegedly concocts a rich variety of schemes for profiting from his appointment of a new senator.

I want to make money," he declares, according to court papers. Blagojevich allegedly had a salary in mind: $250,000 to $300,000 a year. (He earns $177,412 a year.)

Even in this city inured to political chicanery — three other governors have been convicted in the past 35 years and numerous officeholders from Chicago have gone to prison for graft — the latest charges were stunning. And not just for the vulgarity, but for the naked greed, the recklessness and the self-delusion they suggest.

He thought that his friend President Obama would give an ambassadorship or a Cabinet post in return for an election of the person that Obama wanted into this key senate seat 'Maybe they'll make me secretary of health and human services.' He also discussed getting his wife, Patti, who has been in the real estate business, on corporate boards where she could earn up to $150,000 a year.

Blagojevich was elected as Mr. Clean, promising to clean up state government, succeeding Gov. George Ryan, now behind bars for corruption.

None of it though is that surprising. The political system is corrupt and inevitably the people who succeed in bending it to their advantage cannot do so without having a pre-disposition to corruption and embracing corruption. Those that are adept do it without falling foul of the law and some become so deluded and reckless that they become unhinged. These are the two extremes of Obama and Blagojevich, colleagues and friends until Obama realized he must distance himself just as he has done with other unsavory characters.

State Senator Barack Obama was intensively involved in the Blagojevich gubernatorial campaign of 2002.

Congressman Emanuel, re-elected to a 4th term, resigned his 5th Congressional Chicago seat (previously held by Gov. Blagojevich) to become Obama's Chief of Staff. Emanuel's seat was also previously held for decades by Congressman Dan Rostenkowski, who lost his seat after he was indicted for public corruption. (Rostenkowski was subsequently convicted but pardoned by President Clinton).

THE FIRST OF THE THREE MUSKETEERS IN TROUBLE

Impeached and ousted Ill. Gov. Rod Blagojevich has been indicted on 16 felony charges alleging he engaged in a wide-ranging scheme to deprive the people of Illinois of honest government.

The Chicago Democrat was arrested in December on allegations that also include trying to auction off President Obama's vacant U.S. Senate seat. Illinois lawmakers impeached him and threw him out of office in January. Blagojevich has repeatedly denied wrongdoing.

OBAMA WAS MUTE ON ILLINOIS CORRUPTION

When Illinois Gov. Rod Blagojevich was arrested on charges that he conspired to sell Barack Obama's U.S. Senate seat, the president-elect tried to distance himself from the issue by saying, "It is a sad day for Illinois. Beyond that, I don't think it's appropriate for me to comment."

The national media continues its willful fantasy that Obama and Chicago's political culture have little to do with each other. Tony Rezko, the political fixer who befriended Obama and helped him in his political ascendancy and was later convicted on 16 corruption counts, is mentioned dozens of times in the 76-page criminal complaint against Mr. Blagojevich.

Mr. Obama has an ambiguous reputation among those trying to clean up Illinois politics. He has been noticeably silent on the issue of corruption in his home state involving mostly Democratic politicians.

One reason for Mr. Obama's reticence may be his close relationship with the powerful Illinois senate president Emil Jones. Mr. Jones was a force in Mr. Obama's rise. In 2003, the two men talked about the state's soon-to-be vacant U.S. Senate seat. As Mr. Jones has recounted the conversation, Mr. Obama told him "You can make the next U.S. senator." Mr. Jones replied, "Got anybody in mind?" "Yes," Mr. Obama said. "Me."

Starting in 2003, Mr. Jones worked to burnish Mr. Obama's credentials by making him lead sponsor of bills including a watered-down ban on gifts to lawmakers. Most of Mr. Obama's legislative accomplishments came as result of his association with Mr. Jones.

In 2002, Mr. Obama turned up to help Mr. Blagojevich, a staunch ally of Mr. Jones, win the governor's mansion. Rahm Emanuel, Mr. Obama's incoming White House chief of staff, told The New Yorker earlier this year that six years ago he and Mr. Obama "participated in a small group that met weekly when

Rod was running for governor. We basically laid out the general election, Barack and I and these two other participants."

Mr. Blagojevich won, but before long, problems surfaced. In 2004, Zalwaynaka Scott, the governor's inspector general, said his administration's efforts to evade merit-selection laws exposed "not merely an ignorance of the law, but complete and utter contempt for the law." Nonetheless, Mr. Obama endorsed Mr. Blagojevich's re-election in 2006.

This spring, many Democrats were so disgusted with Mr. Blagojevich that state House Speaker Michael Madigan drafted a memo on why Democrats should impeach Mr. Blagojevich. But Mr. Madigan's move drew a rebuke from Mr. Jones, saying he thought it was wrong for the speaker to "promote the impeachment of a Democratic Governor ... Impeachment is unwarranted in my opinion, and should not be used as a political tool."

Many people were curious who Mr. Obama would side with in the dispute. Would it be with those Democrats who wanted to move aggressively against an apparently corrupt governor or with his old Chicago ally, Mr. Jones, who preferred to wait? Mr. Obama did neither. He kept silent.

Addressing the scandal involving Illinois Gov. Rod Blagojevich, Barack Obama said he had no contact with the governor's office nor did his office speak with Blagojevich about any deal-making over the appointment of his replacement in the Senate. That would be "a violation of everything this campaign is about," Obama said.

Like many politicians, Obama does not understand the irony of his hypocrisy. As a smart lawyer, Obama will not get caught with his hand in the till, but it would be better if he continued to keep silent rather than pretend he will not expect a quid pro quo from favors given.

DOES OBAMA REALLY WANT TO CHANGE CORRUPT GOVERNMENT?

New Mexico's Governor Bill Richardson was the first casualty of Barack Obama's transition when he withdrew as President-elect Barack Obama's commerce secretary-designate because of a federal investigation involving state contracts. Obama was taken by surprise because he did not know what everyone in New Mexico knew. For months federal prosecutors were looking into the awarding of a lucrative state contract to a California company, CDR Financial that made big contributions to political action committees formed by Richardson. Specifically, prosecutors are looking for any connection between the work CDR Financial Products won in 2004 and the large political contributions that were given to two PACs started by Richardson. The investigation reportedly centers on whether staffers in Richardson's office influenced the hiring of CDR.

One PAC, Si Se Puede! Boston 2004, was formed to pay for the governor and his staff to attend the Democratic National Convention in Boston in 2004. The other, Moving America Forward, was formed to register Latino and Native American voters in the run-up to the 2004 presidential election.

In 2003 and 2004, CDR Financial gave $75,000 to Richardson's political action committee Si Se Puede! and the company's head, David Rubin, gave $25,000 to Moving America Forward, another Richardson PAC.

According to numerous reports, in 2004 CDR made $1.48 million advising a small state agency on interest-rate swaps and restructuring escrow funds for the state's special $1.6 billion transportation program known as GRIP, short for Governor Richardson's Investment Partnership.

LOBBYING

Citigroup, Bank of America and JP Morgan Chase each spent over $5 million lobbying the federal government in 2008. Citigroup has so far received $45 billion in bailout money, while the two others received $25 billion each. You can expect millions of dollars of that money to be spent on wining and dining Washington lawmakers; none of the banks has indicated it plans to cut back on lobbying.

CONFLICTS OF INTEREST

If you have access, it pays well; such is the corruption of our political system.

White House economic adviser Lawrence Summers received $5.2 million over the past year in compensation from hedge fund D.E. Shaw, and also received hundreds of thousands of dollars in speaking fees from major financial institutions. Mr. Summers made frequent appearances before Wall Street firms including J.P. Morgan, Citigroup, Goldman Sachs and Lehman Brothers. He also received significant income from Harvard University and from investments. In total, Mr. Summers made a total of about 40 speaking appearances to financial sector firms.

Mr. Summers is involved in shaping the Obama administration's policy decisions on the financial meltdown as well as the broader recession. Among the many decisions the economic team has wrestled with has been whether to step up regulation of hedge funds.

Mr. Summers joined D.E. Shaw Group in late 2006 as a managing director. He helped develop strategies including new businesses and also helped evaluate investments for the New York firm, which oversees about $30 billion in assets, making it one of the biggest hedge-fund managers in the world.

David Axelrod, the president's top political advisor, will receive $3 million over the next five years from the sale of his two media consulting firms. Mr. Axelrod had a salary of $896,776 last year and $651,914 in partnership income from the two companies.

In total, Mr. Axelrod reported assets valued between $6.9 million and $9.5 million. Mr. Axelrod's clients were mostly political campaigns, including those of Rep. Patrick Kennedy, New York Attorney General Andrew Cuomo, and Chicago Mayor Richard M. Daley. He also reported receiving money from large corporations such as AT&T Inc., Comcast Corp. and the nuclear energy company Exelon Corp.

National Security Adviser James Jones reported $900,000 in salary and bonus from the U.S. Chamber of Commerce as well as director fees from a number of corporations. He received, for example, $330,000 from Boeing Corp. and $290,000 from Chevron Corp.

Gregory Craig, White House Counsel, reported receiving a salary of $1.7 million last year from Williams & Connolly, the high-powered Washington law firm where he had been a partner since 1999.

White House Social Secretary Desiree Rogers collected a $350,000 salary from Allstate Financial as president of the social networking division, as well as $150,000 in board fees from Equity Residential, a real estate investment trust in which she also holds at least $250,000 in stock. She also collected $20,000 in board fees from Blue Cross Blue Shield. Other assets reported in her checking account, stock investments, and mutual funds total at least $2 million.

Valerie Jarrett, assistant to the president for intergovernmental affairs, lists a $300,000 salary and $550,000 in deferred compensation from The Habitat Executive Services, Inc., in Chicago.

Ms. Jarrett also disclosed payments of more than $346,000 for service on boards of directors that reflect her political ties, and work in Chicago real estate and community development.

She was paid $76,000 last year for service as a director of Navigant Consulting, Inc. a Chicago-based global consulting group with governmental clients. She received $146,600 for service on the board of USG Corporation, a building materials manufacturer, and $58,000 to serve on the board of Rreef American REIT II, a real estate investment trust based in San Francisco. The Chicago Stock Exchange, Inc. paid her $34,444 to serve on its board.

Deputy National Security Advisor Tom Donilon earned $3.9 million as a partner at the law firm of O'Melveny & Myers LLP, where his clients include Citigroup, Inc., Goldman, Sachs & Co., and Obama fundraiser and heiress Penny Pritzker.

Carol Browner, assistant to the president for energy and climate change, disclosed earnings of between $1 million and $5 million from lobbying firm Downey McGrath Group, Inc., where her husband, Thomas Downey, is a principal. She states $450,000 in member distribution income, plus retirement and other benefits from The Albright Group, a lobbying firm whose principals include former Secretary of State Madeline Albright.

EARMARKS

The Senate voted overwhelmingly to preserve thousands of earmarks in a $410 billion spending yesterday. The House passed the legislation last week. Senator John McCain's attempt to strip out an estimated 8,500 earmarks failed on a vote of 63-32. Obama intends to sign the legislation immediately.

The outcome reflected the enduring value of earmarks to lawmakers. Local governments and constituents often covet them. At $410 billion, the bill represents an 8 percent increase over last year's spending levels, which is more than double the rate of inflation.

McCain asked, "How does anyone justify some of these earmarks: $1.7 million for pig odor research in Iowa; $2 million 'for the promotion of astronomy' in Hawaii; $6.6 million for termite research in New Orleans; $2.1 million for the Center for Grape Genetics in New York?"

He also noted the legislation includes 14 earmarks requested by lawmakers for projects sought by PMA Group, a lobbying company at the center of a federal corruption investigation.

Taxpayers for Common Sense estimate the legislation contains 8,570 disclosed earmarks worth $7.7 billion.

CHARITABLE GIFTS

They do not seem the most likely classical music patrons: Northrop Grumman, General Dynamics, Boeing and Lockheed Martin. Together, these defense contractors are donating hundreds of thousands of dollars to the symphony orchestra in Johnstown, Pa., underwriting performances of Mozart and Wagner in this struggling former steel town. A defense lobbying firm, the PMA Group, even sprang for a Champagne reception at the symphony's opera festival.

The orchestra is a favorite charity of Representative John P. Murtha, Democrat of Pennsylvania, whose Congressional committee hands out lucrative defense contracts, and whose wife, Joyce, is a major booster of the symphony.

During the first six months of 2008, lobbyists, corporations and interest groups gave approximately $13 million to charities and nonprofit organizations in honor of more than 200 members of the House and Senate. The donations came from firms with numerous interests before the Congress, such as Wal-Mart, the Ford Motor Company, Kraft Foods and Pfizer.

Charities in turn know how to reward those politicians who persuade companies to donate to them.

SENATOR DODD SLEAZE

The Senate Ethics Committee is pretending to look into possible conflicts of interest in Connecticut Senator Chris Dodd's 2003 mortgages. Now questions about another Dodd real-estate adventure, this one in Ireland, should keep them even busier -all the more because Mr. Dodd's cottage purchase involves a crooked stock trader for whom the Senator once did huge political favors. The Senate though is so corrupt that no reprimand, or even a comment, will result.

Mr. Dodd is already under a cloud for receiving what a former loan officer claims was preferential treatment from Countrywide Financial on two mortgage refinancings -- in Connecticut and Washington -- in 2003. Countrywide was an aggressive lender to shaky borrowers and relied heavily on Fannie Mae and Freddie Mac to buy those mortgages in bulk. As a senior Member of the Senate Banking Committee, Mr. Dodd was one of Fannie's greatest promoters.

Mr. Dodd promised last year to disclose mortgage documents to prove he got no special treatment, but so far all he's done is let a few hand-picked sycophantic journalists take a quick peek before he put the papers back in storage. Former Countrywide Financial loan officer Robert Feinberg has said that Mr. Dodd knowingly saved thousands of dollars on his refinancing of two properties in 2003 as part of a special program for the influential.

Mr. Feinberg also reported that he has internal company documents that prove Mr. Dodd knew he was getting preferential treatment as a friend of Angelo Mozilo, Countrywide's then-CEO, and Mr. Feinberg has offered to provide those documents to investigators.

Just before Mr. Dodd made his promise, Bank of America closed its acquisition of Countrywide and Mr. Dodd has continued to oversee Bank of America and the rest of the mortgage industry as Chairman of Senate Banking. He will now play a lead role in drafting legislation affecting the very business that gave him preferential treatment.

Now another suspicious real-estate investment has been uncovered. The story starts in 1994, when the Senator became one-third owner of a 10-acre estate, then valued at $160,000, on the island of Inishnee on Galway Bay. The property is near the fashionable village of Roundstone, a well-known celebrity haunt. William Kessinger bought the other two-thirds share in the estate. Edward Downe, Jr., who has been a business partner of Mr. Kessinger, signed the deed as a witness. Senator Dodd and Mr. Downe are long-time friends, and in 1986 they had purchased a condominium together in Washington, D.C.

The year before the Galway deal, in 1993, Mr. Downe pleaded guilty to insider trading and securities fraud and in 1994 agreed to pay the SEC $11 million in a civil settlement.

The crimes were felonies and in 2001, as President Clinton was getting ready to leave office, Mr. Dodd successfully lobbied the White House for a full pardon for Mr. Downe.

The next year, according to a transfer document at the Irish land registry, Mr. Kessinger sold his two-thirds share to Mr. Dodd for $122,351. The Senator says he actually paid Mr. Kessinger $127,000, which he claims was based on an appraisal at the time. That means, at best, Mr. Kessinger earned less than 19% over eight years on the sale of his two-thirds share to Mr. Dodd. But according to Ireland's Central Bank, prices of existing homes in Ireland quadrupled from 1994 to 2004. In his Senate financial disclosure documents from 2002-2007, Mr. Dodd reported that the Galway home was worth between $100,001 and $250,000. In Roundstone "a two-bed property recently sold for $918,000 and a cottage is currently on offer for over a million dollars. Mr Dodd has been the beneficiary of a large unreported gift under Senate rules.

Mr. Dodd needs to explain why Mr. Kessinger handed the property over for no increase in value and what role Mr. Downe might have played as a middleman. More broadly, Connecticut voters might want to know why their senior Senator has hung around for years with Mr. Downe, the kind of financial scoundrel Mr. Dodd spends so much time denouncing.

THE BILL AND HILLARY SHOW

If US politics were not corrupt, Hillary Clinton could not have become secretary of state. She is dangerously compromised.

Bill Clinton's post-Presidency has been more or less a vast fund-raising operation -- for himself, his library and legacy, and his charitable causes. These buckets flow quite nicely into each other and in other ways that are of benefit to Bill. The 200,000 or so donors to his foundation include Arab sheikhs, Latin American monopolists and assorted dubious characters. Does anyone believe that they give without expecting something in return?

The blatant conflicts of interest with Mrs. Clinton's new role are great, but Mr. Obama is characteristically silent even though he must know the Clinton history with the Riadys of Indonesia, Johnny Chung, the Lippo Group and Arkansas compadre Thomas "Mack" McLarty's business travels through the Americas.

Former President Bill Clinton's foundation has raised at least $46 million from Saudi Arabia and other foreign governments that his wife Hillary Rodham Clinton will negotiate with as secretary of state.

The Kingdom of Saudi Arabia gave $10 million to $25 million to the William J. Clinton Foundation, a nonprofit created by the former president to finance his library in Little Rock, Ark., and charitable efforts to reduce poverty and treat AIDS. Other foreign government givers include Norway, Kuwait, Qatar, Brunei, Oman, Italy and Jamaica. The Dutch national lottery gave $5 million to $10 million.

The Blackwater Training Center donated $10,001 to $25,000. Hillary Clinton will have to decide next year whether to renew Blackwater Worldwide's contract to protect U.S. diplomats in Iraq. Five Blackwater guards have been indicted by a U.S. grand jury on manslaughter and weapons charges stemming from a September 2007 firefight in Baghdad's Nisoor Square in which 17 Iraqis died.

The list also underscores ties between the Clintons and India, a connection that could complicate diplomatic perceptions of whether Hillary Clinton can be a neutral broker between India and neighbor Pakistan in a region where President-elect Barack Obama will face an early test of his foreign policy leadership.

Some of the donors have extensive ties to Indian interests that could prove troubling to Pakistan. Tensions between the two nuclear nations are high since last month's deadly terrorist attacks in Mumbai.

Amar Singh, a donor in the $1 million to $5 million category, is an Indian politician who played host to Bill Clinton on a visit to India in 2005 and met Hillary Clinton in New York in September to discuss an India-U.S. civil nuclear agreement.

David J. Phillips

Also in that giving category was Suzlon Energy Ltd. of Amsterdam, a leading supplier of wind turbines. Its chairman is Tulsi R. Tanti, one of India's wealthiest executives. Tanti announced plans at Clinton's Global Initiative meeting earlier this year for a $5 billion project to develop environmentally friendly power generation in India and China.

Two other Indian interests gave between $500,000 and $1 million each:-

The Confederation of Indian Industry, an industrial trade association.

Dave Katragadda, an Indian capital manager with holdings in media and entertainment, technology, health care and financial services.

Other foreign governments also contributed heavily to the foundation:-

AUSAID, the Australian government's overseas aid program, and COPRESIDA-Secretariado Tecnico, a Dominican Republic government agency formed to fight AIDS, each gave $10 million to $25 million.

Norway gave $5 million to $10 million.

Kuwait, Qatar, Brunei and Oman gave $1 million to $5 million each.

The government of Jamaica and Italy's Ministry for Environment and Territory gave $50,000 to $100,000 each.

The foundation's donor list is heavy with overseas business interests:-

Audi businessman Nasser Al-Rashid gave $1 million to $5 million.

Friends of Saudi Arabia and the Dubai Foundation each gave $1 million to $5 million, as did the Taiwan Economic and Cultural Office.

The Swedish Postcode Lottery gave $500,000 to $1 million.

China Overseas Real Estate Development and the U.S. Islamic World Conference gave $250,000 to $500,000 apiece.

The No. 4 person on the Forbes billionaire list, Lakshmi Mittal, the chief executive of international steel company ArcelorMittal, gave $1 million to $5 million. Mittal is a member of the Foreign Investment Council in Kazakhstan, Goldman Sachs' board of directors and the World Economic Forum's International Business Council, according to the biography on his corporate Web site.

Among other $1 million to $5 million donors:-

Harold Snyder, director for Teva Pharmaceutical Industries, the largest drug company in Israel. His son, Jay T. Snyder, serves on the U.S. Advisory Commission on Public Diplomacy, which oversees State Department activities, and served as a senior U.S. adviser to the United Nations, where he worked on international trade and poverty.

The top ranks of Clinton's donor list are heavy with longtime Democratic givers, including some who are notable for their staunch support of Israel.

TV producer Haim Saban and his family foundation, who donated between $5 million and $10 million, splits his time between homes in Israel and California. "I'm a one-issue guy and my issue is Israel," he told The New York Times in 2004.

Slim-Fast diet foods tycoon S. Daniel Abraham, a donor of between $1 million and $5 million, has been a board member of the American Israel Public Affairs Committee, which promotes Israel's interests before the U.S. government.

ETHICS IN GOVERNMENT

An upstate New York developer donated $100,000 to former President Bill Clinton's foundation in November 2004, around the same time that Senator Hillary Rodham Clinton helped secure millions of dollars in federal assistance for the businessman's mall project.

Mrs. Clinton helped enact legislation allowing the developer, Robert J. Congel, to use tax-exempt bonds to help finance the construction of the Destiny USA entertainment and shopping complex, an expansion of the Carousel Center in Syracuse.

Mrs. Clinton also helped secure a provision in a highway bill that set aside $5 million for Destiny USA roadway construction.

New Mexico Gov. Bill Richardson has withdrawn his nomination to be Barack Obama's commerce secretary. The move comes as a federal grand jury is investigating how a California company that contributed to Richardson's political activities won a lucrative New Mexico state contract.

CHAPTER 8 ... ... DEBT

AUDACITY WITHOUT HOPE

President Obama's budget with its staggering $1.75 trillion deficit, a health-care fund of more than $600 billion, a $150 billion energy package and proposals to tax wealthy Americans even beyond what he talked about during his campaign, underscores the breadth of his aspiration to use his presidency to rapidly transform the country to favor the underdog. Even the super-wealthy Liberal powerbrokers who enabled his rise to power to grasp power themselves, must now question whether they might not also end up under the bus.

CREDIT MESS

The federal government has announced a series of actions in the past few weeks ostensibly designed to make consumer credit more available and invigorate the economy. Obviously, the country is in recession and the recession is likely to get deeper. But will these actions reduce the depth and duration of the recession? Or, in the long run, will they make matters even worse?

Last month the Federal Reserve and the Treasury announced that the government would buy $500 billion in mortgages guaranteed by Fannie Mae and Freddie Mac. They also announced they would lend $200 billion against securities backed by car loans, student loans, credit-card debt, and small business loans. The purpose of both moves is to create lending capacity across key elements of the consumer sector.

Most recently, the government announced that it would subsidize new home mortgages by one percentage point, effectively lowering monthly payments on a 30-year loan by about 10%. The stated reason was to help the housing market, which is crucial to an economic recovery.

With each announcement, the Fed and Treasury were careful to point out they might take additional action in support of these sectors and others as well. And it is a virtual certainty the government will cobble together some program to reduce foreclosures to keep people in their homes. I'm sure that, as other industries or sectors come under pressure, there will be new programs to help. The automobile industry will not be the last to come to Washington.

To begin to understand today's problem, we have to have a sense of how we got there. Between 1994 and second quarter 2008, the U.S, housing stock more than doubled in value from $7.6 trillion to $19.4 trillion. Almost three quarters of that increase was due to a speculative bubble, the root cause of which was government policies designed to increase home ownership, largely among people who would be considered nonprime borrowers -- i.e., people without sufficient documented income or employment history and little or no savings or credit history.

The intellectual start of this mess was in a flawed Boston Federal Reserve study published in 1992 that purported to show that minorities were treated less well than whites. That study led to increased political pressure on banks to modify their standards with increased emphasis through the Community Reinvestment Act, and aided by U.S. Department of Housing and Urban Development regulations in the Clinton administration that required parity of outcomes in the lending process.

The effect of all of this meddling was compounded by the lax or incompetent supervision of Fannie Mae and Freddie Mac. All in all, the government got into the business of encouraging and then forcing lending institutions to make mortgage loans to people who could not pay them back. What we ended up with is a failure of government, which we have erroneously termed a failure of capitalism.

The standards applied to these subprime loans began to be applied to what heretofore had been prime borrowers who also increasingly became overextended. But, as housing prices increased, owners cashed out their equity and bought cars, appliances and other items, including using the freed-up equity to pay for everyday living purchases. Over the past decade alone, U.S. households have taken on some $8 trillion in debt, bringing the nation's current consumer debt load to $14 trillion.

This cynical and unsustainable cycle was abetted by mortgage originators who had little interest in making sure loans were good quality, investment banks that securitized and packaged these loans, rating agencies who forgot fundamental laws of gravity, and purchasers who bought securities they could not possibly understand. This was fueled by borrowers who committed fraud and bought houses, or speculated in them, when there was no realistic chance they could afford them.

All of this led to a huge overleveraging in the consumer market. The increase in debt burden fueled much of the nation's economic growth over recent decades, aided somewhat by increases in productivity and underpinned by easy money from the Federal Reserve. Since consumers represent about 70% of the nation's GNP, and since leverage cannot increase forever, we were bound to see the bubble burst and eventually enter a substantial recession.

So, are the current credit easing actions likely to be helpful or not? In my judgment, measures to create liquidity are likely to be helpful. Financial institutions that lend money to credit-worthy people for reasonable purposes have experienced a substantial reduction in available funding from which they can make loans. Hence the programs to support the securitization markets are sensible because money used for this purpose will be lent and used for purchases. Programs that deliver a short-term reduction in mortgage rates will, at the margin, help absorb some of the available housing stock, reducing the time it will take for housing to reach market-clearing levels.

However, measures intended to reduce foreclosures, per se, are likely to be ineffective at best and morally flawed at worst. When analysts say that people are being foreclosed because house values have declined they are missing the point. A large number of foreclosures are taking place because people can no longer refinance and take value out. They could not afford the houses to begin with and greed or stupidity, not a falling real-estate market, has caused their problems. On the other hand, measures to subsidize homeowners facing foreclosures because they have lost their jobs can be helpful.

In the longer term, our nation must de-lever, either by reducing the amounts of borrowing or by increasing consumer earning power through economic growth. Relying on growth alone implies a growth rate higher than we have ever experienced in our nation's history. Nonetheless, our public policy must encourage economic growth by lowering tax rates for corporations and individuals while at the same time avoiding what would be growth killers, including "card check" legislation and trade restrictions. Public policy should support higher savings rates, and avoid encouraging increased consumer spending funded by further debt, which may be helpful in the short term but catastrophic in the longer term.

It is not only consumers that must de-lever. Governments must as well. State and local governments across the nation have incurred direct and indirect debt or obligations in the tens of trillions of dollars -- obligations that cannot be met under any set of reasonable circumstances without an explosion in growth and tax revenues. In fact, we continue to incur debt for politically palatable ideas, like rebate checks, which have very little stimulative power but increase the depth of the hole we are in.

To solve this problem for ourselves and future generations, we must get back to our historic reliance on personal responsibility and market forces, and get government out of economic management. It doesn't do a good job, as the current economic mess amply proves.

INCREASING DEBT

U.S. debt held by the public has now hit $6.6 trillion up from $5.3 trillion only a year ago. That doesn't count another $5.3 trillion in Fannie Mae and Freddie Mac liabilities that we now know also have a taxpayer guarantee. And it doesn't count the many ways that both the Federal Reserve and Treasury have guaranteed financial assets more broadly such as $29 billion in Bear Stearns paper, $301 billion in dodgy Citigroup assets, and hundreds of billions in Federal Housing Administration loans.

President Obama's stimulus plan and new budget will require additional $3 trillion to $4 trillion in new borrowing over the next two or three years, and that's if the economy recovers smartly. Adding it all up, Federal Reserve Chairman Ben Bernanke last week estimated that U.S. public debt-to-GDP would reach 60% over the next few years, up from 40% before the financial panic hit and the highest level since the aftermath of World War II. He must be an optimist since Obama's budget anticipates a decade of outlays far above postwar spending and revenue averages. And even that assumes, implausibly, that most 'stimulus' spending will be temporary.

That is a lot of T-bills to sell and the world is taking note. The cost to buy insurance against U.S. sovereign debt default has surged in the past year. The spreads on credit default swaps for U.S. government debt hit 97 basis points last week or $97,000 to buy insurance on $10 million in debt, nearly seven times higher than a year ago and 60% higher than the end of 2008.

The Chinese Premier, Mr. Wen called on the U.S. to maintain its credibility, honor its commitments and guarantee the safety of Chinese assets. Little wonder: China, like other trading nations, has a big stake in this fiscal free-for-all. Two-thirds of Beijing's $1.9 trillion foreign-exchange reserves are parked in U.S. Treasury debt.

As the supply of U.S. debt increases, investors will demand a higher yield and interest rates will rise, reducing the tradable value of current Treasury bonds. The other temptation will be to inflate away the debt, which would also devalue dollar-denominated assets.

What Mr. Wen is saying is that even the U.S. national balance sheet has limits. The dollar is the world's reserve currency, so the U.S. has the rare privilege among nations of being able to borrow (and then repay its debts) in its own currency. America also remains the world's main safe haven in a crisis, as the flight to the dollar and T-bills in recent months underscores.

But reserve currency status isn't a birthright and it can vanish when nations are irresponsible. Deficits are sometimes necessary to finance tax cuts and investments that promote economic growth. The tragedy of Mr. Obama's $787 billion stimulus and $410 billion 2009 budget is that they spend principally on transfer payments that have little growth payback. The U.S. received another foreign rebuke on this score when German Chancellor Angela Merkel and other Europeans rejected Mr. Obama's calls for a comparable spending binge on the Continent.

The Chinese Premier is right to warn the U.S. Liberal political class that the global demand for American debt will continue only if the U.S. runs economic policies that make U.S. dollar assets worth the risk.

David J. Phillips

DEBT TIME BOMB

President Barack Obama and his Liberal super majority Congress will increase the national debt by $2 trillion this year, an unprecedented increase that could test the world's appetite for financing U.S. government spending.

For now, investors are frantically stuffing money into the relative safety of the U.S. Treasury, which has come to serve as the world's mattress in troubled times. Interest rates on Treasury bills have plummeted to historic lows, with some short-term investors literally giving the government money for free. The market for U.S. Treasurys is by far the largest and most liquid bond market in the world, and big institutional investors have few other places to safely invest large sums of reserve cash.

A problem is that 40 percent of the debt held by private investors will mature in a year or less. When those loans come due, the Treasury will have to borrow more money to repay them, even as it launches the most aggressive expansion of U.S. debt ever.

Even before the Obama administration started its spending spree, Washington had already approved $168 billion in spending to stimulate economic activity, $700 billion to prevent the collapse of the U.S. financial system, and multibillion-dollar bailouts for a variety of financial institutions, including insurance giant American International Group and mortgage financiers Fannie Mae and Freddie Mac.

National debt is now $10.7 trillion, of which about $4.3 trillion is owed to other government institutions, such as the Social Security trust fund. Debt held by private investors totals nearly $6.4 trillion, or a little over 40 percent of gross domestic product.

Foreign investors held about $3 trillion in U.S. debt at the end of October. China, which in October replaced Japan as the United States' largest creditor, has increased its holdings by 42 percent over the past year; Britain and the Caribbean banking countries more than doubled their holdings.

The good news is that the United States is currently in relatively good financial shape compared with other industrial nations, such as Japan, where the public debt equaled 182 percent of GDP in 2007, or Germany, where the debt was 65 percent of GDP. A $2 trillion increase would push the U.S. debt to about 53 percent of the overall economy.

The deepening global recession will force some of the largest U.S. creditors to divert cash to domestic needs, such as investing in their own banks and economies. Even if demand for U.S. debt keeps pace with supply, investors are likely to demand higher interest rates, driving up debt-service payments, which last year stood at $250 billion. There could come a time when we can't even pay the interest on the money we've borrowed. That's default.

Even a $2 trillion increase in borrowing would not greatly diminish the U.S. financial condition. That could change. Nearly a year ago, Moody's raised an alarm about the skyrocketing costs of Social Security and Medicare as the baby-boom generation retires, saying the resulting budget deficits could endanger the U.S. bond rating threatening continued confidence in the dollar.

FOREIGN CAPITAL FLEES

Foreigners withdrew funds from U.S. assets in record amounts in January, even though China continued to add to its stockpile of U.S. government debt.

Already the largest foreign creditor to the U.S. government, China raised its Treasury holdings another $12.2 billion in January, taking its total holdings to $739.6 billion. China held $492 billion in Treasurys in January 2008.

Foreigners sold a net $60.9 billion in long-dated U.S. securities in January, after buying $24.3 billion in December. Including changes in banks' dollar holdings, short-term securities and non-market transactions, net foreign capital outflows totaled a record $148.9 billion in January, compared with $86.2 billion in inflows in the previous month.

Dumping Treasurys would hurt both the U.S. and China. Were China to sell a substantial amount of Treasurys, bond yields would jump, while Treasury prices and the value of the U.S. dollar would plunge.

Chinese Premier Wen Jiabao has expressed concern about the safety of U.S. government debt, but he has not as yet signaled any moves by China to unload Treasury holdings.

PRINTING MONEY

The Fed has pledged to print dollars in unlimited volume and to trim its funds rate, if necessary, all the way to zero and will continue to consider ways of using its balance sheet to further support credit markets and economic activity. President Obama is an advocate of massive money-printing.

The Fed's declaration of inflationary intent has knocked the dollar down against gold and will continue to weaken the dollar against other currencies. Now that the dollar yields so little, why will foreigners want to own it once they have found a safe alternative?

On Oct. 6, 1979, then-Fed Chairman Paul A. Volker vowed to print less money to bring down inflation. On so doing, he closed one monetary era and opened another. With the promise to print much more money, the Federal Reserve of Ben S. Bernanke has opened its own new era to do the work of Liberal ideology short term with very negative consequences subsequently.

The Fed must deal with a basic contradiction. The dollar is the world's currency, yet the Fed is America's central bank. Mr. Bernanke's remit is to promote low inflation, high employment and solvent finance in the USA. A problem is that the USA needs foreigners to continue to buy U.S. Treasury's bonds. If the Fed is going to create huge amounts of depreciating, non-yielding dollar bills, who will absorb them? Who will finance the Obama administration's looming titanic fiscal deficits? Who will finance America's annual surplus of consumption over production (after 25 continuous years, now a national trait)? Inflation which is a government sanctioned theft from the American people will be one answer.

The underlying issue is the dollar and the central bank that manipulates it. At one time our central bankers had one job only, and that was to assure that the currency under his care was exchangeable into gold at the lawfully stipulated rate. It was his office to make the public indifferent between currencies or gold. In a crisis, the banker's job description expanded to permit emergency lending against good collateral at a high rate of interest. None arrogated to himself the job of steering the economy by fixing an interest rate or improvising monetary solutions to a credit crisis.

When economic crises hit in the 1870s and again in the 1890s, Americans repeatedly spurned the Populist cries for a dollar you didn't have to dig out of the ground but could rather print. "If the Government can create money," as a hard-money advocate put it in an 1892 broadside entitled "Cheap Money," "why should it not create all that everybody wants? Why should anybody work for a living?" "Why should we have any limit put to the volume of our currency?"

The Federal Reserve came into being in 1913. Promoters of the legislation to establish America's new central bank protested that they wanted no soft currency. The dollar would continue to be exchangeable into gold at the customary rate of $20.67 an ounce. But, they added, under the Fed's enlightened stewardship, the currency would become "expansive." Accordion-fashion, the number of dollars in circulation would expand or contract according to the needs of commerce and agriculture. That was the start of Liberal double talk.

Anticipating the credit inflations of the future and recalling the disturbances of the past, A Conservative, Elihu Root, attacked the bill in this fashion: "Little by little, business is enlarged with easy money. With the exhaustless reservoir of the Government of the United States furnishing easy money, the sales increase, the businesses enlarge, more new enterprises are started, and excessive optimism pervades the community. Everyone is making money. Everyone is growing rich. It goes up and up, the margin between costs and sales continually growing smaller as a result of the operation of inevitable laws, until finally someone whose judgment was bad, someone whose capacity for business was small, breaks; and as he falls he hits the next brick in the row, and then another, and then another, and down comes the whole structure. That is the history of every movement of inflation since the world's business began, and it is the history of many a period in our own country. That is what happened to greater or less degree before the panic of 1837, of 1857, of 1873, of 1893 and of 1907. The precise formula which the students of economic movements have evolved to describe the reason for the crash following the universal process is that when credit exceeds the legitimate demands of the country the currency becomes suspected and gold leaves the country."

In 1971 the dollar lost its gold backing altogether with nothing behind it more than the good intentions of the U.S. government and (somewhat more substantively) the demonstrated strength of the U.S. economy. The world embraced that uncollateralized piece of paper or to an extent that the United States has borrowed its way to a net international investment position of minus $2.44 trillion ($17.64 trillion of foreign assets held by Americans versus $20.08 trillion of American assets held by foreigners).

Now the Fed is lending freely, but not at the stipulated high interest rate. Instead it is starting to lend at a rate below which there is no positive rate. The gold standard was objective. Modern monetary management is subjective and intuitive. The gold standard was rules-based. The 21st century Fed is base on Liberal ideology and political populist Liberal whim. In the last six months the Fed's assets have zoomed to $2.31 trillion from $905.7 billion. The Fed pays for its assets with freshly made dollars. It conjures them into existence on a computer; even printing is now a figure of speech.

In this crisis, the Fed's assets have grown much faster than its capital. The Federal Reserve is itself a highly leveraged financial institution. The flagship branch of the 12-bank system, the Federal Reserve Bank of New York, shows assets of $1.3 trillion and capital of just $12.2 billion. Its leverage ratio, a mere 0.9%, is less than one-third of that prescribed for banks in the private sector. Such a thin film of protection would present no special risk if the bank which has been managed by Timothy F. Geithner, the Treasury secretary, owned only short-dated Treasuries. However, the toxic assets acquired from Bear Stearns and AIG foots to $66.6 billion. A write down of just 18.3% in the value of those risky portfolios would erase the New York Fed's capital account.

A major disaster looms when the Chinese find a safer investment vehicle than U.S. dollars. They have already been badly bitten and so that day might be closer than our Liberal politicians think.

U.S. INFLATION

Weakening the dollar will help us dig out from a mountain of debt, but it may also hasten an already wary world's move away from the dollar as the currency of choice. It's too soon to bury the U.S. dollar as the global reserve currency, but it is time to start thinking about writing its obituary. The dollar's days as the world's reserve currency are numbered. Obama in his first one hundred days has seen to that.

On top of all other debt, the unfunded liabilities for Social Security and Medicare that we have promised to pay but have not put aside money to cover, came to $102 trillion in 2008.

Even a brilliant Fed chairman (which we do not have) would not be able to remove the $8 trillion or whatever this crisis will finally cost taxpayers from the U.S. money supply, without causing appreciable inflation and without causing the U.S. economy to come to a grinding halt again.

But as difficult as achieving that balance would be in practice, no one in the world really believes that the United States intends to fight inflation too vigorously or support the dollar too strongly. A combination of high inflation and a weak dollar really is the best way to get out from under the mountain of debt that we have now committed to run up.

On a debt of $8 trillion, in a world with no inflation at an interest rate of 2%, interest payments alone come to $160 billion a year in current dollars. Paying down the debt over 30 years would require an additional $267 billion a year in current dollars. That's $427 billion we don't have each year.

Inflation and a declining dollar is the only way out. At 3% inflation, that $160 billion in interest payments is really worth just $155 billion in constant dollars after a year. That's a savings of almost $5 billion in one year. The principal is worth 3% less in constant dollars every year as well. In 30 years, even if we didn't pay down a cent on that amount, the principal would be worth just $3.2 trillion in constant dollars.

The savings are even greater if the United States is paying off some of its interest and debt in depreciating dollars. About 50% of U.S. public debt is held by overseas investors and governments. Assuming roughly the same ownership for the new $8 trillion in debt, a 3% annual depreciation of the dollar would save $2.5 billion in constant dollars in interest costs in the first year and would reduce the value of the 50% of the principal held overseas by about $2.5 trillion.

At a 5% inflation rate, the constant-dollar value of that $8 trillion in debt falls to just $1.7 trillion in 30 years. That's a constant-dollar savings of $6.3 trillion. The savings get even bigger if you combine the effects of inflation and a declining dollar. Following Obama, the United States will have no alternative but to follow a policy to encourage higher inflation and a cheaper dollar. Higher inflation and a depreciating dollar would raise U.S. interest rates as overseas investors demanded higher rates in order to stay even. But the very size of the debt and the ability of the U.S. government to reduce interest payments by locking in lower rates with longer maturity bonds still would make inflation and depreciation a winning combination.

Overseas investors will be worried by our obvious fiscal irresponsibility. In fiscal 2007, the last full boom year before the subprime-mortgage crisis started the economy into a tailspin, the federal government still ran an official deficit of $163 billion and that does not include all the off-budget charges, such as the cost of the war in Iraq. The other deficit, the U.S. trade deficit, came to $712 billion in the 2007 calendar year. A country that shows no inclination to balance its books in boom times does not fill its creditors with confidence.

The Chinese, the world's largest holders of dollars, have begun to do something about their exposure to U.S. currency. First, the Chinese have signed a series of currency swaps with individual countries that provide these trading partners with a reserve of yuan that can be used to pay for Chinese exports instead of U.S. dollars. Since December, the Chinese have signed almost $100 billion in these swap deals with countries such as Malaysia, South Korea, Belarus and Indonesia. The most recent deal was a $10 billion swap with Argentina.

Second, the Chinese have urged an expansion of the International Monetary Fund's special drawing rights. An SDR is a 'currency' based on a basket of dollars, pounds, yen and euros issued by the IMF to individual countries based on the relative size of national economies. Member countries pledge to back SDRs with their full faith and credit and to exchange them for gold or other convertible currencies.

The Chinese have urged turning SDRs into a kind of global reserve currency that would not be under the control of any single government. From the perspective of creditor nations, such a system would limit the ability of a debtor nation that also controlled the global reserve currency from inflating and depreciating its way out of debt. The United States, and only the United States, has that advantage.

Russia, which was also a creditor nation until the collapse of oil prices, has joined China in backing this approach. The writing is on the wall and President Obama put it there in less than a hundred days.

CHAPTER 9 ... ... CHINA

CHINA AND THE DOLLAR

As if the dollar didn't have enough problems, Timothy Geithner took China's bait and said he was "quite open" to its suggestion to displace the greenback with an "international reserve currency." The dollar promptly fell and stocks followed.

CHINA TAKES AIM AT DOLLAR

China has called for the creation of a new currency to eventually replace the dollar as the world's standard, proposing a sweeping overhaul of global finance that reflects developing nations' growing unhappiness with the U.S. role in the world economy. China is on the offensive, backed by other countries such as Russia in making clear they want a global economic order less dominated by the USA. Russia recommended that the International Monetary Fund might issue the currency, and emphasized the need to update 'the obsolescent unipolar world economic order.'

The technical and political hurdles to implementing China's recommendation are enormous and so the proposal is unlikely to change the dollar's role in the short term. Central banks around the world hold more U.S. dollars and dollar securities than they do assets denominated in any other individual foreign currency. Such reserves can be used to stabilize the value of the central banks' domestic currencies.

Chinese officials are frustrated at their financial dependence on the USA, with Premier Wen Jiabao publicly expressing concerns over China's significant holdings of U.S. government bonds. The size of those holdings means the value of the national emergency fund is mainly driven by factors China has little control over, such as fluctuations in the value of the dollar and changes in U.S. economic policies. While Chinese banks have weathered the global downturn and continue to lend, the collapse in demand for the nation's exports has shuttered factories and left millions jobless.

"The re-establishment of a new and widely accepted reserve currency with a stable valuation benchmark may take a long time," Mr. Wen said. China acknowledges that the dollar's dominant position in international trade and investment is unlikely to change soon. Mr. Wen's musing about the safety of China's dollar holdings is a warning to the U.S. that it can't expect China to finance its spending indefinitely. President Obama is not listening.

LESSON FROM CHINA

An embarrassing auditor of American misgovernment is China, whose premier has rightly noted the unsustainable trajectory of America's high-consumption, low-savings economy. He has also expressed fears that his country's $1 trillion-plus of dollar-denominated assets might be devalued by America choosing, as banana republics do, to use inflation for partial repudiation of debts.

CHAPTER 10 ... ... DETROIT

GENERAL MOTORS

General Motors posted a $9.6 billion net loss, or $15.71 a share, in the fourth quarter, and burned through $6.2 billion in cash as it sought government assistance to avoid running out of cash. Excluding special items, the Detroit auto maker's loss was $9.65 per share for the quarter. The company recorded a net loss of $30.9 billion for fiscal 2008 amid a global sales slump and recession.

In addition to seeking as much as $30 billion in U.S. funding, the embattled U.S. auto maker is looking for about $6 billion from governments outside the U.S. Its stock has been trading at historic lows of less than $5 as nationalization rumors swirl around the Dow component.

GM Chief Rick Wagoner said in a statement that he expects "challenging conditions will continue through 2009, and so we are accelerating our restructuring actions."

NO OUTRAGE

General Motors said about 7,500 of its U.S. hourly workers have accepted buyout offers, as the auto maker continues to shrink its operations amid heavy losses and a global slump in demand.

GM said that with the union employees' departure, the company will have tallied 60,500 buyouts since 2006. In the latest round, GM offered retirement incentives to 22,000 of its 62,000 United Auto Worker members.

There is no Obama outrage at these taxpayer funded sweetheart deals.

HOLDING CEOS ACCOUNTABLE

The failure of the General Motors board of directors to fire CEO Richard Wagoner provides a rare glimpse into the inner-workings of big-time corporate boards of directors. When Mr. Wagoner took the helm eight years ago the stock was trading at around $60 per share. The stock had fallen to around $11 per share before the current financial crisis. It's now below $5 per share.

In 2007, Mr. Wagoner's compensation rose 64% to almost $16 million in a year when the company lost billions. The board has been a staunch backer of Mr. Wagoner despite consistent erosion of market share and losses of $10.4 billion in 2005 and $2 billion in 2006. In 2007 GM posted a loss of $68.45 a share, or $38.7 billion, the biggest ever for any auto maker anywhere.

The average pay for chief executives of large public companies in the United States is now well over $10 million a year. Top corporate executives in the United States receive about three times more than their counterparts in Japan and more than twice as much as their counterparts in Western Europe. Executive compensation is too high in the U.S. because the process by which executive compensation is determined has been corrupted by acquiescent and pandering boards of directors. When the CEO is also the Chairman of the Board the problem is exacerbated considerably. Indeed the CEO chooses the directors who will support what he wants including compensation. Mutual back scratching and club like affiliations are the norm.

As board tenure lengthens, it becomes increasingly less likely that boards will remain independent of the managers they are charged with monitoring. Mr. Wagoner has had 10 years to cultivate his board. Of the 13 'independent' directors on the board, eight of them have served with Mr. Wagoner since 2003.

Once an opinion, such as the opinion that a CEO is doing a good job, becomes ingrained in the minds of a board of directors, the possibility of altering those beliefs decreases substantially. All too often, it is only when an outsider takes an objective look does anybody realize that the directors of a company are generally the last people to recognize management failure.

We need to encourage market solutions, not bureaucratic government intervention, as the best strategy for addressing corporate governance failures. Hedge funds and activist investors like Carl Icahn are the solution, not the problem. Little if anything has changed at GM since dissident director H. Ross Perot dubbed his board colleagues "pet rocks" for their blind support of then CEO Roger Smith. The broader problem is that there are far too many pet rocks on the boards of other U.S. companies.

AUTO PARTS BAILOUT

Obama is planning to announce a financing facility that will provide $5 billion in assistance to the country's auto-parts suppliers, many of which are teetering on the edge of bankruptcy.

FINALLY THE TRUTH

GM says in its annual report that its auditors have raised substantial doubts about its ability to continue as a going concern, citing recurring losses from operations, stockholders' deficit and an inability to generate enough cash to meet its obligations.

GM has received $13.4 billion in federal loans, and the company is seeking a total of $30 billion from the government. During the past three years it has piled up $82 billion in losses, including $30.9 billion in 2008.

David J. Phillips

DETROIT PLANS

GM's new restructuring plan seeks another $16.6 billion in government aid -- for now. Chrysler wants an additional $5 billion. The $30 billion that GM has either received or requested since December doesn't count the $8 billion it wants to develop fuel-efficient cars, and another $6 billion it's soliciting from foreign governments.

There have been many bright minds in the American auto industry over the years at the auto makers, the United Auto Workers union, and the components companies. Most of them saw today's troubles coming for decades.

"I frankly don't see how we're going to meet the foreign competition," said Henry Ford II, then chairman and CEO of Ford Motor Co., on May 13, 1971, right after the annual shareholders' meeting. "We've only seen the beginning," he predicted. Regarding American's increasing preference for small cars, Henry II declared: "Mini car, mini profits."

That was a couple years before Detroit agreed to let auto workers retire with full pension and benefits after 30 years on the job, regardless of their age. In practice, that meant a worker could start at age 18, retire at 48, and spend more years collecting a pension and free health care than he or she actually spent working. It wasn't long before even union officials realized they had created a monster.

In 1977, UAW Vice President Irving Bluestone said he was flabbergasted that so many workers were retiring at age 55 or younger. "We were aware that the trend to early retirement was escalating but we were surprised at the escalation in 1976," Mr. Bluestone declared. "It is astounding."

None of this is ancient history. The 30-and-out retirement program persists. It is a sacred part of the inflated cost structure that makes it unprofitable for Detroit to make small cars in America. Another example: Every Detroit factory still has dozens of union committeemen -- the bargaining committee, shop committee, health and safety committee, recreation committee, etc. -- who actually are paid by the car companies. This "legacy cost" is one that the nonunion Japanese, German and Korean car factories in America don't have to carry.

Missing from both restructuring plans proposed by GM and Chrysler are concessions from the UAW to reduce the cost of health care for retirees. Ironically, union retirees over age 65 continue to receive generous, company-paid benefits, while their former bosses in management have to rely on Medicare. The companies could and did unilaterally change the health-care plans for management, but they have to negotiate changes for union workers and retirees.

Other missing links include any agreement with bondholders to substantially reduce the amount of outstanding debt, which is an especially acute issue for GM. And the cost of compensating dealers for killing brands, Hummer and Pontiac, as well as Saturn and Saab, is likely to be substantial.

GM justifies its bailout request by contending that a bankruptcy filing will cost the government $100 billion to guarantee pension payments and other obligations. But here's the thing: The total of nearly $45 billion requested so far from the Treasury Department, the Energy Department and friendly foreigners gets us almost halfway to $100 billion, even if the company doesn't request more money down the road it will. Without a bankruptcy filing, the issues with the UAW, dealers and bondholders are likely to remain unresolved. The same pain-avoidance motive that has kept these issues festering for years will continue.

Chrysler's plan, meanwhile, basically requires constant government subsidies until the benefits of its proposed alliance with Fiat begin to flow, at best a couple years from now. So the taxpayers are being asked to provide funds that neither Chrysler's private-equity owners nor Fiat, which would get 35% of Chrysler's stock, are willing to provide.

As for the auto makers' fear that Americans won't buy cars from a company in bankruptcy, that damage has been done. In fact, bankruptcy will improve their chances of survival by relieving them of financial obligations that they can't afford.

The conclusion that President Barack Obama's new automotive task force should reach is obvious. The purpose of Chapter 11 would give GM and Chrysler the opportunity to survive.

OBAMA AUTO WORKS

The Obama administration used the threat of withholding more bailout money to force out GM Chief Executive Rick Wagoner and administer harsh medicine to Chrysler, marking a dramatic government intervention in private industry.

The Obama administration's auto team announced that it doesn't believe Chrysler is viable as a stand-alone company, and suggested that the best chance for success for both GM and Chrysler may well require utilizing the bankruptcy code in a quick and surgical way.

The move also indicates that the Treasury Department intends to wade more deeply into the affairs of the country's largest and oldest car company.

After over a month of analysis, the administration's auto task force determined that neither company had put forward viable plans to restructure and survive. The verdict was gloomier for Chrysler. The government said it would provide Chrysler with capital for 30 days to cut a workable arrangement with Fiat SpA, the Italian auto maker that has a tentative alliance with Chrysler. That requirement alone puts Chrysler in a very weak negotiating position

President Barack Obama blamed leadership failures in Washington, D.C., and Detroit as a key factor in the auto industry's decline. In prepared remarks, Obama said, "The pain being felt in places that rely on our auto industry is not the fault of our workers and it is not the fault of all the families and communities that supported manufacturing plants throughout the generations. Rather, it is a failure of leadership."

Chrysler said it has agreed to a framework of a global alliance with the Italian auto maker Fiat with the help of the U.S. Treasury.

AUTO TASK FORCE

Steven Rattner, leader of the Obama auto task force, was one of the executives involved with payments now under scrutiny in a state and federal probe into an alleged kickback scheme from New York State's pension fund.

BANKRUPTCY

Failure and bankruptcy are essential to capitalism. Bankruptcy is an orderly way to give an overburdened debtor a fresh start and to decide which creditors are paid back and which are not. Bankruptcy is a means to cope with those times when markets fail to allocate capital wisely and monitor its use.

President Barack Obama has no right or capability to pick GM's chief executive and apportioning losses among auto workers, pensioners, suppliers and lenders. Politics will produce unfair and unwise decisions, such as protecting workers in the domestic auto industry at taxpayer expense while workers in non-unionized industries experience unfair competition.

What about failed Banks? Why should they not go through bankruptcy the way Macy's and Delta Air Lines did? The reason is that a retailer or airline can shed debts and then operate stores and airplanes. Financial institutions have nothing so tangible: They basically have their names, their people and their ability to borrow and lend money short term. All of that can vanish instantly while a bankruptcy judge ponders the matter. So the U.S. devised a bankruptcy substitute for banks: The Federal Deposit Insurance Corp. does the deed quickly without a judge and has done so efficiently until Washington devised the phrase 'Too big to fail' so that they could seize control. Having succeeded with Banks, Obama now has the same game plan for the Auto industry,

BANKRUPTCY IS THE PERFECT REMEDY

Obama hates the idea because he would lose leverage. The Detroit auto makers and the United Auto Workers Union keep insisting that bankruptcy would be the kiss of death. To the contrary a Chapter 11 bankruptcy filing would result in a stronger domestic industry.

Chapter 11 allows a financially failed enterprise to continue in business while reorganizing. Reorganization arose in the late 19th century when creditors of railroads unable to meet their debt obligations threatened to tear up their tracks, melt them down, and sell the steel as scrap. Creditors realized that they would collect more if they agreed to reduce their claims and keep the railroads running and producing revenues to pay them off. The same logic applies to Chapter 11 today.

General Motors must shed labor contracts, retirement contracts, and modernize its distribution systems by closing many dealerships. Bankruptcy provides a mechanism to do all that. Consumers have little to fear. Reorganization will pare the weakest dealers while strengthening those who remain.

So why does Detroit auto management and the UAW insist that bankruptcy is not an option? It is because of the changes that would be imposed upon both. The UAW has paid heavily for Obama's support and stronger unions are part of his master plan.

The bankruptcy code places severe limitations on the compensation that can be paid to a manager unless there is a bona fide job offer from another business at the same or greater rate of compensation. Given the dismal performance of the Detroit Three, their senior management will not be valued on the open market. Incumbent management is also likely to find its prospects for continued employment less-secure. Most importantly Chapter 11 provides a mechanism for forcing UAW workers to take further pay cuts, reduce their gold-plated health and retirement benefits, and overcome their cumbersome union work rules.

Obama and his Washington cronies repeat the mantra that "bankruptcy is not an option" because they want to use free taxpayer money to force Detroit into manufacturing cars which they favor, rather than those cars American consumers want to buy. A Chapter 11 filing would remove these politicians' leverage.

In short, Detroit and the public have little to fear from a bankruptcy filing, but much to fear from the corrupt bargain that is emerging among incumbent management who agree to pay homage to Obama and the UAW. They want to spend taxpayer money to further their Liberal ideology and to control the auto industry.

CHAPTER 11 ... ... DOMESTIC PROGRAMS

GOVERNMENT CREATED FINANCIAL CRISIS

The failure to rescue Lehman did not trigger the panic. The ongoing incompetence and interference of politicians did. Government actions and interventions, not any inherent failure or instability of the private economy, caused, prolonged and dramatically worsened the financial crisis.

The explanation of financial crises is that they are caused by excesses, frequently monetary excesses, which lead to a boom and an inevitable bust. This crisis was no different: A housing boom followed by a bust led to defaults, the implosion of mortgages and mortgage-related securities at financial institutions, and resulting financial turmoil.

Monetary excesses were the main cause of the boom. The Fed held its target interest rate especially in 2003-2005 well below known monetary guidelines that say what good policy should be, based on historical experience. Keeping interest rates on the track that worked well in the past two decades, rather than keeping rates so low, would have prevented the boom and the bust. It is now clear that the greater the degree of monetary excess in all countries, the larger was the housing boom.

The effects of the boom and bust were amplified by several complicating factors including the use of subprime and adjustable-rate mortgages, which led to excessive risk taking. There is also evidence the excessive risk taking was encouraged by the excessively low interest rates. Delinquency rates and foreclosure rates are inversely related to housing price inflation. These rates declined rapidly during the years housing prices rose rapidly, likely throwing mortgage underwriting programs off track and misleading many people.

Adjustable-rate, subprime and other mortgages were packed into mortgage-backed securities of great complexity. Rating agencies underestimated the risk of these securities, either because of a lack of competition, poor accountability, or most likely the inherent difficulty in assessing risk due to the complexity.

Other government actions were at play: The government-sponsored enterprises Fannie Mae and Freddie Mac were encouraged to expand and buy mortgage-backed securities, including those formed with the risky subprime mortgages.

Government action also helped prolong the crisis. The financial crisis became acute on Aug. 9 and 10, 2007, when money-market interest rates rose dramatically. Interest rate spreads, such as the difference between three-month and overnight interbank loans, jumped to unprecedented levels. Diagnosing the reason for this sudden increase was essential for determining what type of policy response was appropriate. If liquidity was the problem, then providing more liquidity by making borrowing easier at the Federal Reserve discount window, or opening new windows or facilities, would be appropriate. But if counterparty risk was behind the sudden rise in money-market interest rates, then a direct focus on the quality and transparency of the bank's balance sheets would be appropriate.

Early on, policy makers misdiagnosed the crisis as one of liquidity, and prescribed the wrong treatment. To provide more liquidity, the Fed created the Term Auction Facility (TAF) in December 2007. Its main aim was to reduce interest rate spreads in the money markets and increase the flow of credit. But the TAF did not seem to make much difference. If the reason for the spread was counterparty risk as distinct from liquidity that is not surprising.

Another early policy response was the Economic Stimulus Act of 2008, passed in February. The major part of this package was to send cash totaling over $100 billion to individuals and families so they would have more to spend and thus jump-start consumption and the economy. But people spent little if anything of the temporary rebate as predicted by Milton Friedman's permanent income theory, which holds that temporary as distinct from permanent increases in income do not lead to significant increases in consumption. Consumption was not jump-started.

A third policy response was the very sharp reduction in the target federal-funds rate to 2% in April 2008 from 5.25% in August 2007. That was sharper than monetary guidelines would prescribe. The most noticeable effect of this rate cut was a sharp depreciation of the dollar and a large increase in oil prices. After the start of the crisis, oil prices doubled to over $140 in July 2008, before plummeting back down as expectations of world economic growth declined. But by then the damage of the high oil prices had been done.

After a year of such mistaken prescriptions, the crisis suddenly worsened in September and October 2008. We experienced a serious credit crunch, seriously weakening an economy already suffering from the lingering impact of the oil price hike and housing bust. Many have argued that the reason for this bad turn was the government's decision not to prevent the bankruptcy of Lehman Brothers over the weekend of Sept. 13 and 14. A study of this event suggests that the answer is more complicated and lay elsewhere.

While interest rate spreads increased slightly on Monday, Sept. 15, they stayed in the range observed during the previous year, and remained in that range through the rest of the week. On Friday, Sept. 19, the Treasury announced a rescue package, though not its size or the details. Over the weekend the package was put together, and on Tuesday, Sept. 23, Fed Chairman Ben Bernanke and Treasury Secretary Henry Paulson testified before the Senate Banking Committee. They introduced the Troubled Asset Relief Program (TARP), saying that it would be $700 billion in size. A short draft of legislation was provided, with no mention of oversight and few restrictions on the use of the funds.

The two men were questioned intensely and the reaction was negative, judging by the large volume of critical mail received by many members of Congress. It was following this testimony that one really begins to see the crisis deepening and interest rate spreads widening. The realization by the public that the government's intervention plan had not been fully thought through, and the official story that the economy was tanking, led to the panic seen in the next few weeks. The panic was amplified by the ad hoc decisions to support some financial institutions and not others and unclear, seemingly fear-based explanations of programs to address the crisis. What was the rationale for intervening with Bear Stearns, then not with Lehman, and then again with AIG? What would guide the operations of the TARP?

It did not have to be this way. To prevent misguided actions in the future, it is urgent that we return to sound principles of monetary policy, basing government interventions on clearly stated diagnoses and predictable frameworks for government actions. Massive responses with little explanation will probably make things worse. That is the lesson from this crisis. It is a lesson which the Obama administration and a Liberal Congress have even now not understood or heeded. The crisis has deepened and Obama Liberals have deliberately stampeded their ideology into law regardless of the consequences. It is the worst possible time to have a Liberal Super-Majority.

The Liberal Congress was more than George W. Bush could resist particularly as he was being hated and blamed for the inevitable landslide for Liberals in the November elections. Now the USA will reap the consequences of too much government and too little free market self-correcting capitalism. The adoring masses are still dancing behind the Pied Piper.

RECESSION

The U.S. entered a recession in December 2007, according to the official recession watchers at the National Bureau of Economic Research economists declared the end of the expansion that began in November 2001, lasting 73 months.

OBAMA WHAT A BUMMER

Barack Obama took the oath of office exactly one month ago, a day where he was greeted by adoring throngs. They expected big things from the golden boy who railed against the last eight years. Already it is clear that the golden glow is foil and not gold at all, with holes already evident.

It has certainly been one whirlwind of a first 30 days. The problem is that President Obama is going off at half cock and does not know what he is doing.

He showed his hypocrisy and inconsistencies immediately. He said he would not hire lobbyists and then blatantly broke the rule the same week by announcing as Deputy Defense Secretary William Lynn, who lobbied for Raytheon. That is not counting Daschle who not only lobbied for health care companies but also married an attractive young lobbyist, as so many of these politicians do. Fortunately, Daschle like many of Obama's appointments had not paid his taxes and so we do not need to worry about him.

He has also showed that he is a vacillator and pacifier. Guantanamo is a classic example. The president pacified the Left and played to our critics and enemies abroad by signing an executive order saying the prison camp will be closed in a year. But no one knows exactly how that's going to happen. He also told the world that we had tortured detainees but that he was above all that. Obama delights in saying how moral he is; a sure indication that we should hold on to our wallets as he steals from us. In Audacity of Hope (what a ridiculous title particularly for a fear monger), he described the Bush tax cuts as immoral. That presumably is why he is revered; he alone knows what the correct level of taxation should be. Or does he? Giving small tax rebates to people not paying taxes as part of his immediate trillion dollar stimulus bill (the amount that he rushed through a complicit Congress in his first month is just a start). Now we know that he does not even have a Plan as to what do with the money although he did tell Federal Agencies, Governors and Mayors that he will call them out if they do not spend it wisely. Are they now quaking in their boots at the tough man in the White House - the guy who jets around the country to states that voted him into power? His game plan is to keep his popularity high by hugging selected people such as a homeless woman in front of the cameras, promising individual help. Meanwhile Washington burns. Senator Dodd slips a zinger into the stimulus package at the dead of night to severely curtail executive pay. We are talking about young up and comers, not the ultra rich who already have their money salted away. The real losers will be the poor. Just watch Manhattan. Tax revenues will plummet and the people employed by executives in their private lives will be thrown out of work. These executives were not putting their money under the mattress.

This White House is good at making it seem as if Obama has made a tough decision, when he is really just buying time to figure out what to do. An example is the blue ribbon task force on what to do about the car industry. Meanwhile he will continue to pour in our tax money to pay their ongoing operating losses. Obama wants to avoid companies going into Chapter 11 as then they will have to reorganize which means that his union buddies who gave him so much to get him elected, will lose their sweetheart compensation deals. The argument is that no one will buy a car from a car company being reorganized under Chapter 11. The opposite is the case. People will not buy cars when they know that they are paying $2000 for each car to subsidize ex-car workers who are sitting at home doing nothing. People flew in planes operated by companies in Chapter 11; that did not stop them flying. They would buy an American car preferentially if they did not think they were subsidizing free loaders.

Obama's subsidy plan to prevent home foreclosures is a cruel and expensive gesture. Again he is at sea as to whom it will help. He is trying to say that free loaders will not benefit as if he has the ability to separate the wheat from the chaff. Accepting that Obama is a neophyte particularly on the economy is not enough to explain his comments. Does he believe what he says or does he believe that he can continue to snow all of the people all of the time?

Most troubling is his fear mongering. He has talked the stock market down to end its worst week in four months while investors sent gold prices to near records. Contrast Obama with Reagan. The Commander-in-Chief has to be optimistic and up beat. Contrast him with Winston Churchill in Britain's darkest hour – "We will never surrender." Contrast him with Ike – "Pessimism never won battles." Our biggest problem is fear itself. Indeed a free market USA is so resilient that we have nothing to fear other than fear. The markets and the economy move on emotion. Contrary to the oft repeated pessimism that there is no liquidity and that we have to get things moving by injecting money, there is plenty of liquidity. The problem is that it is sitting on the sidelines as no one will invest while Obama and his Liberal friends keep saying how bad everything is. President Obama needs to get aboard on believing in the USA free market resilience and our ability to create the best new companies and deploy new technology better than any other country. Or he should at least be quiet. Thank goodness that Michelle Obama is silent. What we do not need is someone who says that she can be proud of the USA for the first time in her life now that her left wing activist husband is President.

In the latest spin, The White House is playing down nationalization talk of banks. Does Obama not know that Citigroup is already effectively nationalized? In the charade of the House Investigative Hearings where corrupt congressmen castigate corrupt bank CEOs as a popularity contest on TV, Citigroup's CEO understood that they had to speak nicely to his new masters. Citigroup's shares closed at $1.95, prompting the comment that it is now cheaper to buy a share in Citigroup than to withdraw cash from one of its ATMs. That costs $3. Somebody must get Obama to understand that we do not have the resources to subsidize all the troubled institutions and that as we prop them up we weaken those that are strong. In the end Mother

Nature will prevail in the form of free market forces. The only way to prevent that happening is to nationalize every part of an industry. That is socialism. President Obama should heed the experience of King Canute when he sat on his throne at the edge of the ocean and showed that he could not turn back the waves.

When it comes to foreign policy, the prospects are even more troubling. On Afghanistan, instead of answering exactly what he will do, the White House prevaricated. Meanwhile Obama has stepped up the covert war of missile strikes against Pakistan and has deployed more troops there. I think that is right but it is hypocritical for holier than thou Obama. A covert war is still war and it is illegal if we adopt being holier than thou as our platform. Plus it gives mixed signals to friends and enemies alike which is also dangerous.

Getting back to Guantanamo, a detainee who is Ethiopian born but who has British citizenship is being returned to Britain where he will be free to disappear into the general population. A Saudi citizen similarly liberated has resurfaced as a country leader for al-Qaeda. The Ethiopian-Briton was an associate of various high profile al-Qaeda figures and will no doubt resume these relationships and terrorists everywhere will claim another victory in outlasting the West over Guantanamo detentions. All of this activity is against a backdrop where several British citizens were arrested recently for plotting to blow multiple planes out of the sky on their way to the USA.

Obama will continually be jumping into other waters he does not understand. He will continue to muddy the housing pool and then turn his attention to health care; climate change; the impending labor-business fight over secret ballots to ensure unionization; the foreign policy entanglements of Iran's larger-than-expected uranium stockpile and ballistic missile technologies; North Korea's long-range missile and satellite tests; and the ongoing Israel-Palestinian conflict. Tough guy Putin must be licking his chops and Chavez is no doubt looking on with amusement while Venezuela continues to go down the tubes. I wonder how long it will take President Obama to realize that our enemies use diplomatic talking as a stalling tactic while they pursue their real agendas which are not peaceful.

David J. Phillips

OBAMA'S RHETORIC

President Barack Obama has turned fear mongering into an art form. He has repeatedly raised the specter of another Great Depression. In his remarks, every gloomy statistic on the economy becomes a harbinger of doom. As he tells it, today's economy is the worst since the Great Depression. Without his Recovery and Reinvestment Act, he says, the economy will fall back into that abyss and may never recover.

This fear mongering may be good politics, but it is bad history and bad economics. It is bad history because our current economic woes don't come close to those of the 1930s. At worst, a comparison to the 1981-82 recession might be appropriate. Consider the job losses that Mr. Obama always cites. In the last year, the U.S. economy shed 3.4 million jobs. That's a grim statistic for sure, but represents just 2.2% of the labor force. From November 1981 to October 1982, 2.4 million jobs were lost -- fewer in number than today, but the labor force was smaller. So 1981-82 job losses totaled 2.2% of th e labor force, the same as now.

Job losses in the Great Depression were of an entirely different magnitude. In 1930, job losses were 4.8% of the labor force, with an additional 6.5% in 1932 and another 7.1% in 1932. Jobs were being lost at double or triple the rate of 2008-09 or 1981-82. U.S. unemployment is currently 7.6%. That is more than three percentage points below the 1982 peak (10.8%) and not even a third of the peak in 1932 (25.2%).

Other economic statistics also dispel any analogy between today's economic woes and the Great Depression. Real gross domestic product (GDP) rose in 2008, despite a bad fourth quarter. The Congressional Budget Office projects a GDP decline of 2% in 2009. That's comparable to 1982, when GDP contracted by 1.9%. It is nothing like 1930, when GDP fell by 9%, or 1931, when GDP contracted by another 8%, or 1932, when it fell yet another 13%.

Auto production last year declined by roughly 25%. That looks good compared to 1932, when production shriveled by 90%. The failure of a couple of dozen banks in 2008 just doesn't compare to over 10,000 bank failures in 1933 or even the 3,000-plus bank (Savings & Loan) failures in 1987-88. Stockholders can take some solace from the fact that the recent stock market debacle doesn't come close to the 90% devaluation of the early 1930s.

President Obama's analogies to the Great Depression are not only historically inaccurate, they're also dangerous. Repeated warnings from the White House about a coming economic apocalypse continue to damage consumer and investor expectations for the future. In fact, they have contributed to the continuing decline in consumer confidence that is restraining a spending pickup. Fear mongering triggers a political stampede to embrace a "recovery" package that will deliver a lot less than it promises. A calmer assessment of the economy's woes would produce better policies. That though is not the aim. The establishment of Liberal ideology with income redistribution and control of free market capitalism is what Obama Liberals are intent on achieving whatever the economic cost. Then Obama says the USA will be stronger than before. What dishonesty! We will be shackled by debt in a society accustomed to free handouts and welfare where entrepreneurial enterprise is punished by confiscatory taxation. The origin of the USA is the model of what happens when one has repressive taxation without representation.

OBAMA'S ACTIVISM

The continued sell-off on Wall Street and the growing fear on Main Street is a consequence of the realization that our new president's policies are designed to radically re-engineer American capitalism.

President Obama is returning to Jimmy Carter's higher taxes. His $3.6 trillion budget blueprint redefines the role of government in our economy and society. The budget more than doubles the national debt held by the public, adding more to the debt than all previous presidents from George Washington to George W. Bush combined.

The pervasive government subsidies and mandates -- in health, pharmaceuticals, energy and the like -- will do a poor job of picking winners and losers and will be difficult to unwind as recipients lobby for continuation and expansion. Expanding the scale and scope of government largess means that more and more of our best entrepreneurs, managers and workers will spend their time and talent chasing handouts subject to bureaucratic diktats, not the marketplace needs and wants of consumers.

New and expanded refundable tax credits would raise the fraction of taxpayers paying no income taxes to over 50%. This most pernicious feature of the president's budget will cement a permanent voting majority with no stake in controlling the cost of general government and who will ensure continuing left wing activism.

Bigger government programs, always deliver less, more slowly, at far higher cost than projected, with damaging unintended consequences. The most recent example was the government's meddling in the housing market to bring home ownership to low-income families, which became the prime cause of the current economic and financial disaster.

The European social welfare states present a window on our future with standards of living permanently 30% lower than ours and economic stagnation.

ECONOMIC PLAN

Why is Geithner unable to articulate the economic recovery plan? Perhaps Keynes has the answer:

"By a continuous process of inflation, governments can confiscate, secretly and unobserved, an important part of the wealth of their citizens. By this method, they not only confiscate, but they confiscate arbitrarily; and while the process impoverishes many, it actually enriches some ... The process engages all of the hidden forces of economic law on the side of destruction, and does it in a manner that not one man in a million can diagnose." - John Maynard Keynes Economic Consequences of the Peace, 1920

BAR STOOL ECONOMICS

If we suppose that every day, ten men go out for beer and the bill for all ten comes to $100. If they paid their bill the way we pay our taxes, it would go something like this:

The first four men (the poorest) would pay nothing.
The fifth would pay $1.
The sixth would pay $3.
The seventh would pay $7.

The eighth would pay $12.
The ninth would pay $18.
The tenth man (the richest) would pay $59.

So, that's what they decided to do.

The ten men drank in the bar every day and seemed quite happy with the arrangement, until one day, the owner threw them a curve. 'Since you are all such good customers,' he said, 'I'm going to reduce the cost of your daily beer by $20.' Drinks for the ten now cost just $80.

The group still wanted to pay their bill the way we pay our taxes so the first four men were unaffected. They would still drink for free.

But what would happen to the other six men who are the paying customers? How could they divide the $20 windfall so that everyone would get his 'fair share?'

They realized that $20 divided by six is $3.33. But if they subtracted that from everybody's share, then the fifth man and the sixth man would each end up being paid to drink his beer. So, the bar owner suggested that it would be fair to reduce each man's bill by roughly the same amount, and he proceeded to work out the amounts each should pay.

And so:

The fifth man, like the first four, now paid nothing (100% savings).
The sixth now paid $2 instead of $3 (33%savings).
The seventh now pay $5 instead of $7 (28%savings).
The eighth now paid $9 instead of $12 (25% savings).
The ninth now paid $14 instead of $18 (22% savings).
The tenth now paid $49 instead of $59 (16% savings).

Each of the six was better off than before. And the first four continued to drink for free. But once outside the restaurant, the men began to compare their savings. 'I only got a dollar out of the $20,' declared the sixth man. He pointed to the tenth man,' but he got $10!'

'Yeah, that's right,' exclaimed the fifth man. 'I only saved a dollar, too. It's unfair that he got ten times more than I got'

'That's true!!' shouted the seventh man. 'Why should he get $10 back when I got only two? The wealthy get all the breaks!'

'Wait a minute,' yelled the first four men in unison. 'We didn't get anything at all. The system exploits the poor!'

The nine men surrounded the tenth and beat him up.

The next night the tenth man didn't show up for drinks so the nine sat down and had beers without him. But when it came time to pay the bill, they discovered something important. They didn't have enough money between all of them for even half of the bill!

That is how our tax system has worked. The people who pay the highest taxes get the most benefit from a tax reduction. Tax them too much, attack them for being wealthy, and they just may not show up anymore. In fact, they might start drinking overseas.

FALLACY OF THE STIMULUS BILL

Our ignorance of what causes economic ailments -- and how to treat them -- is profound. Downturns and financial crises are not regular occurrences, and because economies are always evolving, they tend to be idiosyncratic, singular events.

After decades of diligent research, scholars still argue about what caused the Great Depression -- excessive consumption, investment, stock-market speculation and borrowing in the Roaring '20s, protectionism, or excessively tight monetary policy? Nor do we know how we got out of it: Some credit the New Deal while others say that that FDR's policies prolonged the Depression.

Similarly, there is no consensus about why huge public-spending projects and a zero-interest-rate policy failed to pull the Japanese out of a prolonged slump.

The economic theory behind the nearly $800 billion stimulus package is based on John Maynard Keynes's speculative conjecture about human nature. Keynes claimed that people cope with uncertainty by assuming the future will be like the present. This predisposition exacerbates economic downturns and should be countered by a sharp fiscal stimulus that reignites the "animal spirits" of consumers and investors.

But history suggests that dark moods do change without stimulus. The depressions and panics of the 19th century ended without any fiscal stimulus to speak of, as did the gloom that followed the stock-market crash of 1987. Countercyclical fiscal policy may or may not have shortened other recessions; there are too few data points and too much difference in other conditions to really know.

Unfounded assertions that calamitous consequences make opposition to the rapid enactment of a large stimulus package "inexcusable and irresponsible" are likely to offset any placebo effect the package might have. A president elected on a platform of hope isn't likely to spark shopping sprees by painting a bleak picture of our prospects.

Stimulus therapy poses great risks. Years of profligacy have put the federal government in a precarious financial position. We don't have the domestic savings to finance much larger budget deficits. Unlike the Japanese, Americans don't have much stashed away under their mattresses: We are reliant on capital inflows from abroad. The long-predicted run on the dollar triggered by fears of a flood of new government debt is a real possibility.

Large increases in public spending usurp precious resources from supporting the innovations necessary for our long-term prosperity. Everyone isn't a pessimist in hard times: The optimism of many entrepreneurs and consumers fueled the takeoff of personal computers during the deep recession of the early 1980s.

Hastily enacted programs jeopardize crucial beliefs in the value of productive enterprise. To sustain these beliefs, Americans must see their government play the role of an even-handed referee rather than be a dispenser of rewards or even a judge of economic merit or contribution. The panicky response to the financial crisis, where openness and due process have been sacrificed to speed, has unfortunately undermined our faith. The Fed has refused to reveal to whom it has lent trillions.

The Obama administration assures us that it will only fund "worthwhile" and "shovel-ready" projects. But choices will have to be made in haste which makes this claim not credible. The alternative isn't, as the stimulus scaremongers suggest, to turn our backs to the downturn. We do have mechanisms in place to deal with economic distress. Public aid for the indigent has been modernized and expanded to provide a range of unemployment and income-maintenance schemes. Bankruptcy courts and laws give individuals another chance and facilitate the orderly reorganization or liquidation of troubled businesses. The FDIC has been dealing with bank failures for more than 70 years, and the Federal Reserve has been empowered to provide liquidity in the face of financial panics for even longer.

These mechanisms have been forged through a much more deliberate, open process than the stimulus bill.

OBAMA ENERGY POLICY

Obama will not await passage of a global warming bill before embarking on the new energy and infrastructure spending. House and Senate supporters of a climate bill said they would continue working on legislative language but did not expect quick action on a cap-and-trade law because of the economic emergency. That means that the green-jobs program would not be financed with pollution credits bought by power generators and other carbon emitters, but instead would be added to the budget deficit.

Congressional officials working with the Obama administration said the stimulus program was also likely to involve tax breaks or direct government subsidies for a variety of clean energy projects, including solar arrays, wind farms, advanced biofuels and technology to capture carbon dioxide emissions from coal-burning power plants.

The programs will be a part of a larger economic stimulus package whose outlines are faint but which is expected to cost a trillion dollars. Obama has said that his goal is to create or save 2.5 million jobs in the next two years. He has assigned to his economic and environmental advisers the task of devising a proposal that is expected to combine a shot of new federal money into existing federal and state programs and the possible creation of agencies modeled on New Deal public works programs.

"We'll put people back to work rebuilding our crumbling roads and bridges, modernizing schools that are failing our children, and building wind farms and solar panels, fuel-efficient cars and the alternative energy technologies that can free us from our dependence on foreign oil and keep our economy competitive in the years ahead," Mr. Obama said in a radio address last month, echoing a campaign promise.

The record of government's intervention in energy markets and new technologies is poor. A spectacular example was the Carter-era Synthetic Fuels Corporation, which spent more than $3 billion without producing any commercially usable amount of coal-based liquid fuel. Ethanol even with massive subsidies and other non-oil-based fuels have also not proved their commercial value, in some cases yielding less energy than was needed to produce them, or, in ethanol's case, diverting land to corn and driving up food prices.

Where will the money come from? Will we print it or borrow it? Who will Obama tax?

OBAMA INTERFERENCE

Is there anywhere Obama will not interfere even though he has no clue what he is doing?

President Barack Obama met on St. Patrick's Day with Irish political leaders to give his opinion on violence in Northern Ireland. Obama met with Irish Prime Minister Brian Cowen in the Oval Office, and then with Northern Ireland's First Minister Peter Robinson and his deputy, Martin McGuinness, in his national security adviser's office.

Obama did not ask McGuinness how many people he killed as a terrorist. McGuinness joined the IRA in 1970 at the age of 20. By the start of 1972, at the age of 21, he was second-in-command of the IRA in Derry. McGuinness was responsible for supplying detonators for nail bombs.

OBAMA WANTS PRIVATE EQUITY

The Obama administration has invited private-sector investors to become business partners with the capricious and increasingly anti-constitutional government. This latest plan to unfreeze the financial system is the latest gimmick almost half a year after Congress shoveled $700 billion into the Troubled Assets Relief Program, $325 billion of which has been spent without purchasing any toxic assets.

David J. Phillips

HELP NEEDED FROM PRIVATE SECTOR

The U.S. will use up to $100 billion in funds from the Troubled Asset Relief Program, as well as capital from private investors, in order to generate $500 billion in purchasing power to buy toxic loans and assets. The program could potentially expand to $1 trillion over time.

Treasury Secretary Timothy Geithner said the only way to remove troubled assets clogging banks' balance sheets, which lie at the heart of the financial crisis, is to work with the private sector, even at a time when Wall Street moneymakers are being vilified by the public and politicians.

GREED

Once upon a time, Washington told the nation of economic distress brought on by villainous, greedy Wall Street bankers. It was so much simpler than the real story of societal credit mania, in which the Federal Reserve, Congress, regulators, credit-rating agencies, Fannie and Freddie, and many homeowners and consumers were all complicit.

If we are giving money to greedy bankers, why not give money to hardworking employees of GM and Chrysler and their parts suppliers? If we are stumping up for Wall Street, why shouldn't Barney Frank get to help his friends? If we are doling out for lascivious New York, why not throw billions at homeowners, who were the 'victims'? TARP really is now a bailout machine, spreading moral hazard, even as it misdirects money away from the purpose for which it was intended.

It was inevitable that tales of greed would lead to a bonus blowup. Stoked by President Obama's frequent critiques of shameful Wall Street greed, public anger was rising.

Connecticut Sen. Chris Dodd saw his opening to play off this anger and deflect attention away from his own corrupt and greedy dealings, by inserting bonus caps into the stimulus bill.

Obama jumped on the "outrage" bandwagon over AIG bonuses. Greed, greed, greed, screamed Obama and Washington, hoping nobody would notice their failure to supervise AIG, their botched intervention, or their refusal to come clean about where the AIG money was going.

This spectacle has left the financial community with one impression: Stay away. What healthy bank, what hedge fund, what private equity firm wants to take part in an Obama plan to sell off toxic assets, or to revive consumer lending, with the knowledge that they might be Washington's newest bonfire? Executives are already working to get out of TARP, fearful of political punishment. Meanwhile the economy is collapsing at an ever increasing speed.

Obama has now suggested the banks might need yet more public capital. But just who in Congress is today prepared to vote to provide more funding, with greedy AIG on the public mind? It is too busy passing laws to levy 102% taxes on bankers (90% Federal + State and Local Taxes).

COMMUNITY COLLEGES

Utah's community college enrollment increased to 23,252 this term, up by 12.5 percent in a year. The state's community colleges, like similar institutions across the country, have been swamped with more applications than they can absorb. The situation is similarly difficult for many other community colleges throughout the USA. Almost 1,200 community colleges serve more than 10 million students across the country, according to the American Association of Community Colleges. Tough times are fueling eagerness among workers who have lost their jobs to upgrade their skills and résumés. They also provide something to do for those who cannot find work or do not want to work. Their success as measured by graduation rates is abysmal. The recession should see an improvement in these figures as the student body has fewer distractions or other options currently.

Community colleges are supposed to accepting all comers but the association said that tens of thousands of students have been turned away. The Stimulus Bill is riding to the rescue and jobs at Community Colleges are a good career choice.

David J. Phillips

CALIFORNIA

The recession has created another $8 billion hole in California's budget, the Legislature's budget analyst says in a new report.

Despite a budget deal in March that was meant to close a $42 billion deficit, the Legislative Analyst's Office has projected that state leaders will have to find new solutions as state revenues continue to fall. The report says the additional gap will be $6 billion in the new fiscal year that starts July 1, plus $2 billion that is needed for a cash reserve.

The Golden State, a decade ago, was the booming technology capital of the world. Its prosperity has been destroyed by two decades of chronic overspending, over-regulating and a hyper-progressive tax code that exaggerates the impact on state revenues of economic boom and bust. Total state expenditures have grown to $145 billion in 2008 from $104 billion in 2003 and California now has the worst credit rating in the nation. It also has the nation's fourth highest unemployment rate of 9.3% (after Michigan, Rhode Island and South Carolina) and the second highest home foreclosure rate (after Nevada).

Roughly 1.4 million more nonimmigrant Americans have left California than entered over the last decade. California is suffering more than most states from the housing bust, but its politicians also showed less spending restraint during the boom.

California needs radical tax and spending surgery. Instead its plan is loaded with short-term gimmicks, such as $5 billion of borrowing from future lottery receipts and nearly $10 billion in one-time federal stimulus cash. Even proponents concede the plan doesn't balance spending and revenues 18 months from now.

Unless Gov. Arnold Schwarzenegger and lawmakers take action, the deficit will grow to $12.6 billion in 2010-11.

NEW YORK'S BUDGET

David Paterson took office as governor of New York on March 17, 2008 but he did not initially take the easy route of blaming the state's worsening budget gap, most recently pegged at $17 billion, on outside forces. "It is the result of our increased spending over years and years," the governor said during one of his many fiscal crisis news conferences last fall. He noted that Wall Street had "bailed us out for a number of years," but that now "the well has run dry."

Now the rhetoric has changed and Mr. Paterson has just agreed to a budget that increases spending 9% (including new federal funds flowing to localities) and boosts taxes and fees by a record amount, including a personal income-tax hike. Any pressure for structural reform was diminished in February, when the Obama administration served up a stimulus package promising New York nearly $25 billion over two years.

Meanwhile, public-sector unions bankrolled a campaign to raise taxes on the wealthy, defined as anyone earning over $250,000, and they didn't let up even when the federal stimulus billions materialized. Mr. Paterson publicly refused to bite, repeatedly warning that higher income taxes would weaken the tax base by driving high-income residents away. But he never ruled out an income tax hike, either, strengthening a widespread impression that he would eventually cave in.

With revenues still eroding as the April 1 start of the 2009-10 fiscal year approached, Mr. Paterson and Democratic leaders last week agreed to a budget deal that approached the worst of all worlds. The $132 billion plan will increase state spending by at least $11 billion from 2008-09, including $6.2 billion of temporary stimulus aid that will be built into future budgetary baselines. It also calls for over $6 billion in higher taxes and fees, half again as much as Mr. Paterson's original plan. This increase includes $4 billion to come from an income tax hike that will raise the state's top rate by 31% and kick in at $200,000 for single filers.

Asked if it made sense to raise taxes in a recession, Mr. Paterson replied "none of this makes sense." That's for sure. New York State has already lost 150,000 jobs since last summer, with roughly 130,000 more job losses projected through the end of the year. Tax receipts are plunging, and the governor himself says he doesn't think they've hit bottom yet.

New York's Medicaid program is still by far the most costly in the country, spending nearly twice the national average per recipient, and it will continue to grow at an unsustainable pace. Indeed, at the governor's behest, the budget also eliminated financial-asset tests and face-to-face screening interviews to determine Medicaid eligibility. As if to ensure a steady flow of new customers for publicly subsidized health care, the budget also raises state taxes and fees on employer-provided coverage by $850 million.

The new budget generally represents a huge victory for the leaders of New York's public-sector employee unions, who won their soak-the-rich income tax while brushing off Mr. Paterson's call for a pay freeze and other contract concessions. While government workers in California and Ohio are taking cuts in the form of payless furloughs, more than 160,000 New York State government employees will receive an average 3% pay hike this month.

TAXES AND SPENDING

Obama now wants to turn to new issues of education, health care and green jobs. His problem is that many Americans are anxious and angry about a set of old issues: deficits, taxes and the national debt. Mr. Obama's radical budget, his administration's slapdash operating manner, and hate politics have revived animosity over government's size and cost.

In response, tea parties are sprouting up, and opposition is growing to more bailouts, more spending, higher taxes and larger deficits, even among Congressional Democrats.

Last fiscal year, the deficit was $459 billion. For this fiscal year, it was $569 billion when Mr. Obama took office. Under his proposals, another $1.276 trillion will be added to the deficit this year, for a total of $1.845 trillion. Even without including interest on the mushrooming debt. Mr. Obama is violating every tenet of his campaign promises 'to spend wisely, reform bad habits, and do our business in the light of day.'

Americans are also worried about Mr. Obama's plans for $1.9 trillion more in taxes. These tax hikes won't just affect the rich as he claims. His cap-and-trade carbon tax will hit everyone who consumes energy, that is, every American. Taxes on the top 5% of filers will result in lost jobs and wages for small businesses and less charitable giving. The administration claims higher taxes are required for deficit reduction. But its spending increases are half again as large as its tax hikes.

Nothing has deterred the administration from pursuing its staggeringly expensive agenda. Mr. Obama has brushed off any concerns. He is quite openly using the economic crisis to launch a massive, permanent expansion of government financed by ever-more borrowing and ever-higher taxes. His goal is to cause taxes to rise to European levels, transforming America into a European-style social democracy.

In his third month on the job, Obama is now a fluid, self-assured president, but one who thinks that repeating a false argument will make it true. The man who promised to end finger-pointing is blaming everyone who came before him. Invoking the language of fiscal responsibility, he is engineering prosperity-killing deficits and bankrupting spending.

RETURN OF WELFARE

The House stimulus bill will end Clinton's biggest reform. Twelve years ago, President Bill Clinton signed a law that he correctly proclaimed would end welfare as we know it. That sweeping legislation, the Personal Responsibility and Work Opportunity Act, eliminated the open-ended entitlement that had existed since 1965, replacing it with a finite, block grant approach called the Temporary Assistance to Needy Families (TANF) program.

TANF has been a remarkable success. Welfare caseloads nationally fell from 12.6 million in 1997 to fewer than five million in 2007. Despite this achievement, President Obama and his Liberal cohorts will undo Mr. Clinton's reforms under the cover of the stimulus bill.

Currently, welfare recipients are limited to a total of five years of federal benefits over a lifetime. They're also required to begin working after two years of government support. States are accountable for helping their needy citizens in the transition from handouts to self-sufficiency. Critically, the funds provided to states are fixed appropriations by the federal government.

Through a little noticed provision of the stimulus package, the bill creates a fund for TANF that is open ended in the same way Medicare and Social Security are.

In the section of the House bill dealing with cash assistance to low-income families, the authors inserted the bombshell phrase: 'such sums as are necessary.' This change is a profound departure from the current statutory scheme, despite the fact that, in this particular bill, state TANF spending would be capped.

The 'such sums' appropriation language is deliberately obscure. The provision in line with Liberal ideology is intended to reverse Clinton-era legislation and create a new template for future TANF reauthorizations.

HOMELESS WITH HOMEWORK

Nine-year-old Daniel Valdez lives in a seaside town northwest of Los Angeles.

Daniel, his mother and five brothers, ages 1 to 17, live in a garage without heat or running water in a modest, low-lying neighborhood that sits between celebrity-owned mansions in the hills and the Pacific Ocean. They have been sleeping in the garage for more than a year.

In Vista, California, about 35 miles north of San Diego, the population of homeless children in the local school district reached 2,542 this year, which is 9 percent of the student body and nearly 10 times the number two years ago

Homelessness is a growing issue nationally with serious ramifications for both a future generation and the overburdened public school system. The turmoil of homelessness inevitably hinders children's ability to socialize and learn. Many are plagued by hunger, exhaustion, abuse and insecurity. Homeless children are confronted daily by extremely stressful and traumatic experiences that have profound effects on their cognitive development and ability to learn. They have high rates of developmental delays, learning difficulties and emotional problems as a product of precarious living situations and extreme poverty.

Under federal law, schools are charged with keeping homeless students like Daniel from falling behind their peers academically by providing a wide range of services, including transportation, free lunches, immunizations, gym uniforms and referrals to family services. With insufficient federal funding and budgets that are severely strained, many schools are struggling to meet the rising need.

Now stimulus funds will provide the answer. Social Services are a burgeoning secure career opportunity. The only risk is whether there are enough fat cats to pay for it all or whether they might move to Mexico in an attempt to escape increasingly onerous taxation being levied to pay for the consequences of illegal immigration and other self imposed social ills.

HEALTHCARE

Americans spend $2.4 trillion a year on health care. Americans in 2006 spent $1,928 per capita on health care, at least two-and-a-half times more per person than any other country. Other countries spend less on health care and people overall are relatively healthier.

In comparing statistics on life expectancy, death rates and even cholesterol readings and blood pressures, factored together with costs into a 100-point value scale, the results show the USA in a poor light. The United States is 23 points behind five leading economic competitors: Canada, Japan, Germany, the United Kingdom and France. The cost-benefit disparity is even wider at 46 points when the U.S. is compared with emerging competitors, China, Brazil and India.

Medical costs have long been a problem for U.S. auto companies. General Motors spends more per car on health care than it does on steel. But as more American companies face global competition, the value gap is being felt by more companies.

Obama and other Liberals will mandate at a government-run health care system that will increase costs and lower health care quality at the top end except for those who will be given special privileges such as the political class. Instead health care should cease to be an entitlement and should stay in private hands, with a limited government-funded safety net for all people. Liberal ideology will prevent that happening.

HEALTH AND HUMAN SERVICES

Kansas Gov. Kathleen Sebelius, after being tapped for the top post for Health and Human Services in the Obama cabinet, filed amended tax returns for 2005 onwards.

Sebelius and her husband, Gary, a federal magistrate judge in Kansas, agreed to pay $7,040 in back taxes and $878 in interest on charitable donations, a home loan and other business expenses.

Sebelius is the President's second pick for the top HHS post. In February, the former Sen. Tom Daschle withdrew from consideration over tax problems.

HEALTH CZAR

Obama appointee Nancy-Ann DeParle has many conflicts of interest.

After years as a top state and federal healthcare official, Nancy-Ann DeParle has served as a board member for more than a dozen companies and managed a private equity portfolio over the last eight years. In 2006 and 2007 alone, DeParle collected at least $3.5 million in fees and the sale or awards of stock from healthcare firms. Now DeParle is the White House czar for healthcare reform, charged with fulfilling President Obama's promise to make healthcare more affordable and broadly available. Once again that raises questions about Washington's revolving door, greed of politicians and Obama not meaning what he says about cleaning up Washington's corrupt practices.

Four companies where DeParle was a director, pharmacy benefits manager Medco Health Solutions Inc., health information technology firm Cerner Corp., cardiac device maker Boston Scientific Corp., and dialysis provider DaVita Inc., are among the largest firms in their fields. These firms will undoubtedly feel the effects of DeParle's healthcare overhaul efforts.

In the latter years of the Clinton presidency, DeParle, one time commissioner of the Tennessee Department of Human Services, oversaw Medicare and Medicaid as administrator of the Health Care Financing Administration.

In the Obama administration, she is to serve as an advisor to and work with Kathleen Sebelius, current Democratic governor of Kansas and Obama's nominee for Health and Human Services secretary. Unlike Sebelius, DeParle will not have to undergo the scrutiny of a Senate confirmation. That allows Obama to play games. Neither DeParle nor the White House has released an accounting of her finances. DeParle isn't legally required to make public a personal financial disclosure statement until 60 days after her March 2 appointment. Delayed disclosure, makes it much harder to raise objections. No one can evaluate whether there's a conflict of interest or how deep it is.

CHAPTER 12 ... ...
FOREIGN POLICY

NAIVETY AND DISINFORMATION

President Obama sent a secret letter to Russia's president last month suggesting that he would back off deploying a new missile defense system in Eastern Europe if Moscow would help stop Iran from developing long-range weapons. He is leaking this information to the public in a style reminiscent of the Clinton White House through an anonymous source. After then gauging the public response, the technique is to then claim credit for or deny the accuracy of the leaked information. In this case Obama received some criticism for his naivety and so said the leaked information was inaccurate but without giving any more specifics other than that there was no coupling of the two issues – the US backing off the missile defense system and Russian help in thwarting Iran.

The letter to President Dmitri A. Medvedev was hand-delivered in Moscow three weeks ago. Moscow has not responded, but a Russian official said Monday that Foreign Minister Sergey V. Lavrov would have something to say on missile defense to Secretary of State Hillary Rodham Clinton when they meet Friday in Geneva. The Russians will play Barack/Hillary as a cat plays a mouse.

David J. Phillips

GAUCHE FOREIGN POLICY

Secretary of State Clinton was so enamored with Vice President Biden's call to "press the reset button" on the relationship with Russia that she decided to go one step further. In greeting Sergey V. Lavrov, the Russian foreign minister, she presented him with a red plastic button emblazoned with the English word "reset" and the Russian word 'peregruzka'.

"We worked hard to get the right Russian word," Mrs. Clinton said, handing the button to Mr. Lavrov. "Do you think we got it?"

"You got it wrong," he replied, explaining that the Americans had come up with the Russian word for overcharged.

Consistent with how the Obama administration does everything, in distancing themselves from the Bush administration, blaming Bush wherever possible, reset gives the Russians a free pass on invading Georgia and their return to a hostile anti –democratic stance with Putin veering towards dictatorship and a return to the cold war. Russia will seize on reset as Bush wrong Putin right. Next we will hear Barack Obama using Margaret Thatcher's words in saying, "We can do business with Mr. Gorbachev, I mean Putin."

Unlike the sloppy Obama administration, the Russian political machine will already have worked out how they can use the divisions and weaknesses in the USA to their advantage. They will not try to curry favor or break the ice with cheap plastic gifts and they will certainly not commit the unacceptable gaffe of misusing the language of the other country as if it not important.

Russia has signed a contract to supply Iran with long-range S-300 missiles. After the meeting, Mr. Lavrov, said, "I think we can manage to arrive at a common view, both in the context of strategic offensive weapons and missile defense," he said. Asked whether he and Mrs. Clinton got along, he smiled and said, "I venture to say we have a wonderful personal relationship."

He and Mrs. Clinton agreed on a 'work plan' that would set the stage for a treaty to replace the Strategic Arms Reduction Treaty, or START, the 1991 pact that expires this year. Mr. Lavrov and Mrs. Clinton also discussed Mr. Obama's recent offer in a letter to Mr. Medvedev, of flexibility in the deployment of a missile defense system in Poland and the Czech Republic, while seeking increased support from Russia in constraining Iran's nuclear program. Barack Obama has denied that he connected the two issues. Perhaps he did not tell Hillary Clinton.

The Russians are 'thinking very carefully' about ways to cooperate, said a senior administration official, who spoke on condition of anonymity (we will hear these words again and again from the Obama White House as it is a way to say something and then being able to say one never said it if the remark bombs), citing the delicacy of the matter. "We're not talking about their good will in helping us to diminish this threat," he said. "We're talking about diminishing the threat."

MRS. CLINTON IN EUROPE

Mrs. Clinton has promised a rejuvenated trans-Atlantic relationship. At a town hall meeting with 500 interns and others at the European Parliament in Brussels, she called Europe the "essential partner" for the United States in climate change and fighting terrorism. The Obama administration presumably thinks that the USA and Europe alone hold the key to cooling the world and defeating terrorism.

It is not clear why only interns wanted to listen to Mrs. Clinton.

OBAMA PUMP PRIMING

Barack Obama's spending on infrastructure such as roads, bridges and spending on jobless benefits is slated to cost $1 trillion over the next two years.

Keynesian "pump-priming" in a recession has often been tried, and as an economic stimulus it is overrated. The money that the government spends has to come from somewhere, which means from the private economy in higher taxes or borrowing. The public works are usually less productive than the foregone private investment.

Japan during its "lost decade" of the 1990s, tried this stimulus cure. In 1992, Japanese Prime Minister Kiichi Miyazawa faced falling property prices and a stock market that had sunk 60% in three years. Mr. Miyazawa's Liberal Democratic Party won re-election promising that Japan would spend its way to becoming a "lifestyle superpower." The country embarked on a great Keynesian experiment:

August 1992: 10.7 trillion yen ($85 billion). Japan passed its largest-ever stimulus package to that time, with 8.6 trillion yen earmarked for public works, 1.2 trillion to expand loan quotas for small- and medium-sized businesses and 900 billion for the Japan Development Bank. The package passed in December, but investment kept falling and unemployment rose. By the end of the year, Japan's debt-to-GDP ratio was 68.6%.

April 1993: 13.2 trillion yen. At exchange rates of the day, this was a whopping $117 billion giveaway, again mostly for public works and small businesses. Tokyo erupted into domestic politicking over election practices, the economy went sideways, and the government fell. New Prime Minister Morihiro Hosokawa floated tax cuts, deregulation and decentralization to spur growth. But as the economy worsened -- inflation-adjusted GNP shrank 0.5% in the April to June quarter -- the political drumbeat for handouts increased.

September 1993: 6.2 trillion yen. Mr. Hosokawa announced a compromise "smaller" stimulus of $59 billion, along with minor deregulation. He dropped plans for an income-tax cut. The stimulus included 2.9 trillion yen in low-interest home financing, one trillion yen for "social infrastructure," and another trillion for business. The economy didn't respond. By the end of the year, Japan's debt-to-GDP reached 74.7%.

February 1994: 15.3 trillion yen. This stimulus included 5.8 trillion in income-tax cuts, 7.2 trillion in public investment, 1.5 trillion for small business and employment-support, 500 billion for land purchases and 230 billion for agricultural modernization. The income tax cut was temporary, effective only for 1994. The economy stagnated and Prime Minister Hosokawa resigned amid a corruption scandal. By the end of the year, debt-to-GDP was 80.2%.

September 1995: 14.2 trillion yen. The Socialist government of Tomiichi Murayama, with a wobbly coalition, rolled out a $137 billion plan, with 4.6 trillion in public works, 3.2 trillion for government land purchases, 1.3 trillion in business loans, and more. Mr. Murayama resigned in early 1996, and in June Prime Minister Ryutaro Hashimoto agreed to raise consumption taxes to 5% from 3%, starting in April 1997, to reduce the fiscal deficit.

In 1994 and 1995, Japan spent 3.1% and 2.9% of its annual GDP, and (helped by central bank easing) the economy did respond with modest growth for about two years. Debt-to-GDP hit 87.6%.

April 1998: 16.7 trillion yen. With growth slowing again, the re-elected LDP turned to old medicine: 7.7 trillion yen for public works. The $128 billion grab-bag also included 2.3 trillion for the disposal of bad loans. The government announced four trillion yen in (again) temporary income-tax cuts, spread over two years. Mr. Hashimoto resigned in July after voters registered their discontent at the polls.

November 1998: 23.9 trillion yen. Desperate to get the economy moving, Prime Minister Keizo Obuchi rolled out Japan's largest-ever stimulus, valued at $195 billion. The giveaway included 8.1 trillion yen in social public works, 5.9 trillion for business loans, one trillion for job-creation programs, 700 billion in cash handouts to 35 million households, and more. By the end of the year, debt-to-GDP hit 114.3%.

November 1999: 18 trillion yen. In a "last push," Mr. Obuchi's government spent 7.4 trillion yen to prop up businesses, 6.8 trillion yen for social infrastructure projects like telecommunications and environmental projects, and two trillion yen for housing loans, among other things. Debt-to-GDP reached 128.3%.

Japan's economy grew anemically over that decade, but its national debt exploded. Only in this decade, with a monetary reflation and Prime Minister Junichiro Koizumi's decision to privatize state assets and force banks to acknowledge their bad debts did the economy recover. Yet recent governments have rolled back Mr. Koizumi's reforms and returned to their spending habits. But Japan does have better roads.

Now Obama's advisors are telling him and he is telling us that a similar spending program -- a New Deal -- will revive the U.S. economy.

EUROPE DISAGREES

G-20 finance officials do not agree with a US led push for more coordinated government spending. Treasury Secretary Timothy Geithner has unsuccessfully lobbied for a global stimulus from the G-20 countries White House economic czar Larry Summers has also called for a global stimulus and has been rebuffed by leaders in Europe.

German Chancellor Angela Merkel and the other Europeans know whereof they speak, since a number of countries have decades of experience trying to spend in a vain effort to boost growth. The Obama Administration came into office promising to listen to its friends and allies, so when Europe rejects gargantuan spending, the President and his advisers should listen.

Luxembourg's Jean-Claude Juncker delivered the Continent's verdict on global stimulus. "American appeals insisting that Europeans make an additional budgetary effort to combat the effects of the crisis were not to our liking," he said. When the European Union established the euro in 1999, it put in place strict limits on deficit spending and debt-to-GDP ratios. For decades, countries like Greece, Italy and Belgium had run up huge national debts trying to pay for social-welfare programs and keep their economies afloat at the same time. The chief result of these policies was a huge pile of IOUs. In Italy, the national debt stood at 107% of GDP in 1999. In Belgium and Greece it was 104%. So from its founding, the euro zone insisted that countries not respond to economic downturn by piling up debt. Budget deficits are supposed to be limited to 3% of GDP, and total debt to 60% of GDP. Debt ratios have come down. Italy's debt-to-GDP ratio is now 96%. Greece is at 105%, while France and Germany have hovered around 50% and 40%, respectively. U.S. debt stood at 36% of GDP at the end of 2007, before the financial stimulus started. The U.S. has run up $1 trillion in publicly held debt in the past six months alone, which is an additional 7% of GDP.

The White House is promoting the idea of a 1.5 Keynesian multiplier. The thought is that every $1 of deficit spending yields $1.5 in economic growth. If that were true, Italy would be the richest country in Europe, instead of merely one of the most indebted.

The White House estimates of 3.6 million new jobs are based on a flawed Keynesian model on the impact of government spending. Leading international economists have new models which adjust for the rational behavioral response to stimulus by businesses and consumers. The White House figures, by their own inexperienced economists Christina Romer and Jared Bernstein, also assume zero interest rates for a minimum of four years. The alternative assumes, more reasonably, that as growth returns interest rates will also rise.

By new model estimates, that the US stimulus bill will produce, at most, 600,000 jobs ($1.3 million in spending per job) and add perhaps 0.6% to GDP at its peak. The $800 billion would have been better devoted to business tax cuts and marginal rate tax cuts on income and investment, so changing incentives to work and invest.

CAPITALISM REVISITED

Heads of state, perplexed finance ministers, inflated retinues and journalists from 20 nations arrived in London to address "the greatest financial crisis since the Depression." A day later they went home with smiling, hugging, media photos all done and success claimed in meaningless press conferences. Best photo was Michelle hugging the Queen and the Queen reciprocating even though a thousand years of royal protocol were swept away in a moment. Even the Queen knows that she has to bow to the Obama phenomenon if she wants to stay relevant in our increasingly devalued world. Second best photo was when Berlusconi persuaded Obama and the guy from Russia who speaks for Putin, to do a three way hug, while he told them about his latest sexual exploits or was it how his latest corrupt scheme for personal enrichment.

The G-20 kept it short to minimize the ruin visited on London by the professional street fighters fronting the anti-capitalism mobs on global TV screens. The event was a great opportunity for the anti-globalization crowd.

In truth, the G-20's goal was accomplished before the first plane landed. The mere announcement of the meeting brought forth a torrent of pent-up global agendas. China wants a new global currency to replace the inflatable dollar. The International Monetary Fund has said the world financial system needs an early warning system. Perhaps he was thinking of something like radar, which saved the UK in World War 2. France's Nicolas Sarkozy wants a global financial regulator and then adopted a Napoleonic pose, threatening to walk out because he was not receiving the attention that he deserved. At least Obama and the multi-gowned Michelle as his adornment, both have the advantage of size so that they do not get lost in the crowd. US Liberals pontificated that the crisis has led to a fundamental rethinking of the American way as a model for the rest of the world, increasing Obama's popularity as they hate the thought that the USA might have something that they do not.

David J. Phillips

G-20 PROTESTERS HAVE WRONG TARGET

Anti-capitalist protesters gathering in London for two days of demonstrations missed the point. If there is one myth the credit crunch has exploded, it is that the financial system is a free market. The world is in a mess because the financial system wasn't capitalist enough.

There were some terrible regulatory failures because of poor regulation, not because regulations did not exist. Politicians then lacked the stomach to stop excess as bubbles formed. But successive bailouts over many years also distorted the banking system to the point where real price signals were swamped. Nothing in the current global recovery proposals suggests this lesson has been learned.

In a capitalist system, prices are set in the free market and providers of capital bear responsibility for their losses. Neither of these characteristics hold true of the banking system. The price of credit, the basic commodity of the financial system, was distorted first by implicit government guarantees to depositors and other providers of capital, and second by government cutting interest rates at the first sign of financial trouble.

Financial theory says the cost of capital to an enterprise should rise in line with risk. But banks during the boom were able to leverage themselves more than 50 times yet see their cost of funding fall. That is hardly the sign of a well-functioning free market. Those who provided funding to banks correctly gambled that governments would ride to their rescue. Since the crisis began, implicit guarantees have become explicit and thresholds have been raised. The U.K. is even proposing to raise depositor protection in certain circumstances to £500,000 ($717,360), further undermining the principle of personal responsibility.

This government protection effectively extends to wholesale funding, too. With a few exceptions, including Lehman Brothers, bondholders have been spared losses as a result of bank failures. Indeed, it has been axiomatic of the policy-maker response that bondholders should be kept whole to avoid the threat that the banking system would seize up completely or that the insurance industry, with large bond portfolios, would become the next domino to fall. Most Western bank bonds are now issued with an explicit government guarantee. The result is a distorted global financial system in which the true cost of capital is obscured. In a fully capitalist system, there would be no guarantees. The market would ensure banks didn't become too big or too leveraged.

At least the current crisis is sure to lead to higher common-equity buffers for all. But since removing the guarantees and breaking up the banks is outside the realm of political reality, an alternative solution is to charge banks explicitly and upfront for all guarantees. The charges would rise in line with leverage. That at least would raise the cost of funding, helping to generate a price signal to the market. Instead, global governments are taking the opposite tack. Unable to remove the guarantees and unwilling to properly charge for them because the banks remain too weak, they will try to limit the risks through more intrusive regulation. The consequences will be lower bank profits, less capital generated, less credit created, lower economic growth and more bureaucratic control over the banks and the wider economy.

LESSON FROM SWEDEN

TARP funds have been used for the partial purchase of GM and Chrysler and some of their parts suppliers. That unlikely tutor of America regarding capitalist common sense has said, through a Cabinet minister, that the ailing Saab automobile company is on its own. "The Swedish state is not prepared to own car factories."

INTERNATIONAL MONETARY FUND

Treasury Secretary Timothy F. Geithner is now pressing for a sweeping plan that calls on the United States and other nations to offer billions more to bail out economies in crisis and prods a reluctant Europe to prop up the reeling world economy with more aggressive government spending.

Europe doubts the wisdom of falling deeply into debt in a questionable effort to create jobs and halt the plunge in consumer demand, as the United States is doing. Even on Capitol Hill, some members of Congress have grown wary of approving still more money.

Geithner said the administration will ask Congress to make $100 billion more available, doubling the current U.S. commitment, to the International Monetary Fund to aid struggling nations. U.S. lawmakers are already bracing for Obama to request hundreds of billions of dollars in more rescue funds for U.S. financial firms and possibly a second massive economic stimulus package as well.

Obama will claim success in persuading other G-20 countries to pony up equal amounts of money and there will be talk of a trillion dollar commitment in total. The reality as in troop deployments is that the USA is largely on its own other than vocal support backed by a little window dressing. A weak US President is easily flattered particularly when a compliant Liberal media goes along with the charade. Both Obama and the media know that all that really matters is the votes back home from a populace which is easily duped.

ISLAM

Barack Obama, making his first visit to a Muslim nation as President, declared that the United States "is not at war with Islam" and called for a greater partnership with the Islamic world in an address to the Turkish parliament.

"Let me say this as clearly as I can," Obama said. "The United States is not at war with Islam. In fact, our partnership with the Muslim world is critical in rolling back a fringe ideology that people of all faiths reject."

"America's relationship with the Muslim world cannot and will not be based on opposition to al-Qaeda," he said. "We seek broad engagement based upon mutual interests and mutual respect."

"We will convey our deep appreciation for the Islamic faith, which has done so much over so many centuries to shape the world for the better, including my own country," Obama said.

AFGHANISTAN AND PAKISTAN

A disastrous new era is dawning in Afghanistan and in Pakistan's Swat Valley, where a top Islamist militant leader, emboldened by a peace agreement with the federal government, laid out an ambitious plan to bring a complete Islamic system to the surrounding northwest region and the entire country.

Speaking to thousands of followers in an address aired live from Swat on national news channels, cleric Sufi Mohammed bluntly defied the constitution and federal judiciary, saying he would not allow any appeals to state courts under the system of sharia, or Islamic law that will prevail there as a result of the peace accord signed by the president With tacit Obama support.

"The Koran says that supporting an infidel system is a great sin," Mohammed said, referring to Pakistan's modern democratic institutions. He declared that in Swat, home to 1.5 million people, all "un-Islamic laws and customs will be abolished," and he suggested that the official imprimatur on the agreement would pave the way for sharia to be installed in other areas.

Mohammed's dramatic speech echoed a rousing sermon in Islamabad by another radical cleric, Maulana Abdul Aziz, who appeared at the Red Mosque in the capital after nearly two years in detention and urged several thousand chanting followers to launch a crusade for sharia nationwide.

These rallying cries create radical energy between the turbulent, Taliban-plagued northwest region and the increasingly vulnerable federal capital, less than 100 miles to the east. They also appeared to pose a direct, unprecedented religious challenge to modern state authority in the Muslim nation of 176 million.

The Pakistani government, with support from Obama's week kneed policies, made a critical mistake in giving the Taliban and Islamic clerics legal cover for their agenda. Now they are going to be battle-ready to struggle for the heart of Pakistan as well as making Afghanistan a losing cause. A further surge in suicide bombings will now occur. Two recent bombings at security checkpoints in the northwest killed more than 40 people. The decision by insurgents to keep fighting in spite of the peace deal showed that you cannot deal with the Taliban by giving away territory. That will only encourage them to move closer and closer to the populated centers of the Punjab and Islamabad.

An Obama sanctioned U.S. missile strike killed three people at a Taliban compound in the South Waziristan tribal region. Such attacks, designed to keep U.S. troops out of harm's way while waging war, have become a powerful recruitment tool for extremist groups in Pakistan as anti-American sentiment builds.

David J. Phillips

OBAMA AS COMMANDER-IN-CHIEF

After years of often testy cooperation with NATO and resentment over unequal burden-sharing, the United States is taking unabashed ownership of the Afghan war.

U.S. intelligence officials are drawing up targets for Predator drone strikes along the Pakistan-Afghanistan border, to kill without risking being killed in return.

President Obama's decision to deploy an additional 17,000 troops to Afghanistan this year will bring the number of foreign troops there to nearly 90,000, more than two-thirds of them Americans. Many will report to NATO commanders. The number of American civilian officials will also grow by at least 50 percent to more than 900. American diplomats and development experts plan to spread into relatively peaceful western and northern regions of Afghanistan that until now were left to other NATO governments. In Afghanistan, Obama will continue to characterize the effort untruthfully as multinational. There will continue to be a few thousand troops from NATO, but increasingly the burden will fall on the USA.

The increasing U.S. dominance is both by default and by design. The United States has far more troops, equipment and money and more willingness to use them than the rest of NATO. Although European governments have been asked to send up to four additional battalions of 800 to 1,000 troops each to boost security for Afghan elections in August, they will be temporary additions. Britain, whose 8,000 combat troops make it the second-largest NATO contributor, is considering whether it can send more after its withdrawal from Iraq this year. Germany, the third largest, has authorized 4,500, although they are restricted from certain combat areas and duties; France fields nearly 3,000 unrestricted troops.

The Netherlands plans to end its 1,700-troop combat mission in Afghanistan next year; Canada will bring its 2,800 troops home in 2011. With the arrival of new forces this year, U.S. troops will number more than 55,000.

Rather than expecting more combat forces, Obama has asked NATO to say what more they can contribute in terms of financing, training for Afghan forces, and civilian experts in every sector, from agriculture to governance. A NATO trust fund established last year to pay for equipment and transportation for Afghan security forces set a goal of about $1.5 billion; contributions to date total less than $25 million. Plans to double the size of the Afghan army to 134,000 by 2011 will require an additional 29 NATO training teams. The U.S. will provide them. American trainers outnumber their NATO counterparts three to one.

Some NATO members restrict their troops to certain areas of the country, trainers often cannot move with redeployed Afghan forces, leaving U.S. forces to pick up the responsibility to transport the Afghans and their equipment from one region to another.

The Americanization of the war under Obama is visible in the turbulent south, where the regional NATO command, led by a Dutch general, with Dutch, British, Danish and U.S. troops, faces the primary Taliban threat. Most of the additional U.S. troops will deploy there, and dozens of C-130 transport aircraft land at the Kandahar air field every day with pallets of supplies. A British general will take over the southern command this fall. The USA will have almost three times as many troops as any other NATO member reporting to this British general.

Obama's war will be different to what Americans have experienced before.

WILL ISLAM RETURN OBAMA RESPECT?

The experience of Arab Christians living now amid majority Islamic populations is often repression, arrest, imprisonment and death.

Coptic Christians in Egypt have been singled out for discrimination and persecution. Muslim rioters often burn or vandalize their churches and shops.

In Turkey, the Syriac Orthodox Church (its 3,000 members speak Aramaic, the language of Christ) is battling with Turkish authorities over the lands around the Mor Gabriel monastery, built in 397.

Pakistan's recent peace deal with the Taliban in the Swat Valley puts at risk the 500 Christians still trying to live there. Many fled after Islamic extremists bombed a girls' school late last year. Pakistan has never let them buy land to build a church.

In 1995, the Saudis were allowed to build a mosque in Rome near the Vatican, but never reciprocated with a Christian church in their country. Saudi Arabia even forbids private worship at home for some one million Christian migrant workers.

In Iraq, the situation for small religious minorities has become dire. Reports emerge regularly of mortal danger there for groups that date to antiquity -- Chaldean-Assyrians, the Yazidis and Sabean Mandaeans, who revere John the Baptist. Last fall the Chaldean-Assyrian archbishop of Mosul was kidnapped and murdered. Some Iraqi Christians believe the new government won't protect them, and talk of moving into a "homeland" enclave in Nineveh.

The respect Mr. Obama is giving Islam will go only in one direction as he knows. We need a stronger, more principled and less sycophantic President.

Mr. Obama should make formalized tolerance of Christian sects in the Middle East the basis for arriving at what he called common ground with Islam. In churches in the rest of the world this weekend, that common ground was first walked in the Middle East 2,000 years ago.

LESSON FROM MEXICO

From Mexico, the USA is receiving needed instruction about fundamental rights and the rule of law. Obama and his Liberal fellow travelers want to abolish the right of workers to secret ballots in unionization elections. The secret ballot is absolutely necessary in order to ensure that workers are not intimidated into voting for a union they might not otherwise choose. Last year, Mexico's highest court unanimously affirmed for Mexicans the right that Liberals want to strip in the USA.

MEXICO FIGHTS BACK

Mexico plans to boost tariffs on about 90 U.S. products in retaliation for the decision to cancel a pilot program that allowed some Mexican trucks to transport goods within the U.S. Mexico says the U.S. decision violates a NAFTA provision to open cross-border trucking.

OBAMA JOINS TEAMSTERS' WAR

President Obama campaigned as a trade warrior, and now he's getting his wish. Mexico has announced that it will raise tariffs on 90 U.S. products, affecting some $2.4 billion in goods across 40 states. The move was retaliation for the recent decision by Congress, signed into law by Mr. Obama, to close the Southern U.S. border to Mexican trucks.

Proponents cloaked the decision in safety language, insisting that the Mexican trucks are a road hazard. However, a federal pilot program has shown that Mexican trucks actually have fewer violations than do American. The real hazard here is the new Administration's obeisance to the Teamsters, who endorsed Mr. Obama early in the 2008 Democratic primaries and demanded the trucking shutdown.

By rejecting Mexican trucks, the Administration violated the North American Free Trade Agreement and picked a needless fight with our southern neighbor.

AMERICAS SUMMIT

President Barack Obama's goal at the fifth Summit of the Americas in Trinidad and Tobago was to be better liked by the region's dictators and left-wing populists than his predecessor George W. Bush. He succeeded. He allowed the USA to be lambasted by Venezuela's Hugo Chávez, Bolivia's Evo Morales, and Nicaragua's Danny Ortega, at the same time as he shared smiling, double hand clasp, and photo opportunities with these left wing enemies of the USA. Mr. Obama passed up the opportunity to defend freedom and our democratic principles.

The subject of Cuba was a softball that the American president could have hit out of the park. He knew well in advance that his counterparts would pressure him to end the U.S. embargo. He even prepared for that fact a few days ahead of the summit by unconditionally lifting U.S. restrictions on travel and remittances to the island and offering to allow U.S. telecom companies to bring technology to this backward country.

Raúl Castro responded with a long diatribe against the Yankee oppressor. The Castro brothers want credit from U.S. banks because they have defaulted on the rest of the world, and no one will lend to them anymore. They also want foreign aid from the World Bank.

Venezuelan has supported Colombian terrorists, drug trafficking and Iran's nuclear ambitions. Mr. Obama said nothing. He could have neutralized Venezuelan tyranny by announcing a White House push for ratification of the U.S.-Colombia Free Trade Agreement. That didn't happen either. His strategy is to offend no one and accomplish nothing.

Chapter 13 ... ... Housing

Building Flawed American Dreams

A grandson of Mexican immigrants and a former mayor of San Antonio, Henry G. Cisneros spent years trying to make the dream of homeownership come true for low-income families. As the Clinton administration's top housing official in the mid-1990s, Mr. Cisneros loosened mortgage restrictions so first-time buyers could qualify for loans they could never get before.

Then, capitalizing on a housing expansion he helped unleash, he joined the boards of a major builder, K B Horne, and the largest mortgage lender in the nation, Countrywide Financial — two companies that fueled the housing boom, through abusive business practices. Mr. Cisneros became a developer himself building the Lago Vista development in San Antonio. Joining with KB, he built 428 homes for low-income buyers in what was a neglected, industrial neighborhood. Much of Lago Vista is now in foreclosure.

Mr. Cisneros left government in 1997 after revelations that he had lied to federal investigators about payments to a former mistress. He reinvented himself as a well-regarded advocate and builder of urban, working-class homes. He has financed the construction of more than 7,000 houses.

For the three years he was a director at KB Home, Cisneros received at least $70,000 in pay and more than $100,000 worth of stock. He also received $1.14 million in directors' fees and stock grants during the six years he was a director at Countrywide. He made more than $5 million from Countrywide stock options.

To-day Cisneros is reflective. "You think you have a finely tuned instrument that you can use to say: 'Stop! We're at 69 percent homeownership. We should not go further. There are people who should remain renters. I'm not sure you can regulate when we're talking about an entire nation of 300 million people and this behavior becomes viral."

Until Clinton was president, getting a mortgage was a challenge for low-income families. Many of these families were minorities, which naturally made the subject of special interest to Mr. Cisneros, who, in 1993, became the first Hispanic head of the Department of Housing and Urban Development.

Thus was born the National Homeownership Strategy, which promoted ownership as patriotic and an easy win for all. Under Mr. Cisneros, there were changes at HUD to inflate property appraisals and make it easier to qualify for mortgages with less proof of income. HUD also became an agency that greased the mortgage wheel for first-time buyers by insuring billions of dollars in loans. A later HUD inquiry uncovered appraisal fraud that imperiled the federal mortgage insurance fund.

Lenders sprang up to serve those whose poor credit history made them ineligible for lower-interest "prime" loans. Countrywide, which Angilo R. Mozilo Angelo co-founded in 1969, set up a subprime unit in 1996. It made for a cozy network. Fannie bought or backed many mortgages received by home buyers in the KB Home/American CityVista partnership. And Fannie's biggest mortgage client was Countrywide, whose board Mr. Cisneros had joined in 2001.

To get things rolling in Lago Vista, traditional bars to homeownership were lowered to the ground. Fannie Mae, CityVista and KB promoted a program allowing police officers, firefighters, teachers and others to get loans with nothing down and no closing costs.

Victor Ramirez and Lorraine Pulido-Ramirez bought a house in Lago Vista in 2002. "This was our first home. I had nothing to compare it to," Mr. Ramirez says. "I was a student making $17,000 a year, my wife was between jobs. In retrospect, how in hell did we qualify?"

KB and Cisneros eventually built more than a dozen developments, primarily in Texas.

Officials at HUD uncovered problems with KB's lending. In 2005, about two years after Mr. Cisneros left the KB board, the agency filed an administrative action against KB for approving loans based on overstated or improperly documented borrower income, and for charging excessive fees. KB Home paid $3.2 million to settle the HUD action without admitting liability or fault, one of the largest settlements collected by the agency's mortgagee review board. Shortly afterward, KB sold its lending unit to Countrywide. Then they set up a joint venture: KB installed Countrywide sales representatives in its developments.

By 2007, almost three-quarters of the loans to KB buyers were made by the joint venture. In Lago Vista, residents secured loans from a spectrum of federal agencies and lenders.

During years of heady growth, and then during a deep financial slide, Countrywide became a lightning rod for criticism about excesses and abuses leading to the housing bust — which Countrywide routinely brushed off.

Still, Countrywide expanded subprime lending aggressively while Cisneros served on its board. In September 2004, lending audits in six of Countrywide's largest regions showed about one in eight loans was "severely unsatisfactory" because of shoddy underwriting.

Today in Lago Vista, crime has risen sharply, and with association dues unpaid, there is no security. Salvador Gutierrez, a truck driver, woke up recently to see four men stealing the tires off his pickup.

Countrywide was eventually bought at a fire-sale price by Bank of America but not before they had given sweetheart mortgage deals to influential politicians including Senator Dodd. In turn these politicians failed to act to correct their corrupt practices and thwarted regulatory changes. To-day Dodd is slipping zingers into bailout legislation to punish up-and-comers on Wall Street and is castigating CEO's from his Senate bully pulpit.

FORECLOSURE PREVENTION PLAN

The three-part plan will help four million borrowers that are "underwater" refinance through the Government Sponsored Enterprises (GSE's), help five million additional borrowers through the creation of a $75 billion Homeowners Stability Initiative, and provide additional support to Fannie Mae and Freddie Mac.

The plan includes an additional $100 billion of funding to Fannie and Freddie in addition to the $75 billion stability initiative, which includes a $10 billion loan guarantee plan with the Federal Deposit Insurance Corp.

The plan's centerpiece is the Homeowners Stability Initiative, which is designed to help borrowers who have defaulted on their mortgages or are at imminent risk of default. Under the initiative, Treasury will partner with lenders to reduce the monthly payments of a loan. The plan requires the lender to reduce monthly mortgage payments to no more than 38% of a borrower's income. After that point, the government will match further reductions by the lender to bring payments down to a 31% debt-to-income ratio. Lenders will keep the modified payments in place for five years; after that interest rates may be gradually increased. Lenders may also choose to reduce mortgage principal, with Treasury sharing in the cost.

The plan provides numerous incentives for lenders to perform modifications and borrowers to stay current on loans. For example, servicers will receive a $1,000 fee for each eligible modification meeting the regulators' guidelines. Servicers will also receive "pay for success" fees for each month the borrower stays current on the modified loan, up to $1,000 a year for three years. The government will provide an incentive payment of $1,500 to mortgage holders and $500 for servicers for modifications made while a borrower at risk of imminent default is still current. For borrowers who stay current on their mortgage, they will receive a monthly balance reduction payment of up to $1,000 each year for five years to reduce the principal balance of the loan.

The Obama administration has developed a $10 billion partial guarantee program with the FDIC to discourage lenders from foreclosing on mortgages. Treasury will give a 50% partial guarantee to loans modified through the initiative to be paid if home prices depreciate.

The government is also allowing underwater borrowers to refinance through the GSEs if their loan is already owned or guaranteed by Fannie or Freddie. Previously, the GSEs could not accept a loan with a greater than 80% loan-to-value ratio. To do so Treasury will double its funding commitment to $200 billion each for Fannie and Freddie. In September, Treasury purchased preferred stock purchase agreements in each enterprise worth $100 billion. Treasury will continue to purchase the GSEs' mortgage-backed securities, and will increase the size of the enterprises' retained portfolios by $50 billion to $900 billion.

In short bloated GSE's, notably Fanny and Freddy, will not be reined in but will become increasingly bloated at increasing cost to taxpayers to prop up homeowners who would do better as renters. The increased bureaucracy alone will be overwhelming.

OBAMA HOUSING PLAN

Housing experts caution that US President Barack Obama's plan to revive the US housing market is not likely to help most homeowners at risk of foreclosure, may even worsen their debt loads and aggravate the mortgage finance crisis.

In late February, the Obama administration proposed its Homeowner Affordability and Stability Plan, a three-part approach meant to ease, if not halt, the rash of mortgage defaults and resulting foreclosures that are flooding the already swollen housing inventory with more homes for sale.

The fate of the US housing sector and hopes for its revival is seen by many as fundamental to a general economic recovery for the nation as a whole. The housing market collapse and the attending mortgage credit debacle are seen as the factor underlying the credit crisis and resulting recession.

The housing sector, especially new home construction, is also a crucial downstream consuming industry for a wide variety of chemicals and plastics.

In the first part of the Obama plan, the government-authorized secondary-mortgage-market firms, Fannie Mae and Freddie Mac, are directed to ease their lending rules so that homeowners who owe more on their mortgage than their home is worth can refinance their loans.

In the second part, private banks and other lenders will be encouraged to modify mortgages on primary residences held by owners at risk of default so that the borrower can have more affordable terms.

Banks that agree to participate would have to rewrite mortgage terms - the duration of the note and monthly payments - so that the borrower would not have to use more than 31% of his or her income to service the debt.

The government would pay up to half of the difference between the previous loan payments and the revised schedule, with the bank required to absorb the other half.

Lastly, Obama's plan asks Congress to revise US bankruptcy law so that bankruptcy court judges may unilaterally adjust the value of a mortgaged primary residence and adjust terms of the mortgage.

The housing rescue plan would, in fact, add new and more costly debt burdens on the very people who got into financial trouble by taking on more debt than they could handle.

Worse, the value of the benefits to at-risk mortgage holders will vary in direct proportion to the degree of borrower financial irresponsibility. In addition, the first phase of the Obama plan is likely to benefit mostly high-end homeowners, not lower income and middle class mortgage holders. Homeowners with a first mortgage as large as $729,750 are eligible for the initiative, meaning that the well-to-do will receive more financial benefits than those of modest means. The mortgage modifications would go disproportionately to borrowers who overstretched and who lied about their income. A clear message is being sent to the American people: The worse the behaviour, the greater the reward.

The second part of the Obama plan, requiring banks to accept half the losses in rewriting at-risk loans, could freeze out those troubled mortgage holders most in need of rescue. Because the investor/lenders will be responsible for a portion of the mortgage rate reduction, this program will deter private sector investment in all but the best mortgages.

The bankruptcy court "cram-down" provision would undermine basic contract law and is likely to make it harder for people other than the rich to get home loans. This cram-down provision will increase the risk to lenders of all mortgages. It will make banks increasingly less likely to issue loans to borrowers with less-than-pristine credit histories or to those, such as first-time home buyers, with minimal credit records.

The most troubling part of the plan is the increased reliance being placed on the now federally controlled Fannie Mae and Freddie Mac. The Obama plan will discourage private bank mortgage lending, the study contends, while establishing Fannie Mae and Freddie Mac as the 900-pound gorillas in the residential financing market. This plan substantially advances the de facto nationalization of America's housing finance system for all but jumbo mortgages. There is little indication that President Obama's Homeowner

Affordability and Stability Plan will provide any relief, either short term or long term, to the beleaguered housing market.

MORTGAGE BAILOUT DOWNSIDE

It is one of the biggest and most popular bailouts. But who will pay for it later?

The Federal Reserve is buying hundreds of billions of dollars of low-interest-rate mortgages guaranteed by Fannie Mae and Freddie Mac. The purchases, which so far amount to $250 billion and could grow to $1.25 trillion, have driven mortgage rates to historical lows, inducing house purchases and sparking a refinancing wave.

Of course, printing money carries inflation risk. The Fed's aggressive actions, led by Fed Chairman Ben Bernanke, interfere with market pricing. The mortgage purchases could help increase assets on the Fed's balance sheet to $3 trillion, equivalent to more than 20% of gross domestic product. So when it stops buying, mortgage rates could rise sharply.

The size of the Fed purchases are already overwhelming private markets. Right now, there is limited investor demand for Fannie and Freddie mortgages with coupons under 5%, due to the risks of holding such low-yielding paper. Filling that gap, the Fed purchased $192 billion of 4% and 4.5% conforming mortgages, on a gross basis, in the four weeks ended March 25.

Holding this risky paper could damage the Fed later on. If it wants to sell 4% mortgages to private investors, it would likely have to do so at a price that creates a yield above 5%, potentially triggering a loss for the Fed. It could, of course, choose to hold the mortgages to maturity, with any credit losses covered by Fannie and Freddie.

The mortgage buying also could alter the Fed's core mission in a detrimental way. In an unusual joint statement last month, the Fed and Treasury said the Fed's job wasn't to 'allocate credit to narrowly defined sectors or classes of borrowers.' Yet focusing so much money on residential mortgages, and thus homeowners, seems to do just that. Investors might come to expect support-purchases every time an asset gets into trouble.

Chapter 14 ... ... Liberal Ideology

HIGH INCOME WARFARE

President Lyndon Johnson's administration was known for his War on Poverty. President Obama's will become notable for his War on Prosperity.

Obama plans to hike income taxes on the wealthiest 5 percent of the nation. He is not just raising the top rate to 39.6 percent; he is also disallowing about one-third of top earner's deductions, whether for state and local taxes, charitable contributions or mortgage interest. The effective hike in their taxes is an average of about 20 percent.

He will also apply the full payroll tax to all income over $250,000 a year. At present, the 15.3 percent Social Security tax only applies to the first $106,800 of income; you neither pay the tax on income above that, nor accumulate added benefit. For many taxpayers in this bracket, this hike will raise their total taxes by about half.

He is also raising the capital-gains tax rate to 20 percent.

These increases are politically insignificant: The top 2 percent of the nation casts only about 4 percent of the votes, but they have enormous economic significance. Those who earn more than $200,000 pay almost 60 percent of America's income taxes and account for a third of its total disposable income. If these spenders and investors are hunkering down, their spending will drop and they will invest less except to find new ways to shelter against taxes.

Franklin Roosevelt's presidency was marked by an emphasis on recovery in his first term and class warfare (which he called reform) in his second. Campaigning for re-election in 1936, FDR famously declared, "I should like to have it said of my first administration that in it the forces of selfishness and of lust for power met their match. I would like to have it said of my second administration that in it these forces met their master." Obama seems to have skipped the first-term FDR program and jumped right into the class divisions and warfare of the second.

Roosevelt's assault on the rich led directly to the recession of 1937-39 - when unemployment soared back up to 19 percent. It was brought down only by World War II.

Obama's tax hikes will dampen investment and consumer spending and prolong and deepen the economy's woes. The rich will hunker down even before the coming confiscatory taxes become worse.

Obama's stimulus package, with its massive growth of government, will kindle huge inflation in coming years. He cannot expand government health insurance as massively as he intends without additional large cost increases unless he also intends to ration medical services. He probably does have that in mind. Those who pay the bill through their taxes will probably be those deemed unworthy of treatment.

He knows, but we have a President steeped in class hatred who does not care. Michelle Obama's comment that she can now be proud of the USA for the first time should not have been dismissed so easily, nor should Obama's own past. They were all pointers to an alarming truth. Here is a President who would rather redistribute income than create wealth. He thinks it more important to grow government than to fight inflation. He believes that it is crucial to expand health care to the young and middle aged, even if it means cutting it back for the elderly. He's more committed to effecting broad change as quickly as possible even if he destroys the USA in the process. In short we have a President who will think no further than Liberal ideology regardless of cost to those who pay the bills.

LOST ECONOMIC PRINCIPLES

Practically every day the government launches a massively expensive new initiative to solve the problems that the last day's initiative did not. It is hard to discern any principles behind these actions. The lack of a coherent strategy has increased uncertainty and undermined the public's perception of the government's competence and trustworthiness.

The Obama administration has abandoned two key principles. The first is that government should only intervene where there has been a market failure. The second is that government intervention should be carried out at minimum cost to taxpayers.

How do these principles apply to the present crisis? First, the market economy provides mechanisms for dealing with difficult times. Take bankruptcy. It is often viewed as a kind of death, but this is misleading. Bankruptcy is an opportunity for a company (or individual) to make a fresh start. A company in financial distress faces the danger that creditors will try to seize its assets. Bankruptcy gives it some respite. It also provides an opportunity for claimants to figure out whether the company's financial trouble was the result of bad luck or bad management, and to decide what should be done. Short-cutting this process through a government bailout is dangerous. Does the government really know whether a company should be saved?

As an example of an effective bankruptcy mechanism, one needs to look no further than the FDIC procedure for banks. When a bank gets into trouble the FDIC puts it into receivership and tries to find a buyer. Every time this procedure has been invoked the depositors were paid in full and had access to their money at all times. The system works well.

From this perspective, one must ask what would have been so bad about letting Bear Stearns, AIG and Citigroup (and in the future, General Motors) go into receivership or Chapter 11 bankruptcy? One argument often made is that these institutions had huge numbers of complicated claims, and that the bankruptcy of any one of them would have led to contagion and systemic failure, causing scores of further bankruptcies. AIG had to be saved, the argument goes, because it had trillions of dollars of credit default swaps with J.P. Morgan. These credit default swaps acted as hedges for trillions of dollars of credit default swaps that J.P. Morgan had with other parties. If AIG had gone bankrupt, J.P. Morgan would have become unhedged, putting its stability and that of others at risk.

This argument has some validity, but it suggests that the best way to proceed is to help third parties rather than the distressed company itself. In other words, instead of bailing out AIG and its creditors, it would have been better for the government to guarantee AIG's obligations to J.P. Morgan and those who bought insurance from AIG. Such an action would have nipped the contagion in the bud, probably at much smaller cost to taxpayers than the cost of bailing out the whole of AIG. It would also have saved the government from having to take a position on AIG's viability as a business, which could have been left to a bankruptcy court. Finally, it would have minimized concerns about moral hazard. AIG may be responsible for its financial problems, but the culpability of those who do business with AIG is less clear, and so helping them out does not reward bad behavior.

Similar principles apply to the housing market. It appears that many people thought that house prices would never fall nationally, and made financial decisions based on this premise. The adjustment to the new reality is painful. But past mistakes do not constitute a market failure. Thus it makes no sense for the government to support house prices.

NEW GOVERNMENT HIRES

President Obama's budget will require vast new spending on health care, energy independence, education and services for veterans, requiring huge numbers of new federal government workers. Once they are in place they will not go away and so the 'stimulus' expenses will be a continuing tax burden.

The Obama $3.6 trillion plan proposes spending billions to begin initiatives and implement existing programs, and given President Obama's insistence that he would scale back the use of private-sector contractors, his priorities could reverse a generational decline in the size of the government workforce. Between 100,000 and 250,000 new government workers will be required.

Officials at the Department of Veterans Affairs said they expect to hire more than 17,000 new employees by the end of the year, many at hospitals and other facilities to fulfill Obama's pledge to expand veterans' access to health care. The agency, whose budget will grow by 11 percent, to $56 billion, under Obama's plan, will add about 7,900 nurses, 3,300 doctors, 3,800 clerks and 2,400 practical nurses.

At the Social Security Administration, the budget will increase by 10 percent, to $11.6 billion, enabling the agency to hire new staff on frontline operations, such as local field offices, hearing offices and teleservice centers.

Between 1940 and 1970, the federal civilian workforce swelled from 707,000 to 2.1 million. Starting with Ronald Reagan presidents have limited the size of the workforce. Although President George W. Bush added tens of thousands of airport baggage screeners and other homeland security jobs, he offset much of that increase by limiting hiring at other agencies.

NEW JOBS

The first hiring spree to result from the $787 billion stimulus plan will not involve construction workers or teachers but government auditors, investigators and lawyers who will try to track all of the taxpayer money being spent.

JOHN MAYNARD KEYNES

The government is about to inject $800 billion into our ailing economy. Why are we doing so? The answer is the theory of John Maynard Keynes a disgusting specimen of the worst of humanity. He was educated at Eton and Cambridge and became a destructive force of the British Empire, at the same time as always enriching himself.

A Depression era economist, John Maynard Keynes' basic idea was simple: Massive government spending can lift an economy out of a recession.

Keynes, one of the few openly homosexual/bisexual men of his time, counted with pride his many sexual partners. He detailed his conquests in diaries with explicit portrayals. Keynes was characterized by one favored anal partner, Lytton Strachey, as "A liberal and a sodomite, an atheist and a statistician." His particular depravity was the sexual abuse of little boys. In communications to his homosexual friends, Keynes advised that they go to Tunis, "where bed and boys were also not expensive." As a sodomistic pedophiliac, he ranged throughout the Mediterranean area in search of boys for himself and his fellow socialists. Taking full advantage of the bitter poverty and abysmal ignorance in North Africa, the Middle East, and Italy, he purchased the bodies of children prostituted for very little money.

Such Leftist hypocrites then, as now, issued loud denunciations against poverty, imperialism, and capitalist immorality. However, for their own degenerate purposes, they eagerly sought out the worst pockets of destitution and backwardness to satisfy their perverted purposes through sexual enslavement of youngsters.

Economically his aim was to benefit the common man, even though he was contemptuous of them and believed no one in America was smart enough to run the country.

One of Keynes' most famous homosexual partners was Scottish painter Duncan Grant. The pair was involved with the Bloomsbury Group. Later, however, he became smitten with a Russian ballerina and the two remained married for 20 years.

Keynes was also a supporter of Eugenics, a movement that lost steam after it was used to justify the Holocaust. Eugenics was an international scientific, political and moral ideology and movement which was at its height in first half of the twentieth century and was largely abandoned with the end of World War 2. The movement often pursued pseudoscientific notions of racial supremacy and purity. Its advocates regarded it as a social philosophy for the improvement of human hereditary traits through the promotion of higher reproduction of certain people and traits, and the reduction of reproduction of certain people and traits. Today it is widely regarded as a brutal movement which inflicted massive human rights violations on millions of people.

When it came to economics, one of the ideas that set Keynes apart from his peers was his belief in the role that animal spirits animal played in economics.

In short, Keynes was a nut case and a fruit cake.

KEYNES PART 2

"By a continuous process of inflation, governments can confiscate, secretly and unobserved, an important part of the wealth of their citizens. By this method, they not only confiscate, but they confiscate arbitrarily; and while the process impoverishes many, it actually enriches some ... The process engages all of the hidden forces of economic law on the side of destruction, and does it in a manner that not one man in a million can diagnose." - John Maynard Keynes Economic Consequences of the Peace, 1920

Singing the Red Flag, the highborn sons of the British upper-class lay on the carpeted floor spinning out socialist schemes in homosexual intermission. Sometimes, one of the participants would shout out an obscenity - then, as if on signal, the entire group would join in a frenzied babble of profanity. Here and there individuals would smoke or chew hashish. Most had unkempt long hair, and some sported beards.

The attitude in such gatherings was anti-establishmentarian. To them the older generation was horribly out of date; even superfluous. The capitalist system was declared obsolete, and revolution was proclaimed as the only solution. Christianity was pronounced an enemy force, and the worst sorts of depravities were eulogized as "that love which passes all Christian understanding."

The year was 1904, and the participants were destined to become the intellectual and political leaders of the British Empire. Chief of this ring of homosexual revolutionaries was John Maynard Keynes, who eventually became the economic architect of English socialism and gravedigger for the British Empire. The chief American Fabians, acting as carriers of the Keynesian sickness, were Felix Frankfurter and Walter Lippmann.

Keynes was characterized by his male sweetheart, Lytton Strachey, as "A Liberal and a sodomite, an atheist and a statistician." His particular depravity was the sexual abuse of little boys. In communications to his homosexual friends, Keynes advised that they go to Tunis, "where bed and boys were not expensive." As a sodomistic pedophiliac, he ranged throughout the Mediterranean area in search of boys for himself and his fellow Liberals. Taking full advantage of the bitter poverty and abysmal ignorance in North Africa, the Middle East, and Italy, he purchased the bodies of children prostituted for very little money.

Such Leftist hypocrites then, as now, issued loud denunciations against poverty, imperialism, and capitalist immorality. However, for their own degenerate purposes, they eagerly sought out the worst pockets of destitution and backwardness to satisfy their perverted purposes through sexual enslavement of youngsters. While traveling in France and the United States they complained among themselves of the harassment by the police of practicing homosexuals.

In degenerate areas of the Mediterranean, on the other hand, they found a pervert's Utopia where the bodies of children could be purchased as a cheap part of a cultured holiday.

These Leftist degenerates began to scheme over sixty years ago to secure public acceptance of their depravity. Havelock Ellis, a founder of the Fabian Society, compiled a massive erotic work entitled, Studies in the Psychology of Sex. Ellis was a sexual pervert and drug user. He and a group of fellow Leftists even pioneered in the experimental use of hallucinogens in private orgies. Ellis was definitely a pathological case. He drove his wife into Lesbianism and drug addiction, securing additional erotic excitement by urging her to recite her Lesbian experiences. Mrs. Ellis eventually went insane and died in utmost misery after denouncing her husband as a sexual monster.

The Fabian socialists used the writings of Ellis as a wedge for sex education in the schools. They started in the colleges and gradually eased into the high school level. Ellis complained to his fellow Liberals fifty-five years ago that he found wider acceptance for his books in the United States than he did in England. In fact, he was arrested and tried for obscenity in England, whereas his books were sold in the USA without serious interference by the authorities. Today, his perversions are standard reference material for the sex educators and Havelock Ellis is popularly called "the father of social psychology."

Keynes and his cohorts seized upon the works of Ellis as justification for their depravities. They were also greatly bolstered in their campaign by the theories of an Austrian Leftist named Sigmund Freud. Dr. Freud acknowledged in private correspondence that he copied the thesis of sex as the central determinant in human action from Havelock Ellis. Echoing Ellis, he laid down the premise that homosexuality and carnal depravities are not a matter of abnormality, but merely a case of personal preference. This, plus his declaration of atheism, overjoyed the Liberal Keynesian crowd. John Maynard Keynes audaciously proclaimed, "Sex Questions are about to enter the political arena." He inveighed against "the treatment of sexual offense and abnormalities," adding the charge that "the existing state of the Law and of orthodoxy is still Mediaeval - altogether out of touch with civilized opinion and civilized practice and with what individuals, educated and uneducated alike, say to one another in private."

During the same period (1925) Keynes struck out against drug control. Homosexuals find drugs a useful adjunct in loosening moral inhibitions to perversion. And this ravisher of little boys feigned sympathy for the masses by urging universal rights for users of narcotics. He declared: "how far is bored and suffering humanity to be allowed, from time to time, an escape, an excitement, a stimulus, and a possibility of change?"

Keynes and his conspirators projected homosexuality and drug addiction as an intrinsic part of their collectivist society of the future. His male sweetheart, Lytton Strachey, wrote privately that they would corrupt the whole population, "subtly, through literature, into the bloodstream of the people, and in such a way that they accepted it all naturally, if need be without at first realizing what it was to which they were agreeing." He boasted that he intended "to seduce his readers to tolerance through laughter and sheer entertainment." He pointed out that the object was "to write in a way that would contribute to an eventual change in our ethical and sexual mores - a change that couldn't be done in a minute, but would unobtrusively permeate the more flexible minds of young people."

Keynes put it in the terms of Marxist economics: "When the accumulation of wealth is no longer of high social importance, there will be great changes in the code of morals. We shall be able to rid ourselves of many pseudo-moral principles which have hagridden us for two hundred years."

Keynes and Strachey used their malignant writings to help contaminate the entire English-speaking world. In the United States they both found expression in the New Republic, the New York Times, and the Saturday Review of Literature. In 1939, a comrade of Keynes and Strachey named Bertrand Russell came to America to push their Liberal ideology and was (he says in his Autobiography) legally charged as 'lecherous, libidinous, lustful, venerous, erotomaniac, aphrodisiac, irreverent, narrow-minded, untruthful, and bereft of moral fiber.' His aborted object had been to permeate the College of the City of New York with the corruption of the British Fabians. Immediately, John Dewey and other American Fabians organized to cry that 'Academic Freedom' was under attack. The National Education Association (NEA) and the whole Leftist educational complex began to percolate pervasive degeneracy as being 'Liberal' and 'Progressive.'

The works of Keynes, Lytton Strachey, and Bertrand Russell have been, and are today, required reading in almost every college and university in the United States and Canada.

In the spring of 1905 Keynes and his lavender cohorts had been thrilled by a conference of Russian revolutionaries in London. British Fabians and Joseph Fels, an American soap manufacturer who was also a Fabian, had financed the Russian gathering and furnished them a hall in a Christian church. Key revolutionaries at this London conference included Nikolai Lenin, Leon Trotsky, and Joseph Stalin. The future slaughter of fifty million civilians, and the conquest of one-third of the earth's surface was within this gathering. Shivers of excitement rippled down the spines of the Liberal homosexuals when they heard that Lenin had openly defended the slaughter of bank guards and stealing of bank funds for the Bolshevik coffers.

Keynes and his fellow debauchees became active pacifists and conscientious objectors during World War I. The Liberal position against military service dovetailed perfectly with the homosexual aversion to any kind of physical danger and the manly requirements of military training. Yet, in spite of Keynes' sheltering of "queer conchies," and his own refusal to serve his country, he was made the head of an important division of the British Treasury. During March of 1917 he confided privately that he supported the Bolshevik group among the Russian socialists after the overthrow of Czar Nicholas.

The seizure of power by the Bolsheviks in November of 1917 elated Keynes and the rest of the Fabian coterie. At Leftist parties in London, Keynes and his fellow perverts celebrated by dressing in women's clothes and performing lewd dances. He had as his consort an eighteen-year-old-boy who was ensconced as his assistant in the Treasury Department.

Just before the Bolshevik Revolution, Keynes had made a hurried trip to the United States for the British Government. Here he had a chance to make contact with the American Fabians who were similarly entrenched, via the Frankfurter-Lippmann group, in key positions of the Wilson Administration.

Even the House of Morgan in New York City's financial district trotted out its sissies to welcome Keynes to this country, and gave him an office just for himself. The international grapevine had established the nature of his proclivities. The urbane air of Keynes sent thrills of excitement through the ranks of the financial "giggle gang."

Keynes' deviate Liberal circle was almost completely pro-Bolshevik.

One month after the Revolution, J.M. Keynes wrote to his mother "Well, the only course open to me is to be buoyantly Bolshevik; and as I lie in bed in the morning I reflect with a good deal of satisfaction that, because our rulers are as incompetent as they are mad and wicked, one particular era of a particular kind of civilization is very nearly over."

On February 22, 1918, Keynes proudly boasted of "being a Bolshevik." Yet the British Government blindly sent Keynes to the Versailles peace talks. There he joined forces with his Fabian American comrade, Walter Lippmann, who was among those representing the equally blind U.S. Government. The ensuing pro-Bolshevik and anti-American machinations were largely responsible not only for laying the basis for continuing Red victories, but also for setting off the chain of events that eventually brought Hitler to power.

In 1919 Keynes authored The Economic Consequences of the Peace, which was promptly acclaimed from Moscow by Nikolai Lenin, himself. The Red dictator declared: "Nowhere has the Versailles treaty been described so well as in the book by Keynes." A special edition of The Economic Consequences was printed under the label of the Fabian Society; and, Frankfurter and Lippmann brought the manuscript to the United States and arranged with Harcourt and Brace to publish it here. The volume became required reading among American Socialists and Communists.

A problem was that Keynes' value as a hidden Red was in danger. The Fabians had developed the posture of respectability to a fine art and the value of Keynes' book as an impartial work was in jeopardy. With Keynes' future usefulness in upper-class circles at stake, Lenin had personally come to the rescue. He pulled the classic Leftist double-twist, praising Keynes' book as a model for Communist revolutionaries and at the same time covering for Keynes by labeling him as anti-Bolshevik. Nikolai Lenin rose before the Second Congress of the Communist International and declared: "I will quote another economic source which assumes particularly great significance, the British diplomat Keynes, the author of The Economic Consequences Of The Peace, who on the instructions of his government, took part in the Versailles peace negotiations, watched them directly from the purely bourgeois point of view, studied the subject step by step, and took part in the conference as an economist. He arrived at conclusions which are stronger, more striking and more instructive than any a Communist revolutionary could advance, because they are conclusions drawn by an acknowledged bourgeois."

Thus was launched the career of Fabian leader Keynes as a non-Leftist and non-Communist.

In 1925, John Maynard Keynes was married. It was a bizarre performance. His best man was Duncan Grant, his male lover for many years, and Keynes held Duncan's hand as the marriage vows were spoken. But, the background of the bride was equally odd. She was Lydia Lopokova, the premiere ballerina of the Diaghilev Ballet. She was a habitué of Leftist circles, and had at one time been engaged to Heywood Broun, the well known Socialist and confidant of Leon Trotsky, but had broken the engagement to marry a dwarf named Barocchi. In 1917 Lydia had disappeared in Paris with the top Cossack general of the White Army, returning to the ballet when the general returned to lead his troops against the Bolsheviks. The Bolsheviks had by now, however, acquired advance information and used it to defeat the Cossacks.

Following the wedding to Comrade Lydia, Mr. and Mrs. Keynes were the special guests of the Soviet Government. He and his Russian wife were allowed free access to the Soviet hinterland, even to the extent of visiting her relatives. It was a privilege unheard of at the time, since even members of the Communist International were not then allowed such unlimited travel. It was a time of mass killing of civilians, and ordinarily a Russian national traveling with an Englishman would have been arrested and shot. But, Soviet officials were effusive in their thanks to Keynes for designing the first Soviet currency for them while he was still a member of the British Treasury.

The marriage was an arrangement which allowed Keynes to continue to his sexual perversions with men. They both had separate living quarters, and did not interfere with the personal lives of one another. Lydia was very useful as a go-between since Keynes was in frequent contact with Soviet officials both in Britain and the United States.

J. M. Keynes became the mastermind behind the economic structure of British and American Socialism. Strachey was responsible for writing books that undermined the Christian ethic of the Nineteenth Century and set the tone for the pornographic and depraved literature of today.

LESSON FROM BRITAIN

An "anti-capitalist" terrorist group called "Bank Bosses are Criminals" has vandalized the home of the British Banking Chief, former CEO of RBS. In an email sent to local newspapers, the group called for bank bosses to be jailed and warned: "This is just the beginning".

DANIEL HANNAN MEP

Daniel Hannan's blistering attack on Gordon Brown has become an international hit on the internet. The clip of his three-minute long tirade has attracted more than 750,000 viewers on video streaming website You Tube.

The Conservative MEP accused Mr Brown of being 'the devalued Prime Minister of a devalued Government.' As the Premier watched in person, Mr Hannan ripped apart his economic record and likened him to a 'Brezhnev era apparatchik'.

Daniel Hannan's withering assessment of the Prime Minister's handling of the economic crisis is on course to become one of the most viewed political speeches in the fastest time in internet history. Mr Hannan delivered a scathing riposte to Mr Brown after he delivered a keynote speech to the European Parliament in Strasbourg.

Major broadcasters,including the BBC, predictably failed to report Mr Hannan's onslaught despite giving full coverage to Mr Brown's pro-European speech.

The clip features Mr Brown looking on with a frozen smile, while Mr Hannan warned how Britain was entering the recession in a 'dilapidated condition' with an 'almost unbelievable' deficit.

The speech has an eerie familiarity to the course we are on in the USA. President Obama has done more damage in less than a hundred days than Gordon Brown has wrought in eleven years!

Here is the speech in full:

'Prime Minister, I see you've already mastered the essential craft of the European politician: namely the ability to say one thing in this chamber and a very different thing to your home electorate. You've spoken here of free trade, and amen to that.

Who would have guessed, listening to you just now, that you were the author of the phrase 'British jobs for British workers,' and that you have subsidised - where you have not nationalised outright - swaths of our economy, including the car industry and many of the banks.

Perhaps you would have more moral authority in this House if your actions matched your words, and perhaps more legitimacy in the councils of the world if the United Kingdom were not sailing into this recession in the worst condition of any G20 country.

The truth, Prime Minister, is that you have run out of our money. The country as a whole is now in negative equity. Every British child is now born owing around £20,000. Servicing the interest on that debt is going to cost more than educating the child.

Now, once again today, you have tried to spread the blame around. You spoke about an international recession, an international crisis.

Well, it's true that we are sailing together into the squalls but not every vessel in the convoy is in the same dilapidated condition. Other ships used the good years to caulk their hulls and clear their rigging - in other words, to pay off debt. But you used the good years to raise borrowing yet further.

As a consequence, under your captaincy, our hull is pressed deep into the waterline under the accumulated weight of your debt.

We are now running a deficit that touches 10 per cent of GDP, an almost unbelievable figure - more than Pakistan, more than Hungary; countries where the IMF has already been called in.

It's not just that you are not apologising - like everyone else I've long accepted that you are pathologically incapable of accepting responsibility for these things - it's that you are carrying on wilfully worsening our situation, wantonly spending what little we have left.

In the last year 100,000 private sector jobs have been lost and yet you have created 30,000 public sector jobs. Prime Minister, you cannot carry on forever squeezing the productive bit of the economy in order to fund an unprecedented engorgement of the unproductive bit.

You cannot spend your way out of a recession or borrow your way out of debt. And when you repeat, in that wooden and perfunctory way, that our situation is better than others, that we are well placed to weather the storm, I have to tell you, you sound like a Brezhnev era apparatchik giving the party line.

You know and we know and you know that we know that it's nonsense. Everyone knows that Britain is worse off than any other country as we go into these hard times.

The IMF has said so. The European Commission has said so. The markets say so, which is why the pound has lost a third of its value.

In a few months, the voters will have their chance to say so, too.

They can see what the markets have seen: that you are the devalued Prime Minister of a devalued Government.'

LIBERALS AND PRIVATE ENTERPRISE

The House, Senate and Obama White House act as if the marketplace was the world of an alien tribe, which it has to control through intimidation or demands for protective tribute in the form of campaign contributions or other corrupt payments.

That anti-bonus bill was not unique. Using the private sector as the Liberals' punching bag is now a routine part of the Liberal playbook. Al Gore and John Kerry ran at Big Oil, Big Pharma and Big Insurance. With mercurial shiftiness, so did President Obama. These "big" industries are proxies for the whole world of owners and managers, who somehow now always find themselves beyond acceptable politics as enemies of the people's interests.

Liberal plaintiffs' lawyers meanwhile, continue to assault the private sector, dig cash out and transfer a percentage back to Democratic re-election campaigns. Democrats in Congress then create legislation to make the private sector vulnerable to more such lawsuits. Congress has passed the Lilly Ledbetter Fair Pay Act, with the Paycheck Fairness Act on tap. (Fair and Fairness are their words and in no way reflect reality).

Liberals will increasingly disrupt operations for private companies with a dampening effect on the U.S. growth rate and its ability to create jobs.

BIG BROTHER

Connecticut Attorney General Richard Blumenthal said documents reviewed by his office show that American International Group Inc. paid out $218 million in bonuses, more than the $165 million previously disclosed. Mr. Blumenthal says the documents show that 73 people received at least $1 million apiece, and five of those received bonuses of more than $4 million. His office received the documents after issuing a subpoena.

What are peanuts in the whole scheme of things has distracted Liberal politicians from the larger issue: Any viable enterprise, upon giving a company billions of dollars, would have put some very serious conditions on that investment. One of those conditions would have been, not paying individual bonuses to that it was not happy about.

The tragedy is not that AIG paid out these bonuses, but that government let it happen. Now they are clamoring for the names of the beneficiaries to be made public, irrespective of how good they are at their jobs. Their objective is to make the individuals objects of hatred in their communities. Why do they not spend as much time worrying about the waste and corruption in our local governments?

FREEDOM OF HUMOR

The mayor of California city, Los Alamitos (12,000 people) says he will resign after being criticized for sharing an e-mail picture depicting the White House lawn planted with watermelons under the title "No Easter egg hunt this year."

The mayor came under fire for sending the picture to what he called "a small group of friends." One of the recipients, a local businesswoman and city volunteer, publicly scolded the mayor for his actions.

He will be eligible to attend sensitivity training as that will become a major new program under the Stimulus Bill.

LIBERALS VERSUS CONSERVATIVES

Over the years Conservatives have come to be symbolized by the largest, most powerful land animal on earth, the elephant. Liberals are symbolized by the jackass.

Modern Liberals like imported beer (with lime added), but most prefer white wine or imported bottled water. They eat raw fish but like their beef well done. Sushi, tofu, and

French foods are standard Liberal fare. Another interesting evolutionary side note: Most of their women have higher testosterone levels than their men. Most social workers, personal injury attorneys, journalists, dreamers in Hollywood and group therapists are Liberals.

Liberals invented the designated hitter rule because it wasn't fair to make the pitcher also bat.

Conservatives drink domestic beer and eat red meat. Conservatives are gamesmen, rodeo cowboys, lumberjacks, construction workers, firemen, medical doctors, police officers, corporate executives, athletes, members of the military, airline pilots and generally anyone who works productively. Conservatives who own companies hire other conservatives who want to work for a living.

Liberals produce little or nothing. They like to govern the producers and decide what to do with the production. Liberals believe Europeans are more enlightened than

Americans. They came to the USA after the Wild West was tamed and created a business of trying to get more for doing nothing.

USA DIVIDED

Liberal Government looks after its own, the main bodies of whom are big government advocates, non-producers and free loaders. We live in a polarized society where the capitalist cow is expected to pull the wagon and feed everyone, including free loaders.

We have taxation without representation for those who are not Liberals.

Chapter 15 ... ... President Obama

OBAMANATION

Greed comes in many forms.

Let us define greed as grasping too much money for doing too little of value. Barack Obama has already grasped $8,605,429 and that is but a start. Four years ago, Mr. Obama became a millionaire through the popularity of his somewhat fictional autobiography, which was quickly followed by his second book under the farcical title "The Audacity of Hope."

Mr. Obama has lambasted business executives for creating a culture of runaway salaries and bonuses. He has also signed a new $500,000 book agreement for an adaptation of his autobiography, "Dreams From My Father," for young readers. Mr. Obama profits directly from the reach of his celebrity status. His greed in amassing money will put even Bill Clinton to shame. The $500,000 agreement for a license is so that the President's autobiography can be condensed into a book for middle-school students. Mr. Obama has already signed an additional 50 similar licensing arrangements for the book to be translated into other languages.

When Mr. Obama wrote "Dreams From My Father," which came out in 1995, he did not sell enough books to pay back the advance of $30,817 even though that was in reality the first political payment to Obama as his prize from Democrats for being the first partially black editor of the Harvard Law Review. When the book was reprinted after his speech to the Democratic

National Convention Democratic in 2004 as Presidential Heir Apparent 2008, sales flourished, which led to another book deal worth $1.9 million. For that, Mr. Obama agreed to write another nonfiction book and a children's book.

In 2005, Obama reported royalties of $1.23 million. In 2007, royalties had increased to $4.1 million. They were $2.46 million in 2008. He will continue to receive book royalties while President. That is a lot of greed for books of little or no merit.

POLITICAL POPULISM

President Obama led the anti-AIG bonus charge with instructions to "pursue every legal avenue" to get the money back. The Obama administration's antics around the AIG bonuses are an effort to use political power to contort the law. But rather than doing so for reasons of national security as President Bush was accused of doing, Obama is doing so to pander to the public and to use anger that he is fomenting for his own political advancement even as it hurts the well being of the USA. When the Obama administration and Congress use these tactics, they are creating a new political-risk component to all business activity.

That risk may scare potential investors away from bailout recipients because they cannot trust our government's integrity. It destroys our moral high ground the next time Mr. Obama wants to criticize a foreign country for ignoring the rule of law by nationalizing private assets or repudiating international debt. It will certainly make Mr. Obama's task much more difficult when he tries to sell the public on his administration's ability to manage the rest of the bailout, and when he tries to sell private firms on the public-private partnership that will be needed to make the recovery work.

The administration could have let Congress have its week of grandstanding over bonuses, while issuing a public statement acknowledging the bonuses as deplorable, but not important enough to detract from the real work that lies ahead. The tragedy here is the extraordinary amount of time that is being wasted on this issue when the Treasury Department remains understaffed, a detailed toxic-asset plan remains perpetually forthcoming, and the economy continues to shed jobs.

It's predictable that the Obama administration and Congress would rather abuse an easy target over something every voter can get mad about than actually confront the hard issues of managing the financial crisis, including progress on the "stress test" of banks and the restoration of normal credit operations, establishing genuine oversight of the use of bailout funds, and coordinating international efforts on global economic stimulus and changes to financial-industry regulations. That type of governing is far more troublesome, as it involves making difficult decisions on complex topics and communicating unpopular news to constituents.

Mr. Obama is making a huge mistake in diminishing confidence in the rule of law. That piece of populism will cost the President far more in future credibility than he stands to gain in present popularity.

POLITICS OF HATE

The fact that AIG had a contractual obligation to pay retention bonuses in March 2009 to employees at the financial-products division wasn't a secret. AIG disclosed the retention payment agreements from March 2008, in May 2008 in a securities filing.

The AIG Beltway bonfire was fueled by the spectacle of Ed Liddy, AIG's government-appointed CEO, enduring the wrath of Congress for embarrassing the Members with post-bailout bonuses. What resulted was a full-blown political panic ignited by no less than President Obama himself that is threatening to engulf attempts to revive the financial system, and is further undermining confidence in the USA financial system. It is no way to promote an economic recovery.

White House economist Larry Summers was quickly silenced when he correctly said that the retention bonuses were regrettable but there wasn't much that could be done to stop them. "We are a country of law. There are contracts. The government cannot just abrogate contracts," he said. Of course he was underestimating the chicanery of the Liberals. Assorted Congressmen did what comes naturally, which is declaring their mock outrage. Obama and the White House joined the braying pack.

Speaking of the $165 million paid to members of AIG's Financial Products division, the President asked, "How do they justify this outrage to the taxpayers who are keeping this company afloat?" Treasury Secretary Tim Geithner, who was a party to the payment of the bonuses, was also trotted out to express his "outrage" and declare that Treasury would somehow try to claw back the bonuses. By shouting "greed" in a crowded and panicky Washington, our supposed financial stewards thus gave license to everyone in the media and Capitol Hill to see who could claim to be most shocked and appalled at AIG.

We now have a full-fledged mob on our hands, with Congress inciting the public to string up bankers at their homes. Senator Chris Dodd, down in the 2010 election polls after the latest revelations of his own corrupt greedy deals sweetheart is busy rewriting the TARP compensation limits he only recently stuck in the stimulus bill. His last-minute measure explicitly exempted from compensation limits bonuses agreed to prior to the passage of the stimulus bill: "The prohibition required under clause (i) shall not be construed to prohibit any bonus payment required to be paid pursuant to a written employment contract executed on or before February 11, 2009 ..." So he is now changing the rules yet again.

The Beltway's banker baiting increases in direct proportion to the government's incompetence in nurturing a financial recovery. Anger rises when Americans learn after three bailout revisions that they haven't been told the truth that the AIG nationalization was a conduit to save counterparties, and even hedge funds, which gambled on housing. Americans also wonder why taxpayer guarantees should be provided to Citigroup, a three-time loser, but with little accountability for the board and managers who brought the company down.

Reviving a financial system is a long process that requires a combination of workout ability and discipline for mistakes. The public has to believe the end result will be a better, sturdier system in return for taxpayer support, while at the same time being assured that gamblers aren't saved from their own mistakes.

If this balance is beyond the ability of Mr. Obama's current economic team, he needs a better team. The worst mistake he can make is to deflect attention away from government's mistakes by joining the attack on the very bankers he needs to lead an economic recovery. That's how a deep recession becomes a Depression.

BLAME GAME

In his inaugural address, President Obama proclaimed 'an end to the petty grievances and false promises, the recriminations and worn-out dogmas that for far too long have strangled our politics.'

Unfortunately he did not mean what sounded good to say. He immediately began talking about the unwelcome inheritance of his predecessor. Obama has reminded the public at every turn that he is facing problems inherited from the Bush administration, using increasingly bracing language to describe the challenges his administration is up against. Rhetoric about 'the deepening economic crisis' that the President described six days after taking office is now described as 'a big mess'.

"By any measure," he said during a March 4 event calling for huge government intervention, "my administration has inherited a fiscal disaster."

Obama constantly parrots that former President George W. Bush left behind a trillion-dollar budget deficit, a 14-month recession and a broken financial system. How dishonest and how damaging to the USA are such tactics from a Presidential who built his candidacy on a promise to rise above Washington's divisive partisan traditions, winning over many independent voters and moderate Republicans in the process.

Six days after taking office, Obama kicked off an event on jobs, energy reform and climate change with "a few words about the deepening economic crisis that we've inherited." He lamented announced job cuts at such economic mainstays as Microsoft, Intel, Home Depot and Caterpillar, among others. Just over a week later, Obama, arguing for his stimulus plan, said that "we've inherited a terrible mess," and a few days after that, in the economically depressed city of Elkhart, Ind., he told the audience, "We've inherited an economic crisis as deep and dire as any since the Great Depression." During a prime-time news conference later that day, he used "inherited" twice in the same sentence to describe the deficit and "the most profound economic emergency since the Great Depression."

Unfazed, Obama next lobbied for his $3.6 trillion budget, which proposes sweeping changes in health care, the energy sector and the public education system.

The Obama Cabinet is playing the same partisan game to the detriment of the USA. Referring to the military prison at Guantanamo Bay, Cuba, Vice

President Biden said soon after the inauguration that "we're trying to figure out exactly what we've inherited here." In early February, Secretary of State Hillary Rodham Clinton said that "after I accepted the position, I began looking at the broad array of problems that we were going to inherit," citing the Middle East, Pakistan and Afghanistan in particular.

POSTURING BY OBAMA

Joining the bandwagon on a wave of public anger, President Barack Obama blistered insurance giant AIG for "recklessness and greed" and pledged to try to block it from handing its executives $165 million in bonuses.

"How do they justify this outrage to the taxpayers who are keeping the company afloat?" Obama asked. "This isn't just a matter of dollars and cents. It's about our fundamental values."

In a show of theatrics, he lost his voice at one point and ad-libbed, "Excuse me; I'm choked up with anger here."

"This is a corporation that finds itself in financial distress due to recklessness and greed," Obama declared.

He said he had directed Treasury Secretary Timothy Geithner to block these bonuses and make the American taxpayer whole. Axelrod, Obama's handler said the administration hoped the tough talk would result in voluntary action on the part of AIG and its bonus recipients.

In a move reminiscent of the McCarthy era, New York Attorney General Andrew Cuomo said he would issue subpoenas for information on the bonuses. Cuomo said his office would investigate whether the employees were involved in AIG's near-collapse and whether the $165 million in bonus payments were fraudulent under state law.

The reason that the AIG bonus giveaway is politically troubling for Obama is that it shows that federal bailouts are a mistake. Bailout steps for AIG totaling over $170 billion have effectively left the federal government with an 80 percent stake in the faltering insurance giant. If AIG had been allowed to go bankrupt, all the legal agreements which Obama is now venting about would have been erased. Instead of posturing and making disastrous policy decisions, it is unfortunate that Obama does not reflect on the law which he presumably learned while he was polishing his political credentials at Harvard Law School.

The government-appointed chief executive of AIG, Edward Liddy, is fully aware that the bonuses were legally binding obligations. The government should also have known before their repeated bailouts and Obama should also know. Instead he is now posturing that the government should rework its AIG bailout to make sure the company repays as much of the $170 billion as possible even though he knows that money is gone for ever and even more tax payer money will be required to save AIG from the ignominy of bankruptcy which is seemingly unacceptable to Obama's Liberal ideology.

Without bankruptcy, AIG similarly must honor its contracts with U.S. and foreign banks. The government tacitly agreed to uphold those contracts when it seized control of AIG instead of letting AIG go into bankruptcy. AIG used $90 billion-plus in federal aid to pay off contracts to foreign and domestic banks, some of which had received their own multibillion-dollar U.S. government bailouts. The recipients included Goldman Sachs, at $12.9 billion, and three European banks — France's Societe Generale at $11.9 billion, Germany's Deutsche Bank at $11.8 billion, and Britain's Barclays PLC at $8.5 billion. Merrill Lynch, which also is undergoing federal scrutiny of its bonus plans and which is now part of Bank of America, received $6.8 billion. The money was used by the banks to cover their losses on complex mortgage investments, as well as for collateral needed for other transactions.

Instead of acknowledging government's role in the misuse of taxpayer funds, Obama officials made the rounds of Sunday talk shows to denounce the insurer. Federal Reserve Chairman Ben Bernanke weighed in, saying on CBS' "60 Minutes" that the AIG bailout angered him the most and that he "slammed the phone more than a few times on discussing AIG."

Obama is planning an appearance later in the week on Jay Leno's NBC talk show, to add a lighter touch to his efforts to show himself in command of efforts to resuscitate the economy.

Outcries against the company have also come from Liberal congressional leaders, even though they are even more responsible for the situation than Obama, if only because their ineptitude has been wrought on our federal government for longer.

David J. Phillips

OBAMA LACKS LEADERSHIP

After leading the charge, President Obama has been vague about legislation that would retroactively levy huge taxes on bonuses paid by the largest recipients of government bailout money. He is similarly vague about mutating the tax code is not an effective means for shaping good public policy. At least he knows when to run for cover.

Here are six reasons why he should disassociate himself from the retention bonus lynching.

1. The bills would almost certainly be challenged as an affront to Article I, Section 9 of the United States Constitution, which states that, "No bill of attainder or ex post facto law will be passed."

2. Financial institutions that accepted government funds under government pressure as part of an effort to shore up confidence but now say they didn't really need them would be unfairly punished.

3. A rush to pay back government funds which will be a consequence of the legislation, will remove capital from the banking system when it needs it most. Many of the banks that received money under the Troubled Asset Relief Program (TARP) do not technically need it.

4. By rushing bills through the House and Senate, legislators have undermined government efforts to work constructively with Finance Houses. Castigating Geithner, the Treasury secretary, has damaged confidence in the administration's point man and will make it even more difficult to recruit talent to the shockingly undermanned Treasury Department.

5. Negative Washington behavior also endangers other efforts to shore up the financial system and the economy. The government is urging the private sector to participate in programs intended to invigorate the securitization market (the Term Asset-Backed Securities Loan Facility) and remove dodgy assets from the banks (the Public-Private Investment Fund). Potential participants are now worried that Congress could use the taxpayer financing of these initiatives to impose greater regulation on the programs after the fact, as it has now done for TARP recipients.

6. Foreign banks and bankers will benefit at the expense of United States banks and bankers if they can avoid the clutches of U.S. Government. That could

leave the American banks in even worse shape to pay back the government, create credit and generate tax revenue.

President Obama should think about how to improve the system for the future, not destroy it.

FAILURE IN LEADERSHIP

The Obama led war on private contracts and the financial system is dangerously destructive politics which may define his presidency.

President Obama initiated one of the more amazing and senseless acts of political retribution in American history. In its rage, the House voted, 328-93, to slap a 90% tax on the bonuses of anyone at every bank receiving $5 billion in TARP money who earns more than $250,000 a year. Never mind if the bonus was earned last year or earlier, or under a legally binding employment contract.

Such punitive laws were expressly deplored by America's Founders. James Madison warned that "Bills of attainder, ex post facto laws, and laws impairing the obligation of contracts, are contrary to the first principles of the social compact, and to every principle of sound legislation."

In 1827, the U.S. Supreme Court issued a similar warning about legislative limits under Article I, Section 10 of the Constitution: "The states are forbidden to pass any bill of attainder or ex post facto law, by which a man shall be punished criminally or penally by loss of life of his liberty, property, or reputation for an act which, at the time of its commission, violated no existing law of the land.

Laws of this character are oppressive, unjust, and tyrannical. The House legislation is also unconstitutional on equal protection grounds given that it treats a homogeneous group of individuals differently depending on which companies they work for. It is one thing to treat the companies that receive federal funds differently from those that don't. But the individuals receiving bonuses may have nothing to do with the decision to receive TARP money. The House's 90% tax on some bankers but not others is only a step away from deciding to impose a higher tax rate on employees of any company out of political favor. Congress is introducing an element of political risk to economic decisions that is typical of Argentina or Russia. The sanctity of U.S. contracts has long been one of America's competitive advantages in attracting capital. The 90% tax rate is a revival of the philosophy of redistributionist 'justice' of the 1930s, when capital availability froze for an entire decade.

The financial system will suffer in particular, just when the Obama Administration is desperately seeking more private capital to ride out future losses. Facing such limits on the ability to reward talent, every bank CEO will try to pay off the TARP as soon as possible, whether or not this leaves the bank with a weaker capital base. Hedge funds and other investors that Treasury needs for its new Public-Private Investment Program, or for the Federal Reserve's TALF, will also be wary. Treasury may promise nothing punitive for these programs, but that is also what it said about the TARP.

President Obama has behaved as if he can fuel and channel Congressional anger without being run over himself. In other matters, he has also shown that he is weak. He has failed to stand up to a Congress of his own party on anything difficult, from stimulus priorities, to earmarks, to protectionism against Mexican trucks.

OBAMA AND LENO

Obama introduced another new low in being the first President to demean the office by being a guest on a late night talk show.

President Barack Obama said that he was stunned to hear about the $165 million in bonuses that were paid to employees of troubled insurer AIG, promising to do everything he could to get these bonuses back. "These financial industries are holding us hostage," Obama said in his interview on NBC's "Tonight Show with Jay Leno."

Obama said the AIG payments raised moral and ethical problems, but he stressed that the bigger problem was the culture that allowed traders to claim them. "We need to get back to a place where people know enough is enough," he said. "If we can get back to those values that built America, then we'll be OK."

The interview with comedian Leno was the final stop of the President's two-day visit to Southern California to ensure that his populist support remains intact. The appearance was billed as a chance for the President to reach ordinary Americans to talk about the economy, and Leno played his part as serious interviewer, questioning Obama about the AIG controversy and the economy.

Obama simplistically complained that 'most of the stuff that got us into trouble is perfectly legal,' adding, "That's a sign that we need to change our laws. It's legal to charge 30 percent on our credit cards," he said. "When you buy a toaster, there's a law that says your toaster needs to be safe, but no law that says if your credit card explodes, you're safe."

In attempting to make a joke about his poor bowling performance on a previous TV appearance when he was trying to show how good he is, the President made a misstep when talking about the White House bowling alley.

Telling Leno that he had not removed the alley, Obama said he had recently recorded a 129 game, significantly better than he had in his widely mocked campaign appearance, when he rolled a gutter ball on camera. Then he added: "It was like Special Olympics or something," a reference to the athletic festival held every two years for people with disabilities.

The White House immediately rushed into damage control saying the remark was "in no way intended to disparage the Special Olympics. The spokesmen added that "He thinks that the Special Olympics are a wonderful program that gives an opportunity to shine to people with disabilities from around the world."

Security was expensive and invasive. The Secret Service, which arrived early in the week to make preparations, put parts of the studio on lockdown, with no vehicles or people allowed in or out. Streets around the studio were also shut down. The show's usually busy hallway was blocked by wooden partitions. A ramp leading to the large "elephant doors" from the parking area was closed off. Obama brushed off criticism about all the hoopla, telling reporters: "When you're President, you've got to walk and chew gum at the same time." And throw gutter balls with panache.

OBAMA MAKES IT UP

Barack Obama defended his opposition to the U.S.-Colombia Free Trade Agreement this way: "The history in Colombia right now is that labor leaders have been targeted for assassination, on a fairly consistent basis, and there have not been any prosecutions."

It is true that Colombia has a history of violence. But since President Álvaro Uribe took office in 2002, that violence has been substantially reduced. The homicide rate through the end of 2007 was down by 40.4% and the rate among union members was down almost 87%. As for prosecutions: In union-member killings, there were zero convictions from 1991-2000 and one in 2001. But from 2002-2007, there were 80. According to the Colombian attorney general's office, 29% of those murders were "found to have been results of theft, petty crime and random violence unrelated to union activity." Mr. Uribe has nonetheless created a special investigative unit for crimes against union members, and he expanded a special government protection program for unions.

More broadly, in 2004 Mr. Uribe pushed through congress a judicial reform that has reduced the average time needed to issue an indictment for a homicide to 50 days from 493. He also increased the budget for the attorney general's office to $598 million in 2008, from $346 million in 2002 -- a 73% increase.

If Colombia hopes to keep spending on judicial improvements and better law enforcement, it needs an expanding economy. In addition to misrepresenting the country's progress on reducing violence, Mr. Obama has never explained how denying Colombians the FTA will help the country reduce violence.

OBAMA DIPLOMACY

Obama wrapped up his first overseas visit with a two-day stop in Turkey. In this predominantly Muslim country he held a roundtable with Islamic students.

It is the latest in a diplomatic push for the hearts and minds of the Muslim world. First, there was the President's inaugural speech, in which he declared,

"To the Muslim world, we seek a new way forward, based on mutual interest and mutual respect." Second, he announced he would be closing the Guantanamo Bay prison camp. Then for the Iranian New Year, Obama taped a video greeting distributed to Arabic channels. In that message, he signed off in Farsi, the predominant language in Iran. That overture was received with contempt.

Obama has now granted his first formal TV interview as President to Al-Arabiya, an Arabic television network. In that interview, Obama said that when it comes to Middle East policy, "all too often the United States starts by dictating." He added, "My job to the Muslim world is to communicate that the Americans are not your enemy."

Obama will find that saying that we have been wrong and you are right will not do much good. Platitudes will not persuade repressive Muslim behaviors to be changed, will not lessen hatred against Israel and will not stop terrorism waged in the name of Islam.

OBAMA'S ATTACK MACHINE

The 45-year-old Virginia congressman came to Washington in 2001, and by last year had been unanimously elected Republican Whip, under Minority Leader John Boehner. In recent months, Mr. Cantor has helped unify the GOP against much of President Barack Obama's agenda, in particular his blowout $787 billion stimulus and his blowout $3.6 trillion budget.

Obama's attack machine is being used effectively to kneecap Republicans who might help lead a makeover. Mr. Cantor is the top target. After the GOP's unanimous vote against the stimulus, the Obama White House saw as an opening to brand Mr. Cantor as the public face of partisan opposition to the 'bipartisan' President.

Within days of the vote, the Democratic Congressional Campaign Committee was running radio ads targeting Mr. Cantor. The American Federation of State, County and Municipal Employees (AFSCME) and Americans United for Change, the pro-Obama group, launched their own ads again singling out Mr. Cantor. The groups also ran a national TV spot sporting a picture of the whip with text that read "just saying no" which earned Mr. Cantor a new Liberal nickname: Dr. No.

Mr. Obama joined in at his Fiscal Responsibility Summit. As the TV cameras rolled, he turned his full attention to the whip to say: "I'm going to keep on talking to Eric Cantor. Some day, sooner or later, he's going to say 'Boy, Obama had a good idea.'"

Rush Limbaugh inspired a new AFSCME and American United for Change ad, accompanied by the statement when Rush says jump, "Eric Cantor and other Republicans say 'how high.'" David Plouffe, the President's campaign wizard, followed up with an anti-Limbaugh screed for the Washington Post, zeroing in on "new Republican quarterback Eric Cantor, who says "the GOP's strategy will be to 'Just Say No.'"

Then the goon squad set on Mr. Cantor's wife. An outfit called Working Families Win began running robocalls in key districts noting that Diana Cantor was a top executive at a bank that had received bailout funds and then demanding voters oppose the "Cantor Family Bank bailout." Mrs. Cantor in fact works at a subsidiary of the bank in question and Mr. Cantor led the GOP revolt against the bailout. Truth is obliterated by smear tactics.

DEMOCRATIC CAUCUS

Rep. Peter DeFazio (D-Ore.) is a staunch advocate for more spending on infrastructure projects such as bridges and highways. He pleaded for more funding in those areas at a House Democratic meeting at which President Obama was present.

Obama had already taken note of DeFazio's vote against the stimulus legislation. "I know you think we need more for infrastructure because you voted against it," Obama said. "Don't think we're not keeping score, brother."

OBAMA CONTRADICTIONS

President Barack Obama acts as if no one is watching when he contradicts campaign promises.

Obama, having spent a good portion of the campaign decrying the $2.9 trillion in deficits during the Bush years, thinks that he can now double the national debt held by the public in 10 years. Having condemned earmarks during the campaign, the Obama administration now believes it can wave through 8,500 of them in the omnibus-spending bill, part of the biggest spending increase since World War II.

With the Dow at 7,486 and unemployment at 8.1%, Mr. Obama says the economy is fundamentally sound. He hopes the nation won't recall him attacking John McCain last September for saying the same thing when the Dow was at 11,000 and unemployment at 6.2%?

Candidate Obama vowed to end 'the same partisanship and pettiness and immaturity that has poisoned our politics.' Yet his administration geared up MoveOn.org to lead a left-wing coalition to pressure Republicans and centrist Democrats, organized a daily conference call to coordinate Liberal attack dogs, strategizing with Americans United for Change on ads depicting the GOP as the party of 'no.'

Rather than working with Republicans on the budget, the Obama administration attacked them as mindless obstructionists.

POLLS

President Obama's favorability rating is at an all-time high. Two-thirds feel hopeful about his leadership and six in 10 approve of the job he's doing in the White House. 68 percent have a favorable opinion of the President, including 47 percent whose opinion is "very positive", both all-time highs for Obama in the poll. 57 percent support the stimulus bill, compared with 34 percent who oppose it.

These high marks for Obama come at a time when Americans are increasingly pessimistic about the economy. Only seven percent say they're satisfied about the state of the economy, which is an all-time low in the poll.

The poll unfortunately says more about the American people than it does about Obama other than his populist appeal. Income distribution is such that a substantial majority of people will benefit personally from spending bills that are paid for by high earners through punitive taxation. People are looking for the free handout rather than the prosperity of the USA or the opportunity to become a high earner. It is this attitude reminiscent of Britain at the end of World War 2, which will propel the continuing decline of the USA.

STOCKS SINK

Coming off of its worst performance in more than 75 years since Obama took the helm, the Dow Jones Industrial Average stayed true to form going into March, selling off by another 4% to close at 6,763. The Dow hasn't closed below 7000 since May 1997. NASDQ was also off 4% to close at 1,322. Obama's fear mongering is exacting its toll in all sectors except those that thrive under bloated government and free hand outs.

The pullback, led in part by more selling in financial names, came despite promising government data, which showed consumer spending actually rose by 0.6% in January, a performance that was much better than anticipated. Personal income also rose in January.

Ongoing turbulence in the banking sector paved the way for yesterday's steep stock-market losses. Investors are still grappling with the Treasury's confused plan to stop the bleeding in the housing market, and clean up the sickly assets on many banks' balances sheets.

LISTEN TO INVESTORS

Investors are shunning Obama's words that the Treasury and the Federal Reserve will use all means at their disposal to recapitalize the banking system. They do not believe that after the government has pumped the system full of money it will burst like a piñata, spilling profits in every direction.

The reality is that all that taxpayer money will act more like embalming fluid than artificial respiration, keeping the banks looking eerily lifelike while they stiffen. It's Japan revisited. Obama is repeating the same mistake.

We know that one key error made in the 1930s was the passage of a set of protectionist laws that prevented a free exchange of goods among countries, and they have overtly sworn to prevent that from happening. The Smoot-Hawley Tariff Act in 1930 backfired by smashing world trade and catalyzing a decade-long depression.

President-elect Barack Obama pledged during his campaign to withdraw from the North American Free Trade Agreement until he has a chance to overhaul it. Leaders of the top 20 world economies cannot agree on a plan to coordinate on interest-rate cuts or currency balances. The next steps taken by countries in an attempt to revive domestic economies are to weaken their currencies. This makes exports cheaper, boosting sales, but it cannot be done by every country at the same time, or chaos ensues and sometimes even land grabbing, as Germany did in the 1930s. Obama and the US Treasury have already led a race to the bottom on interest rates. Now Europe is following. Obama introduced protectionist measures on US manufacture in the stimulus bill and Europe retaliated.

French President Nicolas Sarkozy has proposed a socialist path for his country. Barack Obama makes the US look more like France with his every move. Britain is already giving in to protectionist worker unrest undoing what Margaret Thatcher accomplished.

Barack Obama has already put in place in a month the end of what Ronald Reagan accomplished and the welfare reform of Bill Clinton.

The President is arrogant and a neophyte in international matters. That does not matter so much with our allies particularly as they like a malleable USA as it levels the playing field in their favor. The bigger concern is with those who wish us ill. Just for starters, Russia has sworn to prevent its banks from making good on obligations to the United States and the EU. Ecuador's president has said he would ignore Wall Street claims for bond repayments. Dictators and would be dictators around the world are currently silent as they see how our new President handles himself.

We have to accept reality. Obama refuses to face facts. Policymakers throughout history have found no avoidance or protectionism works once the unwinding of debt, known as deleveraging, replaces debt creation as the central theme of global trade. Debt buildup is an unrestrained party that makes borrowers happy and rich on paper; debt unwinding is a wake that leaves ex-borrowers in a bad way once the bubble bursts.

Japan has been able to withstand the past 18 years of extremely slow growth or contraction without social unrest because it was already a homogenous, orderly welfare state in which people were avid savers and accustomed to living in small apartments.

Obama and the Liberal super-majority in Washington have to get beyond politics as usual and shifting from blame tactics to constructive measures. Increased debt will be a short term palliative at best. The present situation is the worst possible timing for unrestrained Liberal ideology. Obama going back to his original political roots of activism will be disastrous. It is the worst possible time for dramatic income redistribution or for expensive new government programs to favor those who have opted out at the expense of those who create wealth in the USA. The latter are already too few as a percentage of those living in the USA.

OBAMA'S TROJAN HORSE

The stimulus is a Trojan Horse. Labeled a bill to help the economy, it is really just an amalgam of the Democratic Party's spending priorities over the past thirty years with some extra pork barrel items thrown in for seasoning. It will not — it cannot — have an appreciable impact.

Due to the overwhelming lack of confidence in the current economic situation (only a third believe the stimulus package will do much to help), consumers and businesspeople are going to sit on any cash the package puts into their hands, either saving it or using it to pay down credit card and other debt. It will have the same lack of stimulus as the Bush stimulus passed last year. Without some longer term confidence, government spending will have very little economic impact.

But the package will park lots of money off to the side of the road. And when the economy shows signs of recovery, it will come out of hiding and flood the economy causing huge inflation and kindling an inflationary cycle leading to another recession as we had in 1980-82.

All of this pain is being caused by Obama's opportunistic attempt to cash in on our concerns and his political capital to trigger a huge increase in government spending, just for the sake of spending.

GOVERNORS VERSUS OBAMA AND CONGRESS

The stimulus sets a long-term budget trap for the states. Debt-laden state governments were targeted to be big winners from the $787 billion economic stimulus bill. Five Republican Governors are declining the $150 billion of "free" money doled out to states, because it will make their budget headaches much worse down the line.

These Governors from Mississippi, Louisiana, Idaho, Texas and South Carolina point out that the tens of billions of dollars of aid for health care, welfare, unemployment insurance and education will disappear in two years and leave states with no way to finance the expanded programs.

Obama is continuing to feed the US debt addiction at an increasing rate. Taking South Carolina as an example, its annual budget is roughly $7 billion and the so-called stimulus will send about $2.8 billion to the state over two years. To spend the hundreds of millions of dollars allocated to the likes of Head Start, child care subsidies and special education, the state will have to enroll thousands of new families into the programs. "There's no way politically we're going to be able to push people out of the program in two years when the federal money runs out," Governor Sanford says.

The Medicaid money for states is also a fiscal time bomb. The stimulus bill temporarily increases the share of state Medicaid bills reimbursed by the federal government by two or three percentage points. High-income states now pay about half the Medicaid costs, and in low-income states the feds pay about 70%. Much of the stimulus money will cover health-care costs for unemployed workers and single workers without children. Then in 2011 almost all the $80 billion of extra federal Medicaid money vanishes according to the charade being played out in Washington. The reality is that our Liberal Congress will simply extend these transfer payments indefinitely, which will triple the 'stimulus' price tag to $3 trillion in additional spending and debt service over 10 years. Additionally, the states will still have to pick up their share of this tab for these new entitlements in perpetuity. The 'stimulus' is simply increased welfare. The inevitable increased taxation to pay for it long term will cause states that adopt it to lose jobs to more fiscally responsible states. Even still, most Governors are praising the 'stimulus' bill as a way to paper over their fiscal holes through 2010.

David J. Phillips

OBAMA'S BUDGET

On Feb. 26, 2009, President Obama delivered Congress a $3.6 trillion budget blueprint with a sharp shift toward expanded government activism, tax increases on affluent families and businesses and spending cuts targeted at those he says profited from "an era of profound irresponsibility."

The plan projects a federal deficit of $1.75 trillion for 2009, or 12.3% of GDP, a level not seen since 1942 as the U.S. plunged into World War II. By 2013, the deficit would drop to $533 billion but begin to climb from there again as the heart of the Baby Boom begins drawing Social Security and Medicare benefits.

There are many worsts about Obama but perhaps the worst worst is that he clearly believes in voodoo economics, no doubt learned when he was discovering his roots in Kenya.

The budget sets aside an additional $250 billion to complete the President's effort to rescue the financial markets by purchasing toxic assets on the banking sector's books.

The blueprint reorders the federal government to provide national health care, shift the energy economy away from oil and gas, and boost the federal commitment to education. To fund it all, families earning more than $250,000 and a variety of businesses will pay a steep price.

President Barack Obama is sending Congress a budget with a deficit for this year which will soar to $1.75 trillion at the same time as he is plunging us deeper into a financial crisis.

His $3 trillion-plus spending blueprint also asks Congress to raise taxes on the wealthy in 2011 and cut Medicare costs to provide health care for the uninsured.

The President's first budget also anticipates spending $250 billion more for additional financial industry bail outs efforts on top of the $700 billion that Congress has already authorized.

Could we be heading for class war fare? Obama plans to raise the tax rate to 39.5 % for those earning over $250,000 and will sharply reduce itemized deductions.

FINE LINE

The Obama administration's auto-rescue plan represents an attempt to find a small patch of middle ground between two giant political forces coursing through the land today.

On one side of President Barack Obama runs a growing populist opposition to bailing out any more big companies. On the other side runs an equally powerful desire to stop a generation-long hemorrhaging of manufacturing jobs.

The President is trying to walk a fine line between being involved enough to show he is protecting taxpayers' dollars, but not so closely involved that Americans will think he is turning GM into a kind of industrial version of the Postal Service.

In his announcement, Mr. Obama said his aides will be working closely with GM to devise a business plan, one involving making many more environmentally friendly cars, irrespective of whether that will be a money making concern. His Liberal ideology prevents him from simply cutting the two auto makers loose. The latest figures from the Bureau of Labor Statistics indicate that the number of manufacturing jobs in America has fallen by more than a third in the past generation, to 12.4 million today from 19.1 million at the start of 1980. President Obama has to posture to be King Canute and pretend to try to turn back the waves. Like Ocean tides the loss of manufacturing jobs in the USA is inevitable unless we are more cost effective manufacturers. That is certainly not the case in Union dominated Detroit. They will go down with all guns blazing rather than bow to economic reality. Their greed over decades in the good times will deprive their families of a future in Detroit unless, of course, they are already retired at 48 and are now in a second career.

PRESIDENTIAL AIDS

When giving a speech President Obama turns his head from right to left, not to look at the audience but to read from two teleprompters strategically set up outside television camera shots. Once he has delivered the set speech written by skilled professionals the teleprompters quietly began retracting into the floor.

Gone are the days of brilliant orators like Winston Churchill and more recently Margaret Thatcher. Presidents have been using teleprompters for more than half a century and even Ronald Reagan avoided non-scripted comments, but none have relied on them as extensively as Mr. Obama. While presidents typically have used them for their most important speeches such as an inaugural, State of the Union or Oval Office address, Mr. Obama uses them for routine announcements and even for the opening statements of his rare news conferences.

He used them during a visit to a Caterpillar plant in Peoria, Ill. He used them to make brief remarks opening his "fiscal responsibility summit." He used them to discuss endangered species, even recalling a visit to national parks as an 11-year-old. "That was an experience I will never forget," he said, reading from the teleprompter.

Like so much else about Obama he is not what the media tells us. He is neither a great orator nor motivational speaker. In a crisis without his aids and words fed to him by others he will fumble. His skill is in using the words of others and in using a teleprompter effectively. That is not easy. He wants to stick to the script. He does so without appearing robotic. In his delivery he is cautious to the maximum. He would be unable to cope with gaffes. When answering questions without a script, his speech is halted and he takes a lot of time to think about what he's going to say.

Harry Truman refused to use teleprompters, concluding it would make him look insincere. Dwight Eisenhower became the first President to use them but he was not a fan either. In 1993, when Bill Clinton addressed Congress on health care, the wrong speech was fed into the teleprompter. It took aides a nightmarish seven minutes to fix the problem while Clinton winged it relying on his customary charisma.

Barack Obama had never used a teleprompter until his keynote address at the 2004 Democratic convention, but he relied on them regularly on the campaign trail, reacting with anger if there was a teleprompter malfunction. Mr. Obama stumbled over words when he did not use a teleprompter. It is working for him. A majority are looking forward to his next staged performance. I prefer to read the words on the internet.

BRAINWASHING PRESCHOOLERS

Nickelodeon's TV Noggin channel advertises itself as preschool on TV. Typically, Noggin features such fare as Dora the Explorer. They are sweet-natured, violence-free, semi-educational programs, even if Noggin's claim to being commercial-free ignores the fact that it is one big advertisement for all the merchandise (dolls, toys, books, DVDs) that goes with the shows.

Now the Noggin channel has a segment which celebrates President Barack Obama. With a voice-over that sounds like a Noggin character and a set of brightly colored illustrations of the 44th president and his family. The Noggin character tells us that:

Barack Obama is the first African-American to be President. That is what's called a historic event. .Leading a country is no easy task. So what does he do to relax you may ask? He loves shrimp linguini and the chili he cooks. He also plays Scrabble; collects comic books. He likes classical and hip hop and jazz music too. He always goes shopping for the same type of shoe! He reads lots of books and writes wonderful speeches. He goes on vacation and takes walks on beaches. He loves basketball; it's his favorite sport. In the White House backyard he'll have his own court. He reads bedtime stories to his daughters at night.

Noggin never had a segment about President Bush with his bike rides, cowboy boots and Scottish terrier. To provide balance, Noggin might consider a few additional comments for their favorite person:

Leading a country is no easy task; if you campaign as a messiah, better not drop the mask. Just don't bankrupt the country, Mr. President, while you bail everyone out.

CHAPTER 16 ... ... WAR ON TERROR

OBAMA AND GUANTANAMO

After arriving here from Guantanamo Bay in November 2005, Abdallah Saleh al-Ajmi was transported by Kuwaiti security agents to a military hospital, where he was allowed to meet with his family. He was soon moved to the city's central jail and placed in a high-security wing.

Every few days, he was taken to a small interrogation room, this time by officials of his own government who wanted to know what he had been doing in Afghanistan. Ajmi insisted that he never traveled to Afghanistan that he never fought with the Taliban and that he had simply gone to Pakistan to study the Koran and that he was apprehended when he traveled toward the Afghan border to help refugees.

After four months, a judge ordered him freed on bail. He was later tried in a criminal court and acquitted of all charges. Then he drove a truck packed with explosives on to an Iraqi army base outside Mosul, killing 13 Iraqi soldiers.

His case illuminates a key challenge facing the Obama administration as it implements its cheap political victory in announcing that it will close the U.S. military prison. Now Obama has to resolve what to do with 245 inmates. Once detainees are sent home, even to friendly nations, the United States has very little influence over what happens to them. Convictions are not guaranteed. Neither is surveillance by home countries.

David J. Phillips

THE IMPORTANCE OF GUANTANAMO

The Taliban's new top operations officer in southern Afghanistan had been a prisoner at the Guantanamo Bay detention center. He is the latest example of a freed detainee who took a militant leadership role and is now a potential complication for the Obama administration's efforts to close the prison. This situation underscores the fallacy of Obama currying favor internationally for his own political ends at the expense of US interests. He will now have to deal with the bloodshed that these people will cause. Obama will have much blood on his own hands.

U.S. authorities handed over the detainee to the Afghan government, which in turn released him. Abdullah Ghulam Rasoul, formerly Guantanamo prisoner No. 008, was among 13 Afghan prisoners released to the Afghan government in December 2007. Rasoul is now known as Mullah Abdullah Zakir, a nom de guerre used by a Taliban leader who is in charge of operations against U.S. and Afghan forces in southern Afghanistan.

Rasoul has joined a growing faction of former Guantanamo prisoners who have rejoined militant groups and taken action against U.S. interests. Pentagon officials have said that as many as 60 former detainees have resurfaced on foreign battlefields. Rasoul is now a key militant figure in southern Afghanistan where violence has been spiking in the last year. Thousands of U.S. troops are preparing to deploy there to fight resurgent Taliban forces. Ironically, Rasoul's mission is to counter the U.S. troop surge.

Although the militant detainees who have resurfaced were released under the Bush administration because of pressure from Liberals like Obama, the revelation underscores the Obama administration's dilemma in moving to close the detention camp at Guantanamo and figuring out what to do with the nearly 250 prisoners who remain there.

In one of his first acts in office, President Barack Obama signed an executive order to close the jail. The order also convened a task force that will determine how to handle remaining detainees, who could be transferred to other U.S. detention facilities for trial, transferred to foreign nations for legal proceedings or freed.

More than 800 prisoners have been imprisoned at Guantanamo; only a handful has been charged. About 520 Guantanamo detainees have been released from custody or transferred to prisons elsewhere in the world. A

Pentagon tally of the detainees released show that 122 were transferred from Guantanamo in 2007, more than any other year.

The Pentagon's preferred option is to hand them over to their home governments for imprisonment. But the Defense Intelligence Agency's growing list of former prisoners that have rejoined the fight shows not surprisingly that system does not work.

According to case documents assembled by the U.S. military for a 2005 review of Rasoul's combatant status at Guantanamo, the Afghan was captured in 2001 in Konduz.

Rasoul was captured while armed with a gun and sitting in the car of an alleged Taliban leader. He insisted to American authorities he was forced to carry the gun by the Taliban. Rasoul told the tribunal in 2005 that in fact he had surrendered with other Taliban members to the Northern Alliance in Konduz on Dec. 12, 2001. The Northern Alliance was involved in a protracted civil war with the Taliban and was allied with U.S. forces in the October 2001 invasion.

Rasoul told the tribunal that he and others were then handed over to the Americans for bounties. According to the U.S. documents, Rasoul was conscripted into the Taliban in 1995, and was seriously wounded in a bombing in 1997. He returned to the Taliban in Kandahar in southern Afghanistan in 1999. Rasoul, who hailed from Helmand province in southern Afghanistan, which is a Taliban stronghold, never attended a Taliban or al-Qaeda training camp. A key piece of evidence against him was that he was captured with two Casio watches similar to those used in al-Qaeda bombings. He said he was holding the watches for a Taliban member who lacked pockets. Clearly Rasoul was not tortured – as Obama would have the world believe happened while Bush was President.

He told the tribunal that he intended to return to a peaceful life in Afghanistan.

WAR ON TERROR

The Obama administration has no clue as to what to do and wants to move on with terrorism undefeated and so has stopped using that phase to describe the effort to fight terrorism around the world. President George W. Bush first used the phrase as a rallying cry after the Sept. 11, 2001, terror attacks.

OBAMASPEAK

'War on terror' is out; 'overseas contingency operations' are in.

'Terrorism,' is out; 'man-caused' disasters are in. Is that not sexist?

ENEMY COMBATANTS

By now, President Obama's approach to the legal war on terror is familiar: He lambastes his predecessor, and then makes cosmetic changes that leave the substance of Bush policy intact. Mr. Obama has decided to renounce the term 'enemy combatant' even though detention of terrorists has not changed.

To avoid using enemy combatants, we instead get "individuals captured in connection with armed conflicts and counterterrorism operations," or "members of enemy forces," or "persons who the President determines planned, authorized, committed, or aided the terrorist attacks that occurred on September 11, 2001, and persons who harbored those responsible for the September 11 attacks."

These gyrations are bizarre because the brief is actually a solid legal argument for detaining enemy combatants. Justice argues that the U.S. has the right to hold indefinitely, without legal charges, those who "substantially supported" al-Qaeda or the Taliban, reserving the right to define what qualifies as "substantial" in each case. It also extends its writ to people who support terror networks away from the battlefield, such as financiers.

The concept of the unlawful enemy combatant is deeply rooted in international law and custom, including the Geneva Conventions. It refers to those who violate the laws of war by killing civilians or fighting out of uniform, and thus are not entitled to prisoner-of-war status.

Barack Obama is doing what George Bush did but has to call it something else to continue to fool his international fan club.

RADICAL CHIC ATTORNEYS

Within our leading law schools and law firms, it would be hard to find a cause more popular than the detainees of Guantanamo Bay. Every lawyer wants his own detainee or detainee group. The result is that dozens of the world's most dangerous men now have their own legal Dream Teams.

The 200 or so Guantanamo detainees filing for habeas corpus in federal district courts are up against 60 or so Justice Department lawyers, who are handling the bulk of the legal load. Against these 60 attorneys are arrayed some of our nation's most prestigious private firms. Last year, at a dinner at Washington's Ritz-Carlton hotel, the National Legal Aide Defender Association bestowed its "Beacon of Justice Award" on 50 law firms for their pro bono work on behalf of the detainees. These firms in turn are joined by law professors from Stanford, Yale, Northwestern and Fordham.

SECRET MEMOS

Bush memos have been made public by Obama. One is a secret legal document from 2001 in which the Bush administration claimed the military could search and seize terror suspects in the United States without warrants.

The legal memo was written about a month after the Sept. 11 terror attacks. It says constitutional protections against unlawful search and seizure would not apply to terror suspects in the U.S., as long as the President or another high official authorized the action. Even after the Bush administration rescinded that legal analysis, the Justice Department refused to release its contents.

What is Obama trying to do other than make himself look good despite the potential damage to the USA? How long will it be before Obama issues apologies to people and countries which wish us harm?

IRAQ

President Obama made an unannounced trip to Baghdad, saying a trip to Iraq was critical because progress in a country rocked by a new round of bombings lies "in political solutions." The visit came at the conclusion of an overseas trip that included economic and NATO summits in Europe, a keynote speech in Prague and two days in Turkey.

IRAN

President Obama has extended a 'hand of friendship' to Iran.

"The Iranian nation welcomes a hand extended to it should it really and truly be based on honesty, justice and respect," Ahmadinejad said in a speech broadcast live on state television.

Ahmadinejad, however, said Obama will meet the fate of former President George W. Bush if he is proved not to be honest. "But if, God forbid, the extended hand has an honest appearance but contains no honesty in content, it will meet the same response the Iranian nation gave to Mr. Bush," Ahmadinejad said.

Diplomatic ties between the U.S. and Iran were cut after the U.S. Embassy hostage-taking that followed the 1979 Islamic Revolution. The revolution toppled the pro-U.S. shah and brought to power a government of Islamic clerics.

It seems that Barack Obama might be an even bigger know-it-all than Jimmy Carter, who never could work out what to do about the hostage crisis which occurred early in his presidency and ended as Ronald Regan took the oath of office as his successor.

WAR FUNDING

President Barack Obama is seeking $83.4 billion for U.S. military and diplomatic operations in Iraq and Afghanistan, pressing for special troop funding that he opposed two years ago when he was a senator and George W. Bush was president.

Obama's request, including money to send thousands more troops into Afghanistan, would push the costs of the two wars to almost $1 trillion since the Sept. 11, 2001, terror attacks against the United States, according to the Congressional Research Service. The additional money would cover operations into the latter months of this year.

Obama was a harsh critic of the Iraq war as a presidential candidate, which attracted support from the Democratic Party's liberal base and helped him secure the party's nomination. He opposed two infusions of war money in 2007 after Bush used a veto to force Congress to remove a withdrawal time line from the $99 billion measure.

He supported a war funding bill last year that also included about $25 billion for domestic programs. Obama also voted for war funding in 2006, before he announced his candidacy for president.

The coming debate in Congress is likely to provide an early test of Obama's efforts to remake the Pentagon and its much-criticized weapons procurement system. He is requesting four F-22 fighter jets costing about $600 million as part of the war funding package but wants to shut the F-22 program down after that.

The special measure will include $3.6 billion for the Afghanistan National Army.

WEAPONS

Defense Secretary Robert Gates unveiled a sweeping overhaul of the Pentagon's top weapons priorities that he said will orient the U.S. military toward winning unconventional conflicts like the one in Afghanistan rather than focusing on war with major powers.

Among the major changes he is proposing includes ending production of Lockheed's F-22 Raptor jets at 187, which outclasses everything in the sky, Original plans called for 750. Gates said funding for another Lockheed program, the Joint Strike Fighter, will be increased in 2010 to $11.2 billion, which will now buy 30 jets, up from 14. The F-35 is a cheaper, more multipurpose plane but it can't begin to compete with the F-22 as a fighter jet.

Pentagon spending is now about 4% of GDP and is expected to decline. Losers in the $1.4 billion in cuts to missile defense include the Airborne Laser, designed to shoot down ballistic missiles in the boost phase, and additional interceptors planned for the ground-based system in Alaska. As North Korea's latest launch showed, rogue regimes aren't far away from securing long-range missiles that could reach the U.S.

Previous Pentagon reforms have faltered thanks mostly to the micromanagers on Capitol Hill who are often more interested in funneling money to their home states than in spending dollars most effectively.

TESTING OBAMA

Maj. Gen. Anatoly Zhikharev, chief of staff of Russia's long-range aviation, said Cuba had air bases with four or five suitable runways and that Russian strategic bombers may be based in Cuba in the future

Zhikharev also said that Venezuelan President Hugo Chavez has offered an island as a temporary base for Russian planes.

The Russians are testing Obama just as they did Kennedy, whom they also considered to be weak. The subsequent stand off over Cuba was the closest that the world has come to nuclear Armageddon.

BAN THE BOMB

North Korea fired a rocket over Japan, defying a warning from President Barack Obama who said that the move would further isolate the communist nation. Tokyo and other world leaders suspected that the launch was cover for a test of its long-range missile technology, bringing it one step closer towards mounting a nuclear weapon on a missile capable of reaching Alaska and beyond. President Obama said, "The U.S. will take appropriate steps to let North Korea know that it cannot threaten the safety and security of other countries with impunity."

President Obama condemned North Korea's missile launch as a direct violation of U.N. resolutions. He used strong words. "Rules must be binding. Violations must be punished. Words must mean something." The Security Council then spent hours debating its non-response, thus proving to nuclear proliferators everywhere that rules aren't binding, violations won't be punished, and words of warning mean nothing. The U.S., Britain and France, each of which holds veto power on the 15-nation council, are unlikely to secure agreement on new sanctions in the face of probable resistance from China, North Korea's closest ally, and Russia, the other two nations with veto power.

Obama has not spoken on the subject since. He perhaps now realizes that his 'moral authority' won't deter Tehran or Pyongyang from their nuclear ambitions.

The President's speech was immediately shown to be words divorced from reality. The President delivered a strong call to banish nuclear weapons at the very moment that North Korea and Iran are bidding to trigger the greatest proliferation breakout in the nuclear age. Mr. Obama also proposed an elaborate new arms-control regime to reduce nuclear weapons, even as both Pyongyang and Tehran are proving that the world's great powers lack the will to enforce current arms-control treaties.

The President went even further in Prague, noting that "as the only nuclear power to have used a nuclear weapon, the United States has a moral responsibility to act." The barely concealed apology for Hiroshima is an insult to the U.S. decision makers in 1945. They saved a million lives by ending World War II without a bloody invasion of Japan. As for the persuasive power of 'moral authority,' U.S. Presidents learned long ago that the concept has no meaning in Pyongyang or Tehran, much less in the rocky hideouts of al-Qaeda.

The choice of Prague for such a speech carried strong symbolism, and Obama didn't ignore it. Decades of communism were toppled in Czechoslovakia through the 1989 Revolution. Obama praised the Czechs for helping "bring down a nuclear-armed empire without firing a shot." He ignored that fact that the Soviets could not ignore the superior weaponry of the USA.

Mr. Obama's nuclear vision has reality exactly backward. To the extent that the U.S. has maintained a large and credible nuclear arsenal, it has prevented war, defeated the Soviet Union, shored up our alliances and created an umbrella that persuaded other nations that they don't need a bomb to defend themselves.

The most dangerous proliferation in the last 50 years has come outside the U.S. umbrella on the South Asian subcontinent, where India and Pakistan want to deter each other. No treaty stopped a Pakistani renegade selling nuclear secrets to anyone who could pay his price.. Meanwhile, the world's most conspicuous anti-proliferation victories in recent decades were the Israeli strike against Saddam Hussein's nuclear plant at Osirak, and the U.S. toppling of Saddam and the way it impressed Libya's Moammar Ghadafi.

Any serious effort at nonproliferation has to begin with North Korea and Iran. They are the urgent threat to nuclear peace, the focus of years of great-power diplomacy and sanctions. If Iran acquires a bomb or North Korea retains one despite this attempt to stop them, then the world will conclude that there is no such thing as an enforceable antinuclear order. It will be every nation for itself.

In the Middle East, a Shiite bomb will send the region's Arab nations scurrying to Pakistan so that they can have a Sunni weapon. Egypt, Saudi Arabia, the Gulf States and Iraq will be in the market for a deterrent. Mr. Obama is offering pleasant illusions, while various enemy forces plot explosive reality.

CHAPTER 17 ... ... UNIONS

LABOR RIGHTS

In the first 50 days of Barack Obama's presidency, Congress approved $1.2 trillion dollars in new spending, or $24 billion a day.

President Obama's agenda centers on vastly expanding entitlement programs, strengthening unions, and increasing government control over the private sector. The stimulus bill contains multiple provisions that burden the already strained unemployment insurance system with new entitlements, such as paying workers who choose to leave the workforce for family-related reasons. States will have to levy higher unemployment insurance taxes on employers and raising taxes on jobs will only lead to fewer job opportunities.

Within days of taking office Mr. Obama issued executive orders rescinding requirements for workers to be informed of their right not to pay portions of union dues attributable to political activities with which they may disagree.

Americans should also be concerned about the protectionist impulses as evidenced by the "Buy American" provision of the stimulus package of Obama and his Liberal cohorts, which run counter to one of the painful lessons of the Great Depression. Impeding international trade will ignite retaliation by America's trading partners, deepening and prolonging the economic downturn. Policy makers should also resist closing America's doors to skilled workers from overseas, many of whom are educated in our universities and whose talent can help make our economy stronger. Yet provisions like the "Employ American Workers Act" in the stimulus package limits banks that receive government funding from employing skilled foreign workers.

European-style interventions to which the Obama administration is inclined will not make America more competitive in the world-wide economy. Such policies will not increase growth, will not decrease unemployment, and will not increase wages for workers. Evidence has been apparent for decades in Europe's declining growth rates, higher unemployment, lower per-capita income, and longer durations of unemployment. Europe's problems are worse.

The Obama administration is intent on radically expanding government's role. Obama wants to exploit the current situation to advance a Liberal agenda unrelated and even antithetical to fixing the economy. Spending trillions of taxpayers' yet unearned dollars is trivial when socialized medicine and rewarding political allies are one's priorities. But it is not the change most Americans had in mind.

UNIONIZE OR DIE

The Employee Free Choice Act is the exact opposite of free choice. It is a bill that would allow unions to organize worksites without secret-ballot elections. It has now been reintroduced in Congress with Obama backing.

Immediately the Service Employees International Union posted a You Tube video about the horrific death of a Tulsa, Oklahoma, man who fell into an industrial-sized clothes dryer while clearing a jam of wet laundry. The accident occurred at a plant operated by Cintas Corp., a large uniform supplier. The implication is that the accident never would have occurred if the worksite had been unionized, and that opponents of the union bill have blood on their hands.

The video's target is Oklahoma Rep. Dan Boren, a Democrat who recently declared that he will vote against labor's top priority. The video concludes by calling for Mr. Boren by name to stop risking workers' lives and support the bill. The political ad also serves as a warning to other Democrats in Congress who have not declared how they will vote. The message is that if they don't sign on, they will be roughed up and face a primary challenge next election.

The bill allows a union to automatically organize a worksite if more than 50% of workers simply sign an authorization card, so pressure for employees to sign in public view would be enormous. The legislation also imposes a contract through binding arbitration if labor and management reach a stalemate.

Less than 8% of private sector workers today belong to unions, a number that has been falling for decades. Labor groups claim that membership is down because companies sack pro-union employees and threaten to shut down if workers organize. But the National Labor Relations Board, which fields these complaints, rejects almost all of the allegations after inspection. In 2005, for example, the NLRB found evidence of illegal firings in only 2.7% of the organizing election campaigns that took place that year.

Andy Stern, who heads the SEIU, has said he expects union membership to grow by at least a million within the first year of the measure's passage. That could translate into billions of dollars in mandatory dues revenue. So it's no wonder that activists have resorted to exploiting tragedies to gin up votes.

What labor activists are unwilling to acknowledge is that membership might be falling because workers are less interested in joining unions. Some employees may view labor unions as corrupt or overly politicized, and not without justification. Others may be scared off by the precarious condition of heavily unionized industries such as autos and airlines. And many workers might plausibly conclude that one-size-fits-all labor contracts hold back the best and brightest in our modern economy.

It is Big Labor's fourth attempt to pass card check since 2003. With Liberals now running Congress and the White House, they are becoming even meaner.

UNIONIZING FIGHT

The battle over a bill that would ease union organizing is zeroing in on lawmakers in three states, Pennsylvania, Arkansas and Colorado. Business and labor are pressuring three key senators who are up for re-election in 2010, sparing little expense as they ratchet up television and radio ads, and recruit well-connected lobbyists.

In Pennsylvania, the state AFL-CIO has discussed having its members register as Republicans to back Sen. Arlen Specter in a tough primary fight he faces next year, if he supports the bill. Sen. Specter reiterated that he supports a labor-law overhaul, but that he has not voted for passage of the bill.

Sen. Specter, knowing that he will lose the Republican primary has switched sides and has become a Democrat. To gain additional favor, he will now do the Unions' bidding. What is amazing is why Republicans did not dump this unprincipled Liberal in their midst long ago.

EMPLOYEE FREE CHOICE ACT

If you never thought your workers would organize a union, think again. In the near future, Congress may pass the Employee Free Choice Act (EFCA), which will make it much easier for employees to unionize. It could happen, and it would mean you'd face the triple threat of: higher wage and benefits costs, stifling bureaucracy and a far less flexible workforce. The Employee Free Choice Act threatens to strip employees of their right to a secret ballot when deciding on union representation. Employers would have to radically alter their responses to unionization, and employees will be subject to open pressures from the unions and their pro-union peers.

CHAPTER 18 ... ... WEALTH REDISTRIBUTION

TAXING MILLIONAIRES

Anyone who was a millionaire at the beginning of 2008, and had a million dollars invested in stocks, has lost at least $350,000. The losses have increased sharply this year as the market has continued its descent. Losses were also sustained in 2007.

This group also pays a disproportionate share of income taxes, even before President Barack Obama's proposed tax increases. The top 1% of earners is expected to pay 25% of all personal-income taxes this year, and the top 5% to pay 40%.

According to Obama the rich are those earning more than $200,000 a year (if single) or $250,000 (if married and filing jointly). These are the new thresholds established by Obama for his tax-increase proposals.

In New York City, home of Wall Street, $200,000 in income yields $100,000 after all taxes (including the unincorporated business tax, which applies to anyone who is self-employed). To be prudent, these people should spend no more than one-third of after-tax income on housing, which is $33,000. That is only enough for rent on a one-bedroom apartment in Manhattan. As for buying, the collapse in stock prices has wiped out much of what many people invested toward a down payment.

CONFISCATORY TAXATION

The House voted 328-93 to approve a bill imposing 90% taxes on employee bonuses from firms which received $5 billion or more under the Troubled Asset Relief Program (TARP). State and local taxes would take the other 10%. If the Senate approves a complementary plan, Obama will apply his signature immediately.

The legislation goes well beyond top executives and applies to individual employees whose total family income exceeds $250,000 adjusted gross income per year. It affects bonuses received after Jan. 1, 2009.

Financial firms that have received $5 billion or more under TARP include: Citigroup, Bank of America, JPMorgan Chase, Wells Fargo, Goldman Sachs, Morgan Stanley, PNC Financial, U.S. Bancorp and GMAC.

Adding retroactive conditions to TARP money will encourage many bankers to return such funds quickly. Previously they had been urged to participate in the capital injection program in order to increase lending. The political punishment for accepting public money is becoming higher than the benefits of the extra capital cushion. Wells Fargo Chairman Richard Kovacevich said, "If we were not forced to take the TARP money, we would have been able to raise private capital." On Tuesday, Bank of America CEO Ken Lewis joined the rush for the TARP exits, saying he hoped to pay back the $45 billion BofA has received by 2010 if not sooner.

For the well being of banking system, it is the wrong time to be shedding capital. The main point of the TARP was to backstop the financial system against systemic failure. Treasury botched the roll out and the execution, but with the economy still in recession and housing prices still falling, banking losses will grow. Mr. Geithner has projected the need for more than $1 trillion more in public capital, and the FDIC has asked Congress to increase its credit line to as much as $500 billion.

Once again, our populist President shows that he has no concept of motivating the horses that pull the cart. Instead he is igniting class warfare.

VOODOO ECONOMICS

President Obama has laid out the most expensive domestic agenda ever and pretends that he knows how to pay for it. He says that we can get there by ending "tax breaks for the wealthiest 2% of Americans," and he promised that households earning less than $250,000 won't see their taxes increased by "one single dime."

Consider the IRS data for 2006, the most recent year that such tax data are available and a good year for the economy and "the wealthiest 2%." Roughly 3.8 million filers had adjusted gross incomes above $200,000 in 2006. (That is 7% of all returns; the data aren't broken down at the $250,000 point.) These people paid about $522 billion in income taxes, or roughly 62% of all federal individual income receipts. The richest 1% (about 1.65 million filers making above $388,806) paid some $408 billion, or 39.9% of all income tax revenues, while earning about 22% of all reported U.S. income.

Federal income taxes are already progressive with a 35% top marginal rate. President Obama is (so far) proposing to raise it to 39.6%, plus another two percentage points in itemized deduction phase-outs. He will also raise capital gains and dividend rates, but those both yield far less revenue than the income tax. These combined increases would not come close to raising the hundreds of billions of dollars in revenue that Mr. Obama will need.

A tax policy that confiscated 100% of the taxable income of everyone in America earning over $500,000 in 2006 would only have given Congress an extra $1.3 trillion in revenue. That's less than half the 2006 federal budget of $2.7 trillion and is small compared to the more than $4 trillion Congress will spend in fiscal 2010. Even confiscating all earnings from everyone earning more than $75,000 in 2006 would have barely yielded $4 trillion.

The assault on executive pay will mean far fewer wealthy taxpayers in future and so tax revenues will be less than 2006. Profits are plunging, businesses are cutting or eliminating dividends, and capital nationwide is on the sidelines. Tax revenues will be considerably lower. The capitalist cow will be giving much less milk.

Obama and his Liberal fellow travelers are assuming that tax increases will not adversely affect growth and job creation. How wrong they are. Small- and medium-sized businesses are the nation's primary employers and lower individual tax rates have induced thousands of them to shift from filing under the corporate tax system to the individual system, often as limited liability companies or Subchapter S corporations. The Tax Foundation calculates that merely restoring the higher, Clinton-era tax rates on the top two brackets would hit 45% to 55% of small-business income, depending on how inclusively "small business" is defined. These owners will find a way to declare less taxable income.

Corporate Tax rates cannot be pushed higher without accelerating the departure of companies from the USA to more tax friendly parts of the world – which is now most other industrialized countries.

The truth is that President Obama is selling the country on a 2% illusion. The natural unwinding of the U.S. commitment in Iraq (for which Obama will take credit) and allowing the Bush tax cuts to expire can't possibly pay for his agenda.

Even worse, Obama's Liberal agenda will require even more subsidies and will be an indirect increased taxation on all Americans. Mandating alternative fuels and systems will require major tax subsidies. Selling the right to emit greenhouse gases amounts is a steep new tax on most types of energy and, therefore, on all Americans who use energy. To usher these in Charlie Rangel's Ways and Means panel, which writes tax law, is holding hearings this week on cap-and-trade regulation.

President Obama portrays his agenda as nothing more than center-left pragmatism. Pragmatists don't ignore data. The reality is that Obama is a left wing activist ideologue who does not care about the cost to enact his revolution of wealth redistribution to the underclass that he represented when he started his political career in Chicago. The Jeremiah Wright Obama is the real Obama.

CHAPTER 19 ... ... WHITE HOUSE

OBAMA WHITE HOUSE

As the first person to honor at the White House, President Obama chose Stevie Wonder. In the spirit of his populist agenda, he wanted someone who would honor him and who would honor black America.

President Barack Obama thanked musician Stevie Wonder for creating "a style that's uniquely American" as he presented the singer-songwriter the nation's highest award for pop music. The Gershwin Prize with its rich history going back all of three years is given for lifetime achievement in popular music. Paul Simon claimed the nation's first prize in 2007.

Obama, who called Wonder the soundtrack of his youth, gave the star the Library of Congress' Gershwin Prize for Popular Song during an East Room tribute. Wonder was emotional at times, thanking Obama for the award and reflecting on what his election as the first black president means to the United States.

"What is truly exciting for me today is that we truly have lived to see a time and a space where America has a chance to again live up to the greatness that it deserves to be seen and known as, through the love and caring and the commitment of a president — as in our president, Barack Obama," he said.

Wonder cited Martin Luther King Jr., his faith and his mother during an acceptance speech that flowed into a set of Obama's favorite songs. The musician joked that he looked forward to writing more love songs — perhaps a soundtrack for "you know, maybe I'll be a part of creating some more of those babies."

Obama praised Wonder's decades-long career and a style that has blended pop and funk, R&B and gospel. "Stevie has always drawn on the incredible range of traditions in his music and, from that, he's created a style that's at once uniquely American, uniquely his own, and yet somehow universal," Obama said. "Indeed, this could be called the American tradition — artists demonstrating the courage, the talent to find new harmonies in the rich and dissonant sounds of the American experience."

First lady Michelle Obama spoke in more personal terms, calling Wonder "one of the world's greatest artists." She recalled how she and her grandfather would listen to Wonder's albums together. "He'd blast music throughout the house and that's where he and I would sit and listen to Stevie's music together — songs about life, love, romance, heartache, despair. He would let me listen to these songs over and over and over and over again," she said. The first album she bought was Wonder's "Talking Book," and she and Barack Obama used "You and I" as their wedding song.

President Obama said he was lucky to have already loved Wonder's music when he first met his mate. "I think it's fair to say that had I not been a Stevie Wonder fan, Michelle might not have dated me, we might not have married," Obama said, with his wife sitting in the front row. "The fact that we agreed on Stevie was part of the essence of our courtship."

THE CHAMELEON

President Barack Hussein Obama hosted close friends and staff at a private White House meal Thursday evening to mark Passover. It's part of the new president's effort to reach out to Jewish voters.

The White House said the Seder meal was traditional, including matzo, bitter herbs, a roasted egg and greens in the family dining room in the executive mansion. The evening also featured the reading of the Haggadah, the religious text of the holiday.

Passover began at sundown Wednesday. It celebrates the Jewish exodus from Egypt after 400 years of slavery.

White House aides said they believe it was the first president-hosted Seder at the White House.

OBAMA TEAM

On Representative Rahm Emanuel as White House chief of staff: Barack Obama's first decision as president-elect undermines his promise to 'heal the divides.' Rahm Emanuel is a partisan insider who played a lead role in breaking Washington.

On David Axelrod, Mr. Obama's campaign strategist, as White House senior adviser: For a president-elect who promised to change the tone in Washington, it's disappointing that he is filling his White House with partisan bomb-throwers. When people think of 'change,' they don't think of political consultants like David Axelrod.

On Tom Daschle, the former Democratic majority leader in the Senate, as secretary of health and human services: For voters hoping to see new faces and fewer lobbyist-connections in government, Daschle's nomination will be another disappointment. Obama promised to change America's health care system, but his nominee to be secretary is no change agent. The only change will be a national health care system that will be quickly forced through without opportunity for disagreement.

On Eric H. Holder Jr., the former deputy attorney general, as attorney general: Instead of bringing the bipartisan 'change' to Washington that he promised voters, Barack Obama is rewarding yet another one of his political loyalists in Eric Holder. The only person who thinks Eric Holder represents 'hope' is Marc Rich, the convicted financier pardoned by President Bill Clinton with Mr. Holder's acquiescence.

On Senator Hillary Rodham Clinton, Obama's pick for secretary of state: she is not the diplomat that Obama promised and has a different foreign policy agenda than does Obama himself.

David J. Phillips

OBAMA'S CONFLICT-OF-INTEREST PLEDGE

President-elect Barack Obama's selection of former Senator Tom Daschle for secretary of health and human services violates his campaign promises to not have potential conflicts of interest among his appointees.

Since leaving the Senate four years ago, Tom Daschle has worked as a board member of the Mayo Clinic Mayo and a highly paid adviser to health care clients at the law and lobbying firm Alston & Bird.

In a detailed list of campaign promises, Mr. Obama pledged that "no political appointees in an Obama administration will be permitted to work on regulations or contracts directly and substantially related to their prior employer for two years."

It is the standard corrupt practice in Washington for politicians like Daschle to spend their years out of power making money for private influence-seekers.

A spokeswoman for Alston & Bird declined to disclose which of the firm's health care industry clients Mr. Daschle had advised; the firm represents dozens of such concerns including pharmaceutical companies, health care providers, and trade groups for nurses and nursing homes.

As examples of the firm's achievements the Web site lists matters involving Medicare and Medicaid reimbursements, approvals of federally regulated drugs and medical products, fraud investigations, medical waste disposal, privacy and other compliance issues.

The Mayo Clinic, where Mr. Daschle is on the board, is itself a major health care provider, research institution, and recipient of grants from the National Institute of Health.

Tom Daschle's wife, Linda Daschle, is a prominent lobbyist for aerospace and military concerns. Barack Obama did not make specific campaign promises related to the occupation of a spouse and so that avenue for corruption is wide open.

DASCHLE

Former Senate Majority Leader Tom Daschle, President Barack Obama's nominee for the secretary of Health and Human Services, paid around $100,000 in back taxes after his nomination to pay for a car and driver he was supplied but did not report as income,

On Feb. 3, 2009, Daschle withdrew his nomination to be secretary of Health and Human Services. President Obama accepted the withdrawal "with sadness and regret." Not only did Daschle fail to pay more than $100,000 in taxes but his relationship with EduCap is under investigation by the Internal Revenue Service.

TIMOTHY GEITHNER

The Senate confirmed Timothy Geithner to become Treasury Secretary on Jan. 26, 2009 despite concerns over his failure to pay past income taxes. The 60-34 vote split largely along party lines. The selection of Geithner, the president and chief executive of the Federal Reserve Bank of New York, to succeed Henry Paulson, hit a speed bump after disclosing that he did not pay roughly $34,000 in income tax associated with his work at the International Monetary Fund from 2001 to 2005. The Treasury Department oversees the Internal Revenue Service. Obama in supporting Geithner's nomination said the nation couldn't afford to wait for him to search for another nominee to run the Treasury Department, showing once again that his concern about having a clean administration is without substance.

Geithner was the director of the IMF's policy development and review department from 2001 to 2003. He joined the Treasury Department in 1988, and climbed the ranks during the Clinton administration to become the Undersecretary for International Affairs in 1999.

Geithner is at the helm of President Barack Obama's plan to revive the economy. The Plan is nothing but a plan to plan and is being panned. The stock market has dropped precipitously as a result. Vast sums of money will be disbursed without much thought to donors and at the behest of lobbyists who were given a seat at the Obama table. These include the likes of well heeled companies such as GE, Microsoft and Google. Money will also be funneled quickly to free loaders and welfare recipients. Tax checks will be sent to low income people many of whom do not pay taxes, the only certainty is that the stimulus package will not stimulate much of anything except Obama's popularity and will destroy the future prosperity of the USA. The inevitable raging inflation will propel the decline of the USA.

On Feb. 13, 2009, the Democratic-controlled Congress passed the $787 billion economic stimulus bill. The Senate approved the measure 60-38 with three Liberal Republicans providing crucial support to prevent debate. Hours earlier, the House vote was 246-183. Not a single House Republican backed the package. The President will sign the bill immediately, less than a month after taking office. Obama, Congress and the people who will disperse the money do not even know what is in the Bill. It has been prepared by staff members and rushed through Government controlled at all levels by Liberals intent on implementing their ideology immediately. The republican opposition did succeed in removing some abusive add-ons, but many more will be added. The $787 billion is only a start of a dramatic escalation of government spending which is already out of control. Liberal ideologists and free loaders, who voted Obama and a Liberal controlled Congress into absolute power, are in their element. Obama will continue to use populist rhetoric to consolidate his popularity with recipients of the free hand outs.

The seeds of the eventual destruction of US prosperity for subsequent generation are now in the hands of the people who will sow these seeds to get a quick fix for US debt addiction.

NANCY KILLEFER AND JUDD GREGG

On Feb. 3, 2009 Nancy Killefer, nominated by President Obama to be the federal government's first chief performance officer, withdrew from the post over a tax problem. on the heels of the tax avoidance issues of Geithner and Daschle.

Separately, Obama nominated Sen. Judd Gregg of New Hampshire as commerce secretary, adding a third Republican to his cabinet. It was the last open spot in the senior ranks of the Obama administration caused by Richardson, his original nominee being charged with corruption Judd found that it would be impossible to work with Obama and quickly rescinded the nomination.

TREASURY STAFFING PROBLEMS

Two candidates for top jobs at the Treasury have withdrawn their names from consideration, complicating efforts by Treasury Secretary Tim Geithner to staff his department. Annette Nazareth, who was tapped as deputy Treasury secretary, and Caroline Atkinson, who was being considered to oversee international affairs, have both withdrwn,

ANOTHER BITES THE DUST

Charles W. Freeman Jr., the Obama administration's choice for a major intelligence post, has withdrawn his name. Mr. Freeman had come under sharp criticism for his association with the Saudi and Chinese governments. A former ambassador to Saudi Arabia, Mr. Freeman had also been deputy chief of mission at the American Embassy in Beijing. Critics in Congress questioned Mr. Freeman's financial ties to China; he had served for four years on the board of the state-owned China National Offshore Oil Corporation. He also led the Middle East Policy Council, a Washington-based group that receives financial support from the Saudi government.

In the intelligence post, Mr. Freeman would have overseen the production of national intelligence estimates, which represent the consensus of the government's 16 intelligence agencies.

PANETTA

The White House's nominee for director of the CIA, Leon Panetta, has earned more than $700,000 in speaking and consulting fees since the beginning of 2008, with some of the payments coming from troubled banks and an investment firm that owns companies that do business with federal national security agencies. Panetta was confirmed by the Senate Intelligence Committee.

David J. Phillips

RAHM EMANUEL

Rahm Emanuel is a former Clinton White House advisor and most recently a four-term Democrat Congressman from Chicago and now the new White House Chief of Staff of Barack Obama. President Obama, himself a connected Chicago insider, benefited from a sweetheart house deal orchestrated by racketeer Rezko, who is now serving time after also working with ex-Illinois governor Blagojevich. Emanuel took Blagojevich's seat when the latter progressed up the Democratic gravy train in Illinois. Emanuel, the third musketeer with Blagojevich and Obama, seems to have used a different type of sweetheart house deal.

Rahm Emanuel's 4228 North Hermitage home is one of the largest in the neighborhood, with a side yard, making the Emanuels' property the largest on the block. Other North Hermitage homes on Emanuel's block are valued in the $500,000 plus range. According to Cook County Treasurer's website, the Chicago owners of nearby 118 year old 4222 North Hermitage pay almost $6800 annually. The family at 4224 North Heritage pays $6000 each year in property taxes. Rahm Emanuel and his wife Amy Rule pay no property taxes. They declared their 4228 North Hermitage home as the office location for their personal non-profit foundation called the Rahm Emanuel and Amy Rule Charitable Foundation. As the non-profit's headquarters, they claim that their home is exempt from paying property taxes.

The Rahm Emanuel and Amy Rule Charitable Trust was formed in 2002, when the Chicago lawmaker was first elected. Emanuel and Rule are its only donors. The trust reported having $2,900 on hand at the end of 2005 after receiving $34,000 from Emanuel (for which Emanuel claims tax relief) and donating more than $31,000. During the past three years, Emanuel's charity gave nearly $25,000 to the Anshe Emet synagogue and school, which is a private school that the Rahm/Rule children attend and $15,000 to the foundation run by former president Bill Clinton (gratefully received by Bill who's other donors include the leaders of most countries seeking a behind the scenes helping hand) It also gave $14,000 to Marwen, a Chicago charity that provides art classes and other educational help to low-income children. Rule is on Marwen's board.

There is no evidence that Rezko is involved in this scheme unlike the Obama house deal.

OBAMA ETHICS

On the campaign trail, candidate Barack Obama vowed to fix Washington's "broken politics". His slogan was: "Change you can believe in." His new ethics and transparency rules were, he ventured, "historic measures".

Now we see the real Obama. His administration is crammed with alumni of Bill Clinton's White House; Hillary Clinton, whom Obama mocked as the epitome of what was wrong with politics, is now secretary of state.

Now it is clear that Obama wants lobbyists to have top jobs in his administration. Tom Daschle, a former senator and the personification of the slick operator richly rewarded for his influence-peddling, was nominated as health secretary. Daschle has made $5 million in the four years since the voters of South Dakota voted him out of office. He had earned some $200,000 from health companies that stand to benefit from Mr. Obama's promise to overhaul the American health system. It also emerged that Daschle had been pushing for a key financial sponsor of his own to become commerce secretary, after the original nominee, Governor Bill Richardson, pulled out to face a corruption investigation.

William Lynn, a lobbyist for the defense giant Raytheon, has been nominated as the deputy Pentagon chief.

The new treasury secretary, Timothy Geithner – who oversees the Internal Revenue Service, failed to pay $34,000 in taxes and survived while Nancy Killefer, who was to be federal "chief performance officer", stood down for failing to pay employment taxes for her house cleaner. Obama and the Liberal super majority in Congress presumably judge Geithner as too big to be allowed to fail the nomination process.

CHAPTER 20 ... ... EPILOGUE

PRIVATE EQUITY UNDER ASSAULT

As the liquidity crunch curbs debt, private equity will shrink dramatically.

In order to understand how the private equity industry got into this predicament and where it goes from here, it is important to go back to the beginning. The American private equity asset class was formalized almost 30 years ago. At that time, the dominant corporate structure was the conglomerate. These conglomerates were run, largely, by managers with a limited economic stake in the performance of the stock of their companies. In addition, the myopic focus on quarterly accounting earnings, as opposed to cash earnings, obscured the true intrinsic value of many companies and precluded any difficult restructurings.

In this context, the rationale for the private equity asset class was simple. Private equity managers would invest long-term capital in poorly run companies, undertake complicated reorganizations that were not possible in prior corporate forms, and would exploit market inefficiencies. This would be accomplished by employing the discipline of debt, relentlessly focusing on cash generation, and creating fundamental operating improvements at these companies. In addition, private equity managers would put their own money into the fund, and get the bulk of their compensation in the form of a percentage of cash profits on the investments, aligning the incentives of managers and investors. If done right, the capital invested would earn above average returns in order to compensate investors for the illiquidity of and increased risk through leverage on their investments.

The attack by lawmakers on AIG pay has provoked renewed concern from financial company executives that government interference in business decisions is making it difficult for struggling firms to return to profitability. In particular, executives say they need to offer bonuses to keep and motivate their most valuable employees and are already seeing an exodus of talent. Obama and Liberal Congress want the financial industry to be smaller and its jobs less lucrative.

It is a critical juncture for the Obama administration. Officials at the Federal Reserve and the Treasury Department are increasingly worried that the controversy will discourage investors from joining a new government effort to revive consumer lending as well as a separate plan that relies on private money to buy toxic assets from banks.

The firestorm over bonuses paid by insurance giant American International Group has triggered alarm at other financial firms, threatening federal efforts to draw private investors into economic recovery programs.

Private equity companies, observing the pressure being exerted on AIG and other big banks, say they are worried about joining in government efforts to rescue the financial system in the newly charged political environment. They are afraid of the populist outrage being generated by Obama and Liberal Congress. Many have said that they would not partner with the government for fear that lawmakers would impose retroactive conditions on their participation, such as limits on compensation.

WALL STREET COMPENSATION FOR 2006

After making record profits, Goldman Sachs paid its employees an average of $622,000 for 2006. That's more than three times the average salary of a Massachusetts surgeon, four times that of a Massachusetts chief executive, six times that of a Massachusetts business professor and nearly 12 times that of a Massachusetts high school teacher. The average annual salary for an economist in Massachusetts is about $70,000.

The average pay of a Goldman employee would allow a Massachusetts school system to hire 12 more teachers, who make an average of $53,000. It's the equivalent of four primary-care physicians, who make around $150,000 a year.

The average Goldman salary is 58 times the annual earnings of a minimum wage worker in the United States.

Even with frequent all-nighters, Goldman employees probably earned the best hourly wages in the world (an average of about $200 per hour, assuming a 60-hour week; the firm's top traders, meanwhile, reportedly made $17,000 to $33,000 an hour.) In a country where people are debating a $1 increase in the minimum wage, such bonanzas provide a startling reminder of the extremes in our free-market economy.

Capitalism works because it encourages and rewards those who successfully take risks, adapt to change and develop profitable opportunities. In 2006, even after paying themselves and their other expenses, Goldman's employees generated an average of about $550,000 of pre-tax profit apiece.

At the heart of Goldman profit is the annual bonus system, which mirrors the dynamics of free-market capitalism. Like workers at other Wall Street firms, most Goldman employees receive the vast majority of their compensation in a single paycheck, the amount of which is based on firm, group and individual performance.

The system gives the firm extraordinary ability to invest its resources in the assets (people) that earn the biggest returns — and to do so without risk, after the fact, when the returns are in the bank. It allows the firm to pay superstars enough that they won't jump to hedge funds and private equity firms, where the upside is even more extreme. It allows the firm to pay free riders and has-beens next to nothing before it shows them the door.

The bonus system also gives the firm the flexibility to cut compensation drastically in bad years without destroying profit margins or firing thousands of loyal employees: Wall Street is notoriously cyclical. The system ensures that ambitious employees have an incentive to give their best every year, instead of resting on laurels. And it enables the company (and its shareholders) to develop new products and businesses without shouldering all of the risks.

Capitalism is also great at generating immense tax revenue. Goldman's employees pump almost as much into city, state and government coffers as they take home.

While the salaries on Wall Street can be outsized, they reflect risk that few other professions face, One year they can make $600,000, the next year, lose their jobs.

At issue now is how Wall Street will apply capitalist principles to compensation to reflect performance in 2008 and 2009.

FIGHTING BACK

For all the toxic assets that reside on the books of major global banks, an even bigger issue is the absolute lack of confidence in our leaders, both hypocritical, financially naive politicians and big company CEOs.

The way forward is to end the vilification of corporate America and Wall Street. The house bought for $178,000 in 2003 never was worth $575,000 three years later. Instead of facing facts it is easier with media help to trash investment bankers, without even knowing what they do. There is a lack of understanding about the financial meltdown and the investment banking industry by the general public, government and news media. (Read USA in Decline). The investment banking community is in disarray and has not sought to change those misperceptions.

It is more than just an image problem. The entire industry is perceived as responsible for everything that has gone wrong in the financial system and everything that is wrong with America and for all the financial evil in the world. Mainstream news coverage and politicians' statements feed this misconception. They represent the crisis in easily digested sound bytes, even though it is much more complicated and technical.

Investment bankers have to talk about their values, processes, intellectual capital and what will make them competitive in the future, as well as their willingness to be scrutinized and stand up to a high international standard of performance.

A hindrance is the lack of effective communicators and critical thinkers in the banking community. Investment banks have traditionally not felt that they need to market themselves to outsiders. Additionally some investment banking values are not acceptable particularly in the present economic environment. That arrogance also affects the quality of the communication. Bankers are good at communicating their victories and their place in the league tables, but they have never been good at explaining matters that have not gone well. Investment bankers tend not to have good management skills either internally or externally. Investment banks have been defined by a lack of transparency, a lack of effort to build trust about their role in society. There needs to be mutual understanding of what different people are going through in this economy.

Previously investment banks have never needed to market themselves to a general audience as their constituency has been CEOs and policymakers. Today they are being splashed across the newspapers, so their visibility is now a mass audience.

Despite the well-publicized problems, the investment banking industry has done a lot of good, particularly in the USA. Investment banks need to rework their definitions and roles, their function and benefits.

The industry also has to remind the public that many bankers themselves have been hurt in the downturn, having lost their jobs and savings. The media portrays every banker and finance industry professional as self-serving and greedy. The common sound byte is that Madoff's criminality is symptomatic of the greed that pervades all bankers and that the problem was lax regulations. Both are outrageous wildly incorrect statements.

Madoff's investment company reported a total balance of $64.8 billion in November even though it actually had only a small fraction of that amount. Bernard Madoff pleaded guilty on March 12, 2009 to all 11 charges in one of Wall Street's largest swindles.

Most investment bankers are high achieving, honorable, hard-working people who are equally victims of this downturn. They are not, except for the few, perpetrators of some dreadful crime.

An industry wide initiative is critical, because of the debate in Congress about executive compensation and the regulations it will place on the industry. Without engagement, the agenda will be defined by others, which is not good for anyone.

WALL STREET NEEDS INCENTIVES

In a last-minute addition to the stimulus bill, Congress imposed tight restrictions on pay arrangements in all financial firms that have or will receive funds from the federal government's Troubled Asset Relief Program (TARP).

They weaken executives' incentives to deliver the long-term performance that is needed to benefit banks, the economy, and taxpayers who have injected vast amounts of capital into these institutions.

Mandating that at least two-thirds of an executive's total pay be decoupled from performance, as the Stimulus Bill does, is typical addled government thinking.

Compensation structures with distorted incentives may have already imposed large losses on investors and the economy. Public officials should be wary of introducing new distortions and perverse incentives. With so much hanging in the balance, ensuring that those running the country's banks have the right incentives is as important as ever.

The last-minute zinger from Senator Dodd in the Stimulus Bill is that it caps incentive payments to the highest paid executives at banks receiving Troubled Asset Relief (TARP) funds. In practice, that means managing directors at, say, Goldman Sachs who are paid about $250,000 in salary, could only make a bonus of $175,000 apparently regardless of whether it comes in cash or in stock that can't be cashed in for years.

The goal of compensation reform should be to ensure that pay is more closely linked to performance, not less so as the Stimulus Bill's provisions would require. Under the new rules, banks will have every incentive to increase salaries across the board to remain competitive with banks at home and abroad that aren't subject to the restrictions.

That would destroy one good thing about Wall Street — its flexible cost structure. By paying relatively low salaries, investment banks have historically adjusted pay according to earnings and economic circumstances. The cap will promote mediocrity. Big potential earners will flee TARP-tainted firms.

The investment banker who works tirelessly to land an advisory deal that requires skill in capital markets deserves to be paid a slice of the fees generated. The same goes for the trader who makes the firm or its clients tens of millions.

An intelligent reform of Wall Street would ensure that the profits these bankers and traders generated were not fleeting, like the ones Merrill Lynch and Citigroup booked on collateralized debt obligations one year that led to billions of losses in succeeding years. Similarly, legislation fostering best practices, like claw-back provisions where an executive has to return money, would have made sense.

ELECTED TOXIC ASSETS

Each day in the age of Obama now takes us further into lawlessness, situational constitutionalism and institutional derangement.

NAFTA, like all treaties, is the "supreme law of the land." So says the Constitution. It is, however, a cobweb constraint on our Liberal Congress.

The Congress has unambiguous stipulations that the House shall be composed of members chosen "by the people of the several states," but is voting to pretend that the District of Columbia is a state. Hence it supposedly can have a Democratic member of the House and, down the descending road, two Democratic senators. Congress rationalizes this anti-constitutional willfulness by citing the Constitution's language that each house shall be the judge of the "qualifications" of its members and that Congress can exercise exclusive legislation over the District.

The Federal Reserve, by long practice rather than law, has been insulated from politics in performing its fundamental function of preserving the currency as a store of value -- preventing inflation. Now, however, by undertaking hitherto uncontemplated functions, it has become an appendage of the executive branch. The coming costs, in political manipulation of the money supply, of this forfeiture of independence will be steep.

Jefferson warned that "great innovations should not be forced on slender majorities." But Democrats, who trace their party's pedigree to Jefferson, are contemplating using "reconciliation", which is a legislative maneuver to severely truncate debate and limit the minority's right to resist, so that they might impose vast and controversial changes on US health care.

When the Congressional Budget Office announced that the President's budget underestimates by $2.3 trillion the likely deficits over the next decade, the comment back from Obama's spokesman is that all long-range budget forecasts are notoriously unreliable.

We are turning into a banana republic where the "rule of law" is replaced by "the tyranny of the majority" and the political machinations by Liberals, in the name of an economic recession that they are manipulating are undermining most of our founding principles.

David J. Phillips

OBAMA OVER HIS HEAD

The $787 billion stimulus, gargantuan as it was, was in fact too small and not aimed clearly enough at only immediate job-creation.

The $275 billion home-mortgage-refinancing plan, assembled by Treasury Secretary Tim Geithner, is too complex and indirect.

The President gave up the moral high ground on spending not so much with the "stim" but with the $400 billion supplemental spending bill, larded as it was with nearly 9,000 earmarks.

The administration is throwing good money after bad in at least two cases— the sinkhole that is Citigroup (there are many healthy banks) and General Motors (they have to go into Chapter 11).

The failure to call for genuine sacrifice on the part of all Americans, despite the rhetorical claim that everyone would have to give up something.

A willingness to give too much leeway to Congress to handle crucial details, from the stim to the vague promise to "reform" medical care without stating what costs could be cut.

A 2010 budget that tries to do far too much, with way too rosy predictions on future revenues and growth of the economy. This led those who fear we are about to go over Niagara Falls to deride Obama as a paddler who'd rather redesign the canoe.

Now is not the time for costly, upfront spending on social engineering in health care, energy and education.

THE BUCK WILL NOT STOP WITH OBAMA

President Barack Obama offered his domestic-policy proposals as a "break from a troubled past." But the economic outlook now is more troubled than it was even in January, despite Obama's bold rhetoric and commitment of more trillions of dollars.

Obama's agenda of increased government activism is the problem, sowing uncertainty among businesses, investors and consumers that will prolong and deepen the recession.

Obama is a master at the blame game. The administration likes to say it inherited the recession and trillion-dollar deficits, ignoring the fact that the economic wreckage has already substantially worsened on Obama's still-young watch. Stocks have tumbled to levels not seen since 1997. They are down more than 50 percent from their 2007 highs and 25 percent since Obama's inauguration.

The President's suggestion that it was a good time for investors with "a long-term perspective" to buy stocks caused the latest big sell-off. The problem is that he has so little useful perspective that anything he says that is not carefully scripted and delivered from a teleprompter is likely to be the wrong thing to say at the wrong time.

Some once mighty companies such as General Motors and Citigroup are little more than penny stocks. Conflicting actions and comments from Obama are exacerbating their problems.

Many health care stocks are down because of fears of new government restrictions and mandates as part a health care overhaul. Private student loan providers were pounded because of the increased government lending role proposed by Obama. Industries that use oil and other carbon-based fuels are being shunned, because of Obama's woolly proposals for fees on greenhouse-gas polluters.

Obama created the national anxiety by warning of catastrophe if his stimulus plan was not passed and in setting high expectations for Geithner, insisting that he be confirmed even though Geithner had neglected to pay his own taxes. In any administration other than Obama's that would make Geithner a poor choice for the Cabinet official responsible for the Internal Revenue Service. Geithner's public performance has been halting and he seems as much at sea as Obama is. Indeed he is probably totally confused as to the real direction that his boss wants to go.

Obama will continue to use weasel words whatever happens. The White House has claimed that its policies will "create" or "save" 3.5 million jobs. If the economy loses 2 million jobs, Obama will claim that it would have lost 5.5 million jobs. If the economy creates a million jobs, Obama will claim that it would have lost 2.5 million jobs.

Obama's proposals, particularly those borrowed from Europe and touted as his own such as "cap and trade" fees on polluters to combat global warming, will raise taxes on everyone.

The trillions of federal dollars being doled out by the administration, Congress and the Federal Reserve will sow the seeds of inflation down the road, whether the measures succeed in taming the recession or not. That is another pernicious tax on everyone. Obama intends to spend unprecedented amounts of money. His $3.6 trillion budget and the $837 billion stimulus package are but a start.

To the notion that he favors a government-operated approach toward fixing problems, Obama says none of it started on his watch — the collapsing economy or the taxpayer-funded bailouts designed to keep matters from getting even worse. "By the time we got here, there already had been an enormous infusion of taxpayer money into the financial system," Obama said. "I think it might be useful to point out that it wasn't under me that we started buying a bunch of shares of banks. It wasn't on my watch. And it wasn't on my watch that we passed a massive new entitlement — the prescription drug plan without a source of funding."

He said his administration has been operating in a way that has been entirely consistent with free-market principles and some of his critics can't say that. He says that he is absolutely not moving away from the free market towards socialism but then changes the subject without elaborating. I suspect that he does not understand the difference. What he does do is to quickly interject that large-scale government intervention in the markets and expansion of social welfare programs began under President George W. Bush.

Mr. Obama said that the end was not in sight when it came to bail outs and that it will take another $750 billion to address the problem of weak and failing financial institutions beyond the $700 billion already approved.

For how long will Obama continue to blame his predecessor and for how long will a complicit Liberal media allow it to happen. It is not credible for Obama to say he is not embracing socialism when he digs a bigger and bigger socialist hole for us all to fall into. If he truly believed in the free market, he would not be putting his foot harder and harder on the bailout accelerator, whoever made the first bailout. Even Obama surely will not be able to look into the mirror and see who he really is after that piece of buck passing.

Mr. Obama urged Americans to be prudent in their personal financial decisions, but not to hunker down so much that it would further slow the recovery. "What I don't think people should do is suddenly stuff money in their mattresses and pull back completely from spending," he said. Obama fails to add that would be wise from their personal perspectives. He wants consumers to continue with their debt addiction and free handouts as that perpetuates their dependency on his Liberal power elite.

In another piece of buck passing, Obama tried to suggest that the real weakness is a floundering Europe having an impact on our markets. He is uncertain about when the economy will begin to rebound in contrast with the projections embedded in the budget he recently released. That plan rested on the assumption that the economy would shrink by 1.2 percent this year, a projection that he knows is a pipe dream perhaps literally.

"I don't think that people should be fearful about our future," President Obama said. "I don't think that people should suddenly mistrust all of our financial institutions." The fear stems from what President Obama will do or say next!

Mr. Obama exhibits confidence and increasing arrogance despite the economic turmoil and the deteriorating situations in Afghanistan and Pakistan. He struck a reassuring tone, saying Americans should not be frightened of the future, and he said he had no trouble sleeping at night. He leaves that to everyone adversely affected by his misconceived Liberal ideology which is the only play book that he understands.

Asked if the United States was winning in Afghanistan, a war he effectively adopted as his own by ordering an additional 17,000 troops sent there, Mr. Obama replied flatly, "No." He is now intent on following advice from the Europeans that we should negotiate with elements of the Taliban. Europeans prefer that approach than to send troops.

Mr. Obama also left open the option for American operatives to capture terrorism suspects abroad even without the cooperation of a country where they were found hastening to add that "we don't torture" and that "we ultimately provide anybody that we're detaining an opportunity through habeas corpus to answer to charges."

In a court filing last month, the Obama administration agreed with the Bush administration position that 600 prisoners in a cavernous prison on the American air base at Bagram in Afghanistan have no right to seek their release in court. That somehow is different or is it that Obama likes to be right all the time and is actually hypocritical and dishonest? He will derive political capital wherever he can at the expense of his predecessor in the White House even though in reality he has no clue how to have any different foreign policy or do anything different other than to say he will close Guantanamo since it makes him look good, to be replaced by other prisons.

THE RECESSION

Bad policies prolong recessions. So far, the current downturn, which officially began in December 2007, isn't much more severe than the average of all recessions since 1970. In March, the downturn turned 15 months old, which is one month less than the recession of 1981-82, though job loss hasn't yet been as severe. The recession of 1973-75 lasted 16 months and job loss was also worse. The last two recessions in 1990-91 and 2001 were only eight months long and shallow.

In all these recessions after 15 months the sources of recovery were forming and the end was in sight. Economies don't spiral down continuously without a reason. The plunge in equities is a consequence of concern about President Obama's radical budget and the unveiling of the President's policy agenda. Equity prices have reacted to those proposals by signaling that they expect a much deeper and longer recession. The choices that Mr. Obama and Congress are making so far are not contributing to confidence, much less to recovery.

EXPANDED EXECUTIVE POWERS

The Obama administration is asking Congress to give the Treasury secretary unprecedented powers to initiate the seizure of non-bank financial companies, such as large insurers, investment firms and hedge funds, whom they do not like. The government at present has the authority to seize only banks.

Giving the Treasury secretary authority over a broader range of companies would mark a significant shift from the existing model of financial regulation, which relies on independent agencies that are shielded from the political process. The Treasury secretary, a member of the President's Cabinet, would exercise the new powers in consultation with the White House and the Federal

Reserve which is becoming increasingly compliant to political pressure and is expanding its own intervention activity.

TERM ASSET-BACKED SECURITIES LOAN FACILITY

The Treasury plans to partner with up to five asset managers to help it manage the extended Term Asset-Backed Securities Loan Facility (TALF) program, which will now accept lower-rated securities. The department would use up to $100 billion from the Troubled Asset Relief Program to leverage $500 billion of toxic asset purchases. Treasury and Fed officials said the program could be expanded to reach $1 trillion.

Treasury Secretary Geithner said the Obama administration will work with Congress on executive compensation measures to strike the right balance. That means that Obama will once again change his own rules, this time on executive compensation where it enables him to buy cooperation.

The Treasury Department said the Fed would accept the toxic assets on bank balance sheets as collateral for loans under the TALF, creating more risk for the Fed while further stripping it of its political independence. The Fed is doing what a central bank should never do which is to take on huge quantities of highly risky assets. The Fed has already sacrificed its independence and is now a lackey to Obama's Liberal ideology.

The question now is whether those assets will end up on the Fed's balance sheet, and whether the central bank will ever be able to sell them. Since there is no market for them, the Fed will be stuck with them until a market evolves. They are stepping into the shoes of the banks.

Under the program the Fed lends against assets offered by banks as collateral. The assets, initially limited to securities backed by auto, credit card, student and small-business loans, stay on the bank's balance sheet unless the Fed decides to call the collateral.

The goal was originally to liquefy the markets for consumer debt by providing investors an incentive to buy the securities. The revamp complements the Treasury's larger plan by allowing banks to tap liquidity while holding on to assets they might not want to sell to the government. Many of these assets are junk or below.

At issue is whether the central bank is capable of managing troubled assets as well as other regulators, like the Federal Deposit Insurance Corporation (FDIC). The Fed, unlike the FDIC, does not have experience of dealing with troubled assets. They will have to contract out and will still have to manage the people they hire. The Fed and Treasury said that tax payer losses will be determined at a later date and will reflect how bad the assets are.

FED ROLLS THE DICE

Doubting other remedies, the Bernanke Fed has thrown itself all in to unlock financial markets and spur the economy. With its plan to make a mammoth purchase of Treasury securities, the Fed essentially said that the considerable risks of future inflation and permanent damage to the Fed's political independence are details that can be put off, or cleaned up, at a later date. Whatever else people will say about his chairmanship, Ben Bernanke does not want deflation or Depression on his resume.

It's important to understand the historic nature of what the Fed is doing. In buying $300 billion worth of long-end Treasurys, it is directly monetizing U.S. government debt. This is what the Federal Reserve did during World War II to finance U.S. government borrowing, before the Fed broke the pattern in a very public spat with the Truman Administration during the Korean War. Now the Bernanke Fed is once again making itself a debt agent of the Treasury, using its balance sheet to finance Congressional spending.

It is also monetizing U.S. debt indirectly with the huge expansion of its direct purchase program of mortgage-backed securities (MBS). It was $500 billion, and now it will add $750 billion more this year. Foreign governments have been getting out of Fannie and Freddie MBSs in recent months and going into Treasurys. Thus the Fed is essentially substituting for this lost business as these foreign governments finance U.S. debt by buying presumably safer Treasurys. The purpose of these actions is to keep rates low on both Treasurys and MBSs, and to keep the cost of funds low for banks and especially for home buyers.

The case for doing so is that the Fed needs to supply dollars at a time when money velocity is low and the world demand for dollars is high amid the global recession. As long as the world keeps demanding dollars, the Fed can get away with this extraordinary credit creation. That said, bear in mind that the Fed's balance sheet has more than doubled since September to $1.9 trillion from $900 billion. These latest commitments mean it may more than double again, close to $4 trillion. That would be about 30% of GDP, up from about 7%.

The market reaction clearly showed the implied risks, with gold leaping and the dollar taking a dive. As the economy improves, and thus as the velocity of money increases, the risk of inflation will soar. Mr. Bernanke says the Fed can remove the money fast, but central bankers always say that and rarely do. The Fed statement isn't reassuring on that point. The Fed seems to be saying it wants a little inflation, which we know from history can easily become a big inflation or another asset bubble. The last time the Fed cut rates to very low levels to fight deflation, we ended up with the housing bubble and mortgage mania.

The other great, and less appreciated, danger is political. The Bernanke Fed has now dropped even the pretense of independence and has made itself an agent of the Treasury, which means of politicians. With its many new credit facilities, the TALF and the others, it is making credit allocation decisions across the economy. If a business borrower qualifies for one of these facilities, it gets cheaper money. If it doesn't, it is out of luck. Thus the scramble is on by so many non-banks to become bank holding companies, so they can tap the Fed's well of cheap credit.

The question is how the Fed will withdraw from all of this uncharted territory now that it has moved into it. How will it wean companies off easy credit, especially since some companies may need it to survive? What happens when Members of Congress lobby the Fed to keep credit loose for auto loans to help Detroit, or credit cards to help consumers? House Speaker Pelosi has given a taste, saying the AIG bailout was the Fed's idea without any prior notification to us. Mr. Bernanke, meet your new partners.

Above all, the Treasury and Congress won't be happy if the Fed decides to stop buying Treasurys and the result is a big increase in government borrowing costs. This was the source of the dispute between the Federal Reserve and the Truman Treasury. The Fed wanted to raise rates amid rising inflation, while the Truman Treasury wanted cheap financing for Korea and its domestic priorities. The Fed prevailed in 1951. That is unlikely to be the case with a Liberal super-majority holding power in Washington.

CAPITALISM REVISITED

The housing bubble that floated into view in 2007 is turning into the blob that ate the world. Real-estate mortgages and their derivative securities are a significant problem. That discrete problem has now been inflated into a crisis of capitalism.

Capitalism didn't tank the U.S. economy. Overbuilt housing did to house those who could not afford the overbuilt housing. Overbuilt housing tanked the economies of the U.K. and Ireland and Spain. Artificially cheap over-designed housing creates limitless moral hazards.

Even the Russians in addition to most other countries, stuffed their balance sheets with securities carved out of the dreams of real-estate developers. The opportunity was too good to even bother about due diligence and risk management. Such is the skill of the traditional US used car salesmen who reinvented themselves as salesman of financial paper when used cars went out of vogue.

In a normal environment, the problems revealed by the crisis in mortgage finance would produce fixes relevant to the problem, such as resetting the ratios of assets to capital for banks and hedge funds, or telling the gnomes of finance to rethink mark-to-market before a worldwide panic developed. Reformers might also have found ways to ensure that compulsive eaters like AIG Citigroup could fit inside their capital base. Instead Liberals saw their opportunity for Big Government to ride to the rescue. At last they had an excuse for limitless spending to fix the problem created by unprincipled US capitalists. All that they needed was someone who could pass as coming from the downtrodden to lead the charge. Enter Obama on to the world stage.

After the full folly of the mortgage plunge became public in September 2008, the Liberal media did their part in the blame game to ensure victory for their Presidential candidate. An unintended consequence was that the broad credit markets locked up, stock indexes fell and the world's economies spiraled into a severe recession. The loss of savings and jobs has been brutal. Someone has to take the fall for this situation, and it had to be more than the boys in mortgage-backed securities. The immediate target conveniently was George W. Bush and that will continue to work for a few months more.

After the inauguration, Obama did not know how to change gears away from campaigning to be a leader and a statesman, as no one had told him how. His Liberal talk and ideology continued to worsen the recession and his inability to move beyond the blame game already threatens his Presidency. His defense is to talk the crisis up into something much bigger and so now the political talk is about the Great Depression and the Reagan Presidency (and in Europe, Thatcherism).

The Depression put in motion an historic tension between public and private sectors over who sets a nation's course. After 50 years of public dominance, Reagan's Presidency tipped the scales back toward private enterprise. The economic life of the ensuing 35 years became "the American model." Ever since, Liberals have wanted to tip the balance back toward public-sector power. The opportunity to achieve that goal was finally presented to them. They have exacerbated the recession of 2008 into a much grander crisis for 2009. The spin now is that an Obama led USA will lead the G-20 to a new Liberal world away from the previous excesses of US capitalism. He will do so by listening and not lecturing. He will be the ideal of the underdog having finally broken through to erase the shameful specter of slavery. The USA can finally take its rightful place in the world order. The problem is that beyond rhetoric everyone has a different perspective as to what that should be.

No surprise that the French and Germans, who for years have wanted to slow such American fast runners as Microsoft, Compaq (Hewlett Packard), Cisco and Intel and to shackle US Private Equity, want ponderous new bureaucracies euphemized as a new global financial architecture. It's been a long time since anyone thought to elevate the IMF as an economic driver.

Meanwhile, the new U.S. President is attempting to replace the American model of some three decades with the Obama model, which promises to grow the U.S.'s $14 trillion GDP (something else he inherited) with government investments in national health insurance and renewable energy technologies after he has spent trillions paying off those who got him into power. He will also spend trillions more in ensuring that he continues to appeal to a majority of the electorate. There is no better way than free handouts to freeloaders. His spin team and a sycophantic Liberal media will continue to do the rest.

The two happiest G- 20 men in London were probably Hu Jintao of China and Lula da Silva of Brazil. Their game is catching up with the West. It's a lot easier to play ball in the G-20 league if in the future the USA will be running backwards.

OBAMA'S BUDGET

President Obama's budget would produce $9.3 trillion in deficits over the next decade, an eye-popping figure that threatens his goals to overhaul health care and explore new energy sources. The Congressional Budget Office (CBO), which is now controlled by Democrats, has developed figures showing a far direr outlook for Obama's budget than the Obama administration predicted with a deficit $2.3 trillion worse. It is a prospect even the President's own budget director, Peter Orszag, called unsustainable.

In his White House run, Obama assailed the economic policies of his predecessor, President George W. Bush. But the dismal deficit figures, if they prove to be accurate, would amount to more than four times the deficits of Bush's Presidency and show that Obama and his Liberal allies controlling Congress would have to continue to raise taxes after the recession ends.

By the auditors' calculation, Obama's budget would generate deficits averaging almost $1 trillion a year of red ink over 2010-2019. Worst of all, the Budget Office says the deficit under Obama's policies would never go below 4 percent of the size of the economy. By the end of the decade, the deficit would exceed 5 percent of gross domestic product, a dangerously high level. Deficits so large put upward pressure on interest rates as the government offers more attractive interest rates to attract borrowers.

Obama's $3.6 trillion budget for the 2010 fiscal year beginning Oct. 1 contains far reaching programs to overhaul the U.S. health care system and initiate new "cap-and-trade" rules to combat global warming. Both initiatives require raising federal revenues sharply higher, but those dollars will not be used to defray the burgeoning deficit. Instead they help pay for Obama's health plan and implement Obama's tax credit for workers.

The 2009 deficit is fueled by the $700 billion bailout, $787 billion economic stimulus measure and $410 billion omnibus spending bill that awarded big increases to domestic agency budgets. Diving tax revenues stemming from the worsening recession will give a deficit four times the previous $459 billion record set last year. That would equal 13 percent of GDP, a level not seen since World War II. After World War II, spending declined rapidly when the country demobilized. In this case, with the bulk of federal spending geared toward income maintenance and transfer payments to political constituencies that will not happen.

The Budget Office's estimate for 2010 is worse, with a deficit of almost $1.4 trillion expected under administration policies, about $200 billion more than predicted by Obama. As a share of GDP, CBO says spending will hit an astounding 28.5% in fiscal 2009, which ends this September, and still be at 25.5% next year, staying at close to 23% to 24% of the economy for the next decade, well above the average of 20.7 percent over the past 40 years. Even CBO's estimate is conservative because it assumes that most of the spending in the stimulus bill will be temporary, though Democrats are already planning to make much of it a permanent part of the budget baseline.

This year's deficit will hit 13.1% of GDP and next year's will still be at 9.6%, assuming a healthy recovery, and then never get below 4.1% for the entire decade. These deficits assume the passage of Mr. Obama's enormous tax increases in 2011 and $629 billion in new cap-and-tax carbon revenues. The share of debt held by the public will double to 82.4% in 2019 from 40.8% in 2008.

All of this expense is without including the costs of Mr. Obama's plan to offer free health care. The White House budget includes only a down payment on health care. The additional cost will be a minimum $1.2 trillion and probably more. Incredibly, Democrats on Capitol Hill and the White House want to jam Health Care reform through Congress with a special procedure that requires only 50 Senate votes.

Obama's real plan is income redistribution regardless of the cost or consequences. One unstated but clearly implicit goal of his budget is to put in place spending programs that make ever-more Americans dependent on government and that will require a permanently higher level of taxation to finance. All is being done in the name of addressing income inequality. Obama's goal is an express train to a European style welfare state. His means to achieve this goal will require that generations to come will have to contend with much higher taxation if they are among the minority who will earn enough to pay income taxes

David J. Phillips

ROAD TO HELL

The prime minister of the Czech Republic described President Barack Obama's economic plan as the road to hell. That presumably is even worse than communism under Soviet occupation.

CHAPTER 21 ... ... ONGOING SAGA

OBAMA'S DOMESTIC AGENDA

President Obama has proposed the most significant shift toward collectivism and away from capitalism in the history of our republic. His budget aspires to lay the groundwork for sweeping expansions of government authority in areas like health care, energy and even daily commerce. Our government is set to become the world's largest health care provider, mortgage bank and car company for starters.

CHRYSLER

Chrysler became the first major American auto maker to file for bankruptcy court protection with Obama still controlling the process.

A New York bankruptcy judge has approved a unique $4.5 billion debtor-in-possession, or DIP, loan from the U.S. government and Canada for Chrysler. The U.S. will also provide a $4.7 billion exit loan.

Fiat will contribute a fee license to use its intellectual property and know-how to capitalize Chrysler in exchange for 20% of the equity of the reorganized Chrysler. Fiat will have the right to select three directors of Chrysler once reorganized. In addition Fiat will have the right to earn up to 15% in additional equity in three tranches of 5% -- each in exchange for meeting performance metrics, including introducing a vehicle produced at a Chrysler factory in the U.S. that performs 40 miles per gallon.

The Obama plan is that the United Auto Workers union would eventually own 55% of the stock in a restructured Chrysler.

Chrysler will be required to have a new chief executive and board of directors appointed by Italy's Fiat and the U. S. government, if Chrysler and Fiat form an alliance.

GENERAL MOTORS

President Obama has proposed a restructuring plan for General Motors that leaves the government with a majority stake. Geithner and his auto task force, led by Steven Rattner, have decided that Treasury and UAW will own a combined 90% of GM. The biggest losers are GM's bondholders. GM has $27.2 billion in unsecured bonds owned by the public as mutual funds, pension funds, hedge funds and retail investors who bought them directly through their brokers. Under the Obama plan, they would exchange their $27.2 billion in bonds for 10% of the stock of the restructured GM, amounting to less than five cents on the dollar.

The Treasury, which is owed $16.2 billion, would receive 50% of the stock and $8.1 billion in debt -- as much as 87 cents on the dollar. The union's retiree health-care benefit trust would receive half of the $20 billion it is owed in stock, giving it 40% ownership of GM, plus another $10 billion in cash over time. That's worth about 76 cents on the dollar.

The Obama manipulation is so devoid of economic logic or fairness that it confirms the fears that the bailout will lead to a nationalized GM run for political ends for the benefit of the UAW, which is closely tied to the Democratic Party. Next will be tax changes and regulations intended to coax Americans to buy these cars designed and built to meet the Liberal agenda.

General Motors Corp. posted a $6 billion loss in the first quarter as revenue fell by $20 billion.

GM has received $15.4 billion in federal loans and faces a June 1 deadline imposed by the government to either finish a restructuring plan or go into bankruptcy protection.

OBAMA EPA

The Obama EPA has enacted its cap and trade play in the form of a ruling that carbon dioxide is a dangerous pollutant that threatens the public and therefore must be regulated under the 1970 Clean Air Act. This so-called "endangerment finding" sets the clock ticking on a vast array of taxes and regulation that EPA will have the power to impose across the economy with little or no political debate. This momentous decision has the potential to affect the daily life of every American. When America's Founders revolted against "taxation without representation," this kind of kingly diktat is what they had in mind.

LATEST SIMULATED CRISIS

Kansas Gov. Kathleen Sebelius won Senate confirmation as the nation's health and human services secretary, thrusting her into the middle of a public health emergency with the swine flu sickening several hundred Americans with one death. As has now become usual, the White House added to the drama by suggesting that schools should be closed and people should not travel on subways or airlines. They then issued the inevitable clarification as they shifted ground. Common flu takes a much bigger toll on an ongoing basis. The 65-31 confirmation vote came after Democrats urged quick action so that Sebelius could get to work leading the federal response to the flu outbreak. Sebelius was the last of Obama's Cabinet nominees awaiting confirmation.

The Senate hasn't acted on Obama's nominees for deputy HHS secretary or commissioner of the Food and Drug Administration, and Obama hasn't even nominated people for other key jobs, including surgeon general, assistant secretary for preparedness and response.

or head of the Centers for Disease Control and Prevention.

Though the swine flu will be an immediate focus, Sebelius will also be charged with shepherding Obama's overhaul of the nation's $2.5 trillion health care system.

STRESS TESTS

The Treasury has directed 10 of the 19 biggest banks undergoing government stress tests to boost their capital. Losses in 2009 and 2010 at the 19 banks could total $600 billion under the government's scenario of a deepening economic downturn. Mortgage loans and consumer loans account for 70% of the potential losses.

Three months ago bankers largely trusted the government's word, knew what it took to be considered well-capitalized and felt confident that any fiats affecting them were dictated by well-known regulators without interference from the White House, Treasury Department or Congress. Those days are over and it's unclear when, or if, they will return. Now, politically motivated stress tests administered by the government will determine how much capital the biggest banks would need under certain, stressed economic conditions. Government regulators have told Bank of America that the company needs to raise $35 billion in capital. The government's findings will set off a scramble over how to fill the capital hole at the nation's largest bank. At least for the largest banking companies, the Treasury is now in charge. The Treasury is far more powerful because they're giving out the Troubled Asset Relief Program money, and as a result of that, power goes with money.

Banks that want to return TARP funds will have to demonstrate their ability to wean themselves off mandated federal programs. A guarantee of debt issuance offered by the Federal Deposit Insurance Corp., allows firms to borrow money relatively inexpensively. Banks have issued more than $332.5 billion under the program since it began last fall. Firms will have to show they don't need the FDIC guarantee to issue debt, such as by raising it without the guarantee.

Treasury Secretary Timothy Geithner has disabused banks from thinking that they decide when they can pay the government back on funds received through the Troubled Asset Relief Program, or TARP. The final call on that, Mr. Geithner made it clear, belongs to the Treasury and the Federal Reserve.

Civil war is breaking out between the banking industry and its regulators. Obama ordered big-bank CEOs to the White House and told them that he was in charge. At the same time, the government needs banks to implement the necessary programs to revive the economy.

LIFE INSURANCE COMPANIES

The Treasury Department plans to extend the Troubled Asset Relief Program to eligible life insurers. The Treasury says it has about $130 billion remaining in TARP funds.

GOVERNMENT PROGRAMS

There is a pattern. The government announces a program designed to stabilize financial markets or kick start lending, but then the program doesn't work as expected and is quietly dropped or changed. What follows is that Obama or the Fed announces another expensive program. The latest example is the Federal Reserve Board's Term Asset-Backed Securities Loan Facility (TALF), which was hailed by the Fed as a way to revive consumer lending when it was unveiled but generated anemic interest when it was launched and has attracted little interest from investors.

ILLEGAL IMMIGRANTS

President Obama plans to address the country's immigration system this year, providing a path for illegal immigrants to become legal.

David J. Phillips

AMERICA LESS SECURE

President Barack Obama is eager to inject hate into the debate and encourage prosecution of Bush administration lawyers who approved so-called enhanced interrogation techniques on terror suspects. His ultimate target is to derive as much political capital as he can by deriding Bush-Cheney national-security policies. In so doing he has lost sight of his obligations to protect Americans.

Obama and his advisors would do well to try to understand that the point of interrogation is intelligence, not confession.

The Obama administration has declassified and released opinions of the Justice Department's Office of Legal Counsel (OLC) given in 2005 and earlier that analyze the legality of interrogation techniques authorized for use by the CIA. Those techniques were applied only when expressly permitted by the director, and are described in these opinions in detail, along with their limits and the safeguards applied to them.

The release of these opinions was unnecessary as a legal matter, and is unsound as a matter of policy. Its effect will be to invite the kind of institutional timidity and fear of recrimination that weakened intelligence gathering in the past, and that we came sorely to regret on Sept. 11, 2001.

Disclosure of the techniques was designed by Obama to create outrage against the Bush Administration to make Obama look good. It will also incur the utter contempt of our enemies. The people who beheaded Nicholas Berg and Daniel Pearl, and have tortured and slain other American captives, will not be shamed into giving up violence by the news that the U.S. will no longer interrupt the sleep cycle of captured terrorists even to help elicit intelligence that could save the lives of its citizens.

Obama released the four Justice Department memos detailing the CIA's interrogation practices while refusing to release information on what the interrogations yielded in actionable intelligence. Obama is indulging in Liberal revenge fantasies against the Bush administration and in so doing is weakening American intelligence capabilities. The risk-averse CIA that so grievously failed in the run-up to 9/11 was a product of a spy culture that still remembered the Church Committee of the 1970s and the Iran-Contra recriminations of the 1980s. It is tragic that Obama and his henchmen are intent on score-settling and so will not release the documents that reveal what the CIA learned from its interrogations, as that does not serve their political ends.

MILITARY COMMISSIONS

The Obama administration is preparing to revive the system of military commissions established at Guantanamo Bay, Cuba, for prosecuting Guantanamo detainees. Obama has previously derided the Bush Administration for military commissions when he wanted to gain cheap political capital

The military commissions have allowed the trial of terrorism suspects in a setting that favors the government and protects classified information, but they were sharply criticized during the administration of President George W. Bush. "By any measure, our system of trying detainees has been an enormous failure," then-candidate Barack Obama said in June 2008.

In one of its first acts, the Obama administration obtained a 120-day suspension of the military commissions; that will expire May 20.

AFGHANISTAN AND PAKISTAN

Afghanistan is sliding back to its pre-9/11 days that allowed the country to become a safe haven for al-Qaeda leaders plotting attacks.

Defense Secretary Robert M. Gates is expected to bolster the U.S. military leadership in Afghanistan by appointing a three-star general to Kabul, according to senior defense officials. The move underscores growing concern in the military over the course of the conflict and marks the first time since the seven-year war began that the U.S. will have two senior commanders there.

The appointment of Lt. Gen. David M. Rodriguez, who holds the military's second-highest rank, hasn't been announced publicly, and his exact role in Kabul is still being discussed. What it does underscore is the inherent conflict of Obama's own conflict in being Commander-in-Chief when he does not believe in what he is doing. More top brass peering into computer screens to order air strikes on a helpless populace will mean fewer US body bags. Obama gave the green light for the media to report individually on body bags as an embarrassment to George Bush over the Iraq conflict. Now he has to suffer the embarrassment to himself in his war in Afghanistan. Typically and cowardly, he will want the war fought from a safe distance in the hope that our troops will have less engagement with the enemy on the ground with fewer US casualties. Almost unreported by the US media was the consequence of a single air strike recently where over a hundred Afghan civilians were killed. Of course Afghan deaths are not the same as deaths of US soldiers. Obama presumably sees them as expendable collateral damage so long as that damage is not to his popularity at home. That is the thinking of an ugly American.

Obama's soft shoe confusion will also be a disaster in neighboring Pakistan. Already in a few days, half a million Pakistanis are fleeing the Taliban conflict in the Swat Valley and have become refugees. The added concern is that Pakistan is a nuclear power and Obama is out of his depth as al-Qaeda regroups in Pakistan.

OBAMA POLARIZATION

The Pew Research Center reported that President Barack Obama "has the most polarized early job approval of any president" since surveys began tracking this measure 40 years ago. The gap between Mr. Obama's approval rating among Democrats (88%) and Republicans (27%) is 61 points. This gap is 10 points bigger than George W. Bush's at this point in his presidency, despite Mr. Bush winning a bitterly contested election.

Mr. Obama's campaign promised partisanship, but since taking office Mr. Obama has frozen Republicans out of the deliberative process, and his response to their suggestions has been a brusque dismissal that "I won."

Mr. Obama has hastened the decline of Republican support with petty attacks on his critics and predecessor. For a person who promised hope and civility in politics, Mr. Obama has become obsessive in blaming Mr. Bush. Rather than ending "the blame game," he personifies it.

No president in the past 40 years has done more to polarize America so much, so quickly.

CELEBRITY STATUS

A celebrity in the mold of an intelligent, articulate Paris Hilton, not a statesman, today leads our country. That may win short-term applause from domestic and foreign audiences, but do little for what should be the chief preoccupation of any U.S. president, which is to advance America's interests.

Obama never misses a photo opportunity or a chance to advertise his wonderfulness. As he once said to Harry Reid, "I have a gift." A White House aid though had to issue an apology recently after Manhattan residents panicked to a point of evacuating high rise office buildings as the Presidential plane flew low over Manhattan for a publicity shot in line of sight of the Statue of Liberty. Obama was more annoyed with the apology as he promptly blamed the whole incident on the Defense Department and called for an enquiry. Obama is a master at shifting the buck elsewhere.

ARROGANT HUMILITY

When traveling abroad, Obama portrays a proud but flawed United States, using a refrain of humility and partnership in an attempt to rally allies around such issues of mutual concern as the global economy, climate change and nuclear proliferation. He talks about the nation's darker periods of slavery and repression of Native Americans, and its past sanction of torture that he has ended.

CHICAGO POLITICS IN WHITE HOUSE

Senior presidential adviser Valerie Jarrett is in regular contact with MoveOn. Org, Americans United for Change and other Liberal interest groups.

Americans United is going after Democrats who are skeptical of Mr. Obama's plans to double the national debt in five years and nearly triple it in 10.

Obama is steeped in the ways of Chicago politics. He was trained by Saul Alinsky, the radical Chicago community organizer. Alinsky's 1971 book,

"Rules for Radicals," is a favorite of the Obamas. Michele Obama quoted it at the Democratic Convention. One Alinsky tactic is to "Pick the target, freeze it, personalize it, and polarize it." Alinsky's first rule of "power tactics" is "power is not only what you have but what the enemy thinks you have."

Team Obama wants to remind its adversaries it has plenty of power and will not wield it responsibly as our President should.

THE VERDICT

On his second day in office in a great Liberal media fanfare, President Obama signed an order to close Guantanamo. Obama has now announced that he intends to imprison terror suspects (called by him "individuals captured in connection with armed conflicts and counterterrorism operations") as long as they live, in undisclosed locations on the U.S. mainland, without bringing them to trial.

"Opening and continuing the military prison set back the moral authority that is America's strongest currency in the world. By closing Guantanamo we are cleaning up something that is, quite simply, a mess, a misguided experiment." Obama

"People who consistently distort the truth are in no position to lecture anyone about values. It's easy to receive applause in Europe for closing Guantanamo. But it's tricky to come up with an alternative that will serve justice and national security. The interrogations were legal, essential, justified, successful and the right thing to do. The intelligence officers who questioned the terrorists can be proud of their work and proud of the results, because they prevented the deaths of innocent people." Cheney

Obama says what makes him popular with little thought and no plan. He is a Liberal white man with a black face and a black wife. Barack Hussein Obama has taken full advantage of being half Black with a privileged prep school and Ivy League education to become President of a Liberal guilt ridden USA. As yet he has not become presidential and instead continues to polish his celebrity cult status.

Barack Obama has declared war on prosperity. He will increase the national debt by $2 trillion this year. He is intent on establishing Liberal ideology with income redistribution and control of free market capitalism whatever the economic cost.